DATE DUE

Creating a Successful Marketing Strategy for Your Small New Business

Creating a Successful Marketing Strategy for Your Small New Business

Stanley F. Stasch
Loyola University Chicago

PRAEGER

AN IMPRINT OF ABC-CLIO, LLC
Santa Barbara, California • Denver, Colorado • Oxford, England

Library of Congress Cataloging-in-Publication Data

Stasch, Stanley F.
   Creating a Successful Marketing Strategy for Your Small New Business / Stanley F. Stasch.
     p. cm.
   Includes bibliographical references and index.
   ISBN 978–0–313–38246–8 (hard copy : alk. paper) — ISBN 978–0–313–38247–5
(ebook)
   1. Marketing—Management.   2. Strategic planning.   3. New business enterprises.
4. Small business.   I. Title.
HF5415.13.S8573   2010
658.8′02—dc22   2010004669

ISBN: 978–0–313–38246–8
EISBN: 978–0–313–38247–5

14 13 12 11 10   1 2 3 4 5

This book is also available on the World Wide Web as an eBook.
Visit www.abc-clio.com for details.

Praeger
An Imprint of ABC-CLIO, LLC

ABC-CLIO, LLC
130 Cremona Drive, P.O. Box 1911
Santa Barbara, California 93116-1911

This book is printed on acid-free paper ∞

Manufactured in the United States of America

Julia, Martha, Emil, Matilda, Joseph

Contents

Preface

In a sense, this book was started back in the Fall of 1957 when I entered the Master in Business Administration program at Northwestern University's College of Business Administration, later named the Kellogg Graduate School of Management. At the time, my only background had been in engineering, which was quite different from business administration and marketing. At Northwestern, I quickly discovered that business education very often involved the study and analysis of real-world business and marketing situations. They were called case studies.

In the Northwestern MBA program I was introduced to three professors—Richard M. Clewett, Ralph Westfall, and Harper W. Boyd—who were authors of many, many marketing case studies, including most of those assigned in my marketing classes. Although their names are no longer familiar to students majoring in marketing, back in the 1950s, 1960s, 1970s, and even into the 1980s, their marketing case studies were well known and widely used by college business students throughout the United States. All three were among the top marketing giants of the time.

I was most fortunate to benefit from having Professors Clewett, Westfall, and Boyd as instructors in some of my MBA classes. Later, after entering the Ph.D. program, all three were mentors who helped me gain a greater appreciation of the learning benefits associated with case studies. Upon completing my Ph.D. studies, I received an appointment to the marketing faculty at Northwestern University, where I had the great good fortune to have both Dick Clewett and Ralph Westfall as colleagues. Still later, I was further honored when invited to coauthor publications with all three of those distinguished scholars. Through years of friendship and professional association with them, I absorbed more and more about the learning potential of marketing case studies. Without the case study background that Clewett, Westfall and Boyd taught me over the years, this book probably could not have been written. I am forever grateful to them!

I have been learning from marketing case studies ever since I was first introduced to them more than fifty years ago. What I now know about successful and unsuccessful marketing strategies for small new businesses I learned almost exclusively from analyzing marketing case studies. This, I believe, is because such case studies are so very rich in detail that they can lead to a better understanding of the phenomenon being studied, and thus help the researcher more clearly identify relationships among the factors involved.

Almost all of my research since the mid-1970s has been based on case studies. By the late 1970s I had become heavily engaged in researching and studying successful and unsuccessful marketing strategies. The objective of the research has been to identify a model that can distinguish between marketing strategies that will be successful and those that will not.

Initially, my research focused on market leader brands that were trying to defend their positions, and medium-sized brands that were trying to increase their market share. My colleagues and I compiled numerous summaries of marketing strategy case histories involving those types of brands.

What was missing in that research were marketing strategy case histories involving small new businesses. That changed in 1986 when Professor Gerry E. Hills, holder of the Coleman Chair in Entrepreneurship at the University of Illinois at Chicago, invited me to participate in a symposium on research at the interface of marketing and entrepreneurship. Fortunately, the symposium became an annual event and I participated in almost all of them over the next two decades. The discipline demanded by those regularly occurring symposia caused me to persevere in my pursuit of understanding how successful marketing strategies for small new businesses differed from unsuccessful marketing strategies. If Gerry Hills had not organized those symposia and invited me to participate, this book would not have seen the light of day. I greatly appreciate Gerry's unsurpassed leadership in the marketing and entrepreneurship field and his contributions toward making this book possible.

During my 20-odd years of studying small new businesses, I learned a great deal that could be helpful to anyone thinking of starting such a business. However, some 10 or 15 years ago I concluded that I had written my last book. But, then, there were those two now world-famous colleagues of mine from my Northwestern days back in the 1960s and 1970s—Philip Kotler and Sidney Levy. Though no longer young, both of them keep going and going and going. It was their very good example that inspired me to go forward with this book, and I thank them very much for that!

Stanley F. Stasch

PART I

INTRODUCTION

1

Poor Marketing Strategies Cause New Business Failures

A 2004 *Wall Street Journal* article reported that 572,900 new businesses were started in the United States in 2003. The same article pointed out that 554,800 businesses failed during that same year.[1] Given that there are approximately 15 million businesses in the United States, the first of the above figures suggests that a significant portion—approximately 4 percent—of all businesses in any year are new businesses. Sadly, but more importantly for this book, the second figure indicates that an almost equal percentage of businesses fail each year.

New business startups have an extremely high failure rate. Clearly, most new businesses fail in a relatively short period of time. The individuals who start them usually incur great financial losses and often bear significant psychological scars related to the failure. Their personal investment in time and money can be huge in comparison to their resources. Often they continue full time in their regular line of employment while working evenings and weekends on their new business startup. Their new business may consume not only their personal savings, but also money set aside for retirement. Homes are frequently mortgaged, and sometimes even money set aside for their children's education is used. Many of these would-be entrepreneurs devote two, three, or even more years to their failing businesses, a period of time that can represent a significant portion of their adult working years.

New business failures can be attributed to numerous causes. Lack of financial resources is often a cause. The new business founder may not be a strong leader or a good manager. Qualified personnel may choose not to join the new venture, forcing the entrepreneur to hire individuals to perform functions for which they are not fully qualified. The technology or physical facilities needed for operations may not be easily obtained or managed. The new business's accounting or information system may be inadequate. There are numerous reasons why new businesses fail, and many of those are not marketing-based causes. This book, however, concentrates only on marketing causes of new business failures.

Among people who have studied this topic, there is a common belief that new business failures are highly correlated with two characteristics frequently displayed by the individuals starting those businesses.

- They did not thoroughly analyze and understand the wants, needs, and buying motivations of their markets and the people constituting those markets. Very often they also did not carefully identify and evaluate the strengths and weaknesses of the competitors they would face in those markets.
- The marketing strategy they used for their new business was inadequate, and in some cases incomplete. This resulted in marginal or poor marketing planning and weak execution of the marketing plan, if one even existed.

Individuals starting new businesses should be aware of these major marketing causes of failure and make every effort to avoid them when they first begin planning their new businesses. This book is designed to help them do so.

What Percentage of New Business Fail? Survive? Succeed?

This question of success and failure is a very important matter to anyone starting a new business. In fact, since there is a widespread belief that some 80–90 percent of all new businesses fail, the issue is quite critical indeed. The following is a typical quote about this topic.

> James Schrager, a professor of entrepreneurship at the University of Chicago, points out that venture capitalists spend considerable time and expertise winnowing a few good business plans from vast mountains of chaff—and nonetheless see nine out of ten of their businesses fail.[2]

The first two sentences in this chapter reported that in 2003 the number of businesses that failed (554,800) was almost as large as the 572,900 new businesses that were started. These figures give support to the quote immediately above, and suggest that in any given year the number of business failures may be almost as large as the number of new business startups. This observation is in agreement with most studies reporting new venture failure rates, namely, that some 80–90 percent of new business startups fail within the first two to three years.

Here it will be helpful to spend a little time discussing the terms fail, survive, and succeed. When can we say that a new business has failed? When can we say that a new business has become successful? It is not always easy to answer these questions. Some new businesses clearly fail when they close their doors and cease to operate. New businesses that are not such clear failures will survive for a while—some may survive for several years or more before they fail. On the other hand, some may survive for the lifetime of the person who started the new business, even though no independent observer is likely to think of it as successful.

Swedish researchers Bjerke and Hultman identified three different types of *surviving* small firms, the first of which they called *marginal firms*.

Marginal firms: "ordinary" new independent business ventures, often started as a means to substitute income, and commonly based on some kind of service orientation—the overwhelmingly majority of small firms.[3]

We can easily see many examples of this type of small surviving firm. They are represented by such establishments as lawn care services, handyman services, storefront restaurants and snack shops, independent gift stores, stores selling used furniture, and others.

The second type of surviving small firms are those Bjerke and Hultman call *lifestyle firms*.

Lifestyle firms: usually started based on the entrepreneur's profession and skills, not aimed at growing, but at providing a good salary, perquisites and flexibility in the lifestyle of the owner.[4]

Obvious examples here are lawyers and medical professionals who go into business for themselves. But small lifestyle firms also include accountants, income tax preparation specialists, and even the more blue-collar occupations of plumber, electrician, house painter, and shoe repair specialist. This second type of surviving small firm might be considered successful, depending upon what the founder' aspirations were when he or she first started the new business.

Bjerke and Hultman call their third type of surviving small firms *high-potential firms*.

> High-potential firms: companies started with the aim of increasing sales and profits and becoming a big corporation (the entrepreneur's big dream), and therefore receiving the greatest investment interest and publicity.[5]

Fifteen or twenty years ago, or even more recently, some of the internet-based companies now well known to the public belonged in this category. Of course, probably most readers are aware that many other internet-based firms came into existence during the 1990s, only to fail during the dot-com bust that occurred in the late 1990s to early 2000s.

How can we use the Bjerke-Hultman classifications to estimate the percentage of small new businesses that are likely to succeed? Here it is important to keep in mind that *all three types of surviving small firms may constitute as little as 10 percent* of the new businesses started in any given year. The other 90 percent (approximately) may have already failed or be well along the path toward failure. Of the 10 percent of small new businesses that become surviving firms, Bjerke and Hultman estimate that approximately ½ percent will enjoy good growth, while about 2 percent can be viewed as growth-oriented survivors. The remaining 7 ½ percent will be low-growth or no-growth small firms. Based on Bjerke and Hultman's estimates, it appears that only about 1–2 percent of all small new businesses will be successful, in the sense that they will become high-potential firms.

David Carson, Stanley Cromie, Pauric McGowen, and Jimmy Hill studied marketing and entrepreneurship in small and medium-sized businesses in Ireland. They, too, found that small new businesses had slim prospects for survival and growth. They reported that only about one-third of all new enterprises survive beyond their first 18 months. Many of those that did survive were reluctant to expose themselves or their enterprises to further risk and uncertainty by seeking ever more growth.[6] Thus, they tend to remain marginal firms or lifestyle firms, rather than try to become high-potential firms.

Based on the findings reported above—and numerous other findings not reported here—it is very reasonable to conclude that probably 90 percent or more of all small new businesses will fail, although there are differences of opinion as to how soon failure will occur. Of the approximately 10 percent that will survive, only a very small number will become high-potential firms that will grow their sales and profits and increase in size. The vast majority of the surviving firms seem destined to fall into the low-growth/no-growth category.

If you are thinking of starting your own new business, you can see from the above that the odds are not in your favor—especially if you want your small new business to become a high-potential firm. To improve your odds of succeeding, you must learn more about the marketing causes of failure and how to avoid them.

What Are Marketing Causes of New Business Failures?

The fourth paragraph of this chapter identified two marketing causes of new venture failure. Poor market and competitive analysis was one of those causes. The second was inadequate marketing strategy and planning.

The Irish researchers (Carson et al.) who studied marketing in small and medium-sized firms reported four findings that provide us with additional understanding of the marketing causes of new venture failure:[7]

- The entrepreneur considers marketing a peripheral rather than a core business activity.
- Marketing opportunities are not analyzed in a meaningful way, but rather in an unstructured manner without clear purpose.
- Marketing planning is intuitive and unstructured.
- Marketing implementation is more like a haphazard use of marketing tactics than a logical process.

These observations imply that the failure of new businesses can often be linked to questionable market analysis, weak or nonexistent marketing strategies, and poor marketing planning and implementation.

My research on successful and unsuccessful small new businesses reported three major marketing strategy causes of failure:

- Almost 90 percent of the small new businesses studied were launched with an incomplete or a poorly designed marketing strategy. Those poor strategies contributed to the failure of all of those new businesses.
- Some 80 percent of the small new businesses utilized marketing strategies that included elements that caused serious delays when the owners tried to execute those marketing strategies. Those delays prevented the small new businesses from generating the sales revenue streams they badly needed to survive.

- More than 70 percent of the small new businesses used one or more elements in their marketing strategies that required a large marketing budget. Since large marketing budgets were not available to those new businesses, their use of those marketing strategies contributed to their failure.[8]

Ninety percent of the small new businesses I studied experienced at least two of the above marketing strategy causes of failure.

All of these observations strongly suggest that small new business failures can often be linked to marketing causes, such as questionable marketing analysis, weak or nonexistent marketing strategies, poor selection of marketing strategies, and poor marketing planning and implementation. The strength of my own research findings and the severity of this problem gave me the motivation to write a book that would help individuals avoid such serious and potentially destructive handicaps when starting a small new business.

The Fundamental Causes of Failure: Two Critical Time Periods

The fundamental causes of most failures are time and money. That is, if we focus on time, we see that most small new businesses allow too much time to elapse between the business's conception and its achievement of a self-sustaining cash flow from sales. If we focus on money, we see that entrepreneurs typically have available very limited amounts of cash and other financial resources when trying to put together their new businesses. Failures occur because they expend all of their resources before the new business is able to generate the sales revenue stream needed to sustain it. *This is the fundamental cause of most new business failures.*

Two time periods are critical to the survival of every new business—the *prelaunch* period and the *launch* period. The prelaunch period begins when the entrepreneur conceives the new business and starts putting together those things (plant, equipment, facilities, people, etc.) needed to make the new business operational. During prelaunch, no sales revenues are being generated, but money and other resources certainly are being expended, often at a rapid pace.

The launch period begins when the new business first opens its doors to potential customers, and ends when it achieves a self-sustaining cash flow from its sales. When a large organization is starting a new business, the length of the launch period may not be especially critical if the organization has deep pockets. Reportedly, Time Inc. continued investing in its new *Sports Illustrated* magazine for some nineteen years before it became profitable.[9]

Sidney Frank was the entrepreneur who introduced the very successful super premium vodka brand, Grey Goose. He believed that practicing patience was an important ingredient when trying to build a market for a new alcoholic beverage.[10] But he had the resources that allowed him such a luxury.

It is quite another matter for small new businesses—the focus of this book. The people who try to launch them tend to have very limited funds and little access to additional resources. For them, the launch period can be characterized as a life or death race between resources being depleted and sales revenues being accumulated. The survival of the new venture hinges on how quickly sales revenues grow large enough to more than offset the rate of resource depletion.

Throughout the book I make reference to both the *prelaunch period* and the *launch period*. Both periods are critical to the issue of a successful marketing strategy, but for slightly different reasons.

Develop the Marketing Strategy in the Prelaunch Period

Along with others who have studied this matter, my research found that people who start small new businesses typically make poor use of marketing. In turn, poor marketing is a substantial and significant con- tributor to the failure of new businesses. Why? The explanation is quite simple. Poor marketing during the launch period is not likely to produce the sales revenue stream a small new business needs to succeed. Thus, it is obvious that the launch period is the make-or-break period for the new venture, the do-or-die time. Yet, if the new business uses poor marketing, what chance does it have to successfully survive its launch period? Very little! Perhaps none!

There is a huge lesson in this observation. If the launch is so crucial to survival, and if the new business employs ineffective marketing programs, one can quickly arrive at the very important conclusion that *the seed of a new business's failure is planted in the prelaunch period*. It is imperative that the entrepreneur recognize that when the new business enters its launch period, it absolutely must hit the ground running—that is, it has to already have in place a well-designed marketing strategy that will be effective from the very first day of the launch period. Such a marketing strategy should very quickly cause a sales revenue stream to begin flowing and to continue growing with the passing of time. The earlier this revenue stream begins and the faster it grows, the sooner will the new business successfully pass through its very critical launch period. What is the implication of this if you are thinking of starting a new business? From the above, it is quite obvious that *you should be creating a successful marketing strategy during the prelaunch period.* If your new business enters its launch period without a marketing strategy, or with a poor marketing strategy, the launch period will grow longer and that will greatly increase the likelihood of failure for the business.

The following descriptions of three new businesses illustrate the importance of establishing a successful marketing strategy in the prelaunch period. Appliance Control Technology, Inc. is an excellent example of a new business that created a successful marketing strategy during its prelaunch period.

APPLIANCE CONTROL TECHNOLOGY, INC.

Appliance Control Technology, Inc. was organized to design and manufacture microprocessor-based controls for major kitchen and laundry appliances in the mid-price market, which had yet to adopt such controls because of their high cost. From the outset of the new business concept, the company founders created a product and marketing strategy that was designed to help their company quickly break into the identified target market. Four months after the company was incorporated, it received a multimillion-dollar order from Tappan, even though production operations were not scheduled to begin for several months. Six months later, when production got under way, the company had already received a second large order, this one from Magic Chef. The company had also signed development contracts with three other large appliance manufacturers.[11] This small new business registered a sizeable sales backlog even before it began producing its electronic controls.

Axiom Legal was some six to twelve months into its launch period before their marketing strategy began to show results. Given the large expenses they incurred after entering into their launch period, it was certainly fortuitous that Axiom's marketing strategy was able to begin generating revenues after only six months. If their strategy had taken as long as 12–18 months to show results, who knows if the new company would have survived.

AXIOM LEGAL

Axiom Legal was formed in 2000 to recruit well-qualified attorneys dissatisfied with law firm practices, and to offer their specialized expertise to companies in need of them. Because this new legal venture did not have traditional law firm partners that had to be financially supported, it could operate at significantly reduced overhead compared to a typical law firm. As a result, Axiom could offer their legal services at a price almost 50 percent lower than traditional law firms. This new legal business expended $1 million during the first six months of its launch period without attracting a major client. Then its marketing strategy began to take effect. It gained more than 10 big clients by mid-2002, added several dozen more in the next year, and began earning a profit in 2003.[12]

Lakland Basses is an example of a small new business entering into its launch period without a successful marketing strategy in place and ready to go. If it had not been for the great generosity of the founder's father, which sustained the new business while it searched for a successful strategy, there is a very good chance that Lakland Basses would have failed.

LAKLAND BASSES

Daniel Lakin started Lakland Basses in the early 1990s to pursue his love—designing and making electric bass guitars. The new business suffered several serious setbacks over its first 7–8 years, but it managed to continue to survive due to the generosity of Lakin's father. Over the first 6–7 years of Lakland Basses' existence, the senior Mr. Lakin contributed some $850,000 to his son's small new business, without expecting to receive any return on his investment. However, by refining its operations and marketing over the years, Lakland Basses was finally able to reach breakeven for the very first time in 2003.[13]

When you start your new business, it will be very helpful to use Appliance Control Technologies, Inc. as a good model to emulate. They clearly had their marketing strategy in place and ready to go before they entered the launch period. You—and everyone else starting a new business—will greatly increase your new business's chances of succeeding if you have designed a complete and effective marketing strategy during your new business's prelaunch period. And, of course, you will certainly want to avoid using Lakland Basses as an example, even if you happen to have a most generous patron supporting you.

How This Book Will Help You Create a Successful Marketing Strategy

Overall, this book describes how you should go about creating a successful marketing strategy for the small new business you are thinking of starting. When I use the phrase, "successful marketing strategy," I am referring to a marketing strategy that creates a sales revenue stream as soon as the new business enters its launch period, and which then continues to grow with each succeeding time period. If you are starting a small new business, this book will (1) help you design a marketing strategy that possesses the characteristics that are strongly associated with successful marketing strategies and (2) help you avoid characteristics that are associated with unsuccessful marketing strategies. More specifically, this book will:

- Make you more aware of the critical role marketing must play if your small new business is to have a reasonable chance of succeeding—a new business needs more than just operations to be successful, it must use effective marketing.
- Make you fully knowledgeable about the composition of a complete and effective marketing strategy, and how to avoid using an incomplete and/ or ineffective marketing strategy.
- Introduce you to a four-stage framework that will guide you through the process of developing a marketing strategy for your business.
- Give you in-depth exposure to the four conditions that your marketing strategy must possess in order for it to have a good chance of being successful, with emphasis on (1) what characteristics must be present in your marketing strategy and (2) the types of barriers and pitfalls that are likely to be encountered and how to avoid or overcome them.
- Help you recognize that if your selected marketing strategy does not possess the required characteristics or cannot overcome the barriers and/or pitfalls it will encounter, the strategy will not succeed and your new business will probably fail. To avoid such failure, you must greatly revise the strategy you have been considering, or possibly even look for a completely new strategy.

A Framework to Use When Creating a Successful Marketing Strategy

For over twenty years I studied numerous small new business startups in great detail in order to identify the difficulties, problems, and barriers those new businesses encountered, and the mistakes their owners made. After carefully studying those many examples, I discovered that the development of a marketing strategy for a small new business could be greatly simplified and more easily understood through the use of a four-stage hierarchical framework. By using that framework, I was able to clearly see where and how the various marketing strategy elements were contributing to the success or failure of small new businesses. More importantly, I was able to see where each marketing strategy element should fit into the overall marketing strategy in order for the new business to have a good chance of being successful.[14] If you are thinking of starting your own small new business, you also can use this four-stage hierarchical framework to evaluate whether your marketing strategy will have a good chance of being successful.

The framework consists of four conditions, each with different requirements. A marketing strategy must be able to satisfy all of the requirements associated with each of the four conditions if it is to have a good chance of being successful. The conditions are hierarchical because, if the marketing strategy does not satisfy the requirements of Condition I, more than likely the strategy will fail even if it possesses the requirements associated with Conditions II, III, and IV. Similarly, if the marketing strategy possesses all of the requirements associated with Conditions I, II, and III, but does not satisfy the Condition IV requirements, the strategy may be successful in the short run, but will almost surely fail in the long run. Stated rather briefly, these four conditions are:

Condition I: The marketing strategy must be a complete one that highly integrates the following five elements: a specific target market, a differentiated product/service that is designed to appeal strongly to the target market, an effective communication which causes the target market to find the new business's product/service especially appealing, a price which makes the product/service appear as a good value to the target market, and distribution which the target market finds very convenient.

Condition II: Even if the marketing strategy satisfies Condition I, it must also be so designed that its execution will not encounter any significant time delays because of competitors' actions or because of barriers in established distribution channels or because of local, state, or federal regulations. If the selected marketing strategy experiences significant delays due to any of the above reasons, the new business will not be able to execute its strategy in a timely manner. The new business will remain in its prelaunch period longer than intended, and it will continue to consume resources while not beginning to create the stream of sales revenues it desperately needs in order to survive.

Condition III: In addition to satisfying Conditions I and II, if the selected marketing strategy uses individual elements that require a larger marketing budget than is available, the strategy is destined to fail. Persons starting a new business must select marketing strategy elements that match the size of the available marketing budget.

Condition IV: A marketing strategy that satisfies Conditions I, II, and III has a good chance of being successful in the short run, but the small new business may not survive in the long run because of counterattacks by large, well-established competitors who feel threatened by the initial successes of the small new business. To succeed in the long run, the new business's marketing strategy should also include (1) a significant and sustainable product/service advantage compared with competitors, (2) something that prevents competitors from being able to negate the effectiveness of its marketing strategy, and (3) a distribution or product or market barrier that provides the new business with longer-term protection against aggressive attacks by established competitors.

As reported at the beginning of this section, I found this four-stage hierarchy of conditions to be very helpful in understanding what small new businesses were doing right and what they were doing wrong with respect to their marketing strategies. In my own research, I found that almost 90 percent of small new businesses did not select a marketing strategy that satisfied the requirements of Condition I. Essentially all of those new businesses failed. I also found that about 80 percent of small new businesses used elements in their strategies that caused very serious time delays when those new businesses tried to execute their strategies (Condition II). Most of those new businesses failed because their prelaunch period lengthened well beyond what was initially anticipated, and they ran out of money. I also estimated that a vast majority of small new businesses opened their doors to the public with strategies that required a much larger marketing budget than was available (Condition III). All those new businesses failed or struggled to barely survive. A few new businesses used marketing strategies that satisfied each of Conditions I, II, and III, but did not include anything that satisfied Condition IV. As their early successes became apparent, and as large, well-established competitors took note and aggressively attacked those new businesses, the latter suffered serious market losses and either failed or significantly retrenched.

If you want your small new business to be successful, your marketing strategy must possess all of the characteristics associated with each of Conditions I, II, III, and IV. Your marketing strategy must also avoid all of the possible mistakes that a small new business entrepreneur can make in regard to each of these four conditions.

Real Examples Are Used as Illustrations

In the remainder of this book, the above four conditions are described and explained by using examples that illustrate the marketing elements and concepts that constitute those conditions.

For over 30 years I have been using real-world examples to study successful and unsuccessful marketing strategies. Initially, market leaders and medium-sized brands were the focus of that research. However, some 20-odd years ago I began including small new businesses in my research activities. Over the last 15 years or so I have concentrated almost exclusively on researching marketing strategies used by small new businesses. Based on my 30 years of studying marketing strategies, I have selected those real-world examples that are without question the most detailed and clearest illustrations of the marketing characteristics present in Conditions I, II, III, and IV above. By using those examples when describing and explaining the four conditions, readers will quickly and easily understand what constitutes each condition and how a marketing strategy can achieve each condition.

What Kind of New Businesses Is This Book About?

So far the only thing that has been said regarding this question is that the book is about small new businesses. It will be helpful if the reader has a better understanding of what I mean by that.

At the beginning of this chapter, I described Bjerke and Hultman's three types of surviving small firms: marginal, lifestyle, and high-potential. This book is about finding successful marketing strategies for small new businesses that can be categorized as high-potential firms—firms that start small, grow their sales and profits, and become noticeably bigger with the passing of time.

The following four characteristics further describe the kinds of new businesses this book is about.

1. This book is about *new* businesses—businesses that did not previously exist, either under some other name or under some other ownership, and

that are being launched by individual entrepreneurs, not by an established corporation or organization, whether for-profit or not-for-profit.

2. The scale of the new business is *small*, at least at its inception. Typically, only one person—the owner—is involved at the beginning of these new ventures, although occasionally one or two others may be included. The new business does not have a plant or physical facility of the type normally associated with an ongoing business. A basement, a garage, or a spare room in the owner's home is most likely to typify the scale of the new business during its prelaunch period.

3. The new business's resources are *limited*, both in terms of money and access to money, and to other resources as well. The resources that are available are first and foremost likely to be used to acquire those things— physical plant, product design, people, and/or other things—that are absolutely necessary if the business is to open its doors to potential customers in the foreseeable future. Among such new businesses it is almost universally true that there is a very limited marketing budget. It is not at all uncommon for there to be no marketing budget at all. Often the only marketing undertaken on behalf of the new business is that which occurs when the owner personally contacts potential customers. Regardless of the resources available, marketing is usually at the bottom of the priority list.

4. Most people starting small new ventures have a business plan to show to potential investors, to bankers being approached for a loan, to prospective suppliers, and to others whose support will be needed to get the business up and running. Such business plans usually identify the product or service the new venture will offer, how it differs from current offerings already on the market, the market to be served (usually in very general terms), where the business will be located, the number and types of employees, projected sales revenues, costs, and profits, and other things. What tends to be absent from those business plans is a clear statement of the marketing strategy that will be used to guide the new business's early marketing efforts, and a specific marketing plan of action that will result in the creation of the sales revenue stream the new business will need in order to succeed. These omissions follow directly from item 3 above. Since there is no marketing budget of any substance, little purpose is served by dwelling on a marketing strategy and marketing plan. It is the presence of characteristics 3 and 4 in most small new businesses that contribute greatly to their likely failure.

Layout of the Book

The book contains six chapters organized into three parts, with Part I consisting of this introductory chapter. Part II consists of Chapters 2 through 5, each of which presents a detailed description of one of the four conditions presented earlier that a small new business's marketing strategy must possess in order for it to have a good chance of being successful. Chapter 2 addresses Condition I, and discusses what a person has to do to achieve a complete and highly integrated marketing strategy for her or his new business. Chapter 3 is concerned with avoiding a marketing strategy that will encounter serious difficulties or barriers that can cause lengthy delays in the new business's ability to begin generating the essential sales revenue stream it needs for survival (Condition II). Chapter 4 addresses Condition III. This chapter helps the reader evaluate his or her marketing strategy to determine if one or more of the strategy's elements will require a marketing budget larger than that which is available. Chapter 5 is based on the fact that some new businesses enjoy modest success initially, but then go into decline. This is likely to occur when a new business uses a marketing strategy that satisfies Conditions I, II, and III, but not condition IV. Such a strategy does not include the characteristics needed to defend against increased pressure from larger, well-established competitors once the latter fully understand the threat presented by the new business's sales and market success. Chapter 5 describes the other characteristics needed in a new business's marketing strategy if it is to satisfy Condition IV and have the capability of defending against counterattacks by strong, well-established competitors.

Part III has only one chapter, Chapter 6. This chapter reviews successful marketing strategies used by three small new businesses. The objective of the chapter is to illustrate how those strategies possessed all of the characteristics of successful marketing strategies, as described in Chapters 2 through 5. Having followed the evaluation of the elements of three successful marketing strategies—relative to Conditions I, II, III, and IV—individuals preparing to launch their own small new business should be quite well prepared to evaluate the marketing strategy they are thinking of using. Such an evaluation will help them have confidence that their marketing strategy has a good chance of being successful, or help them identify where and how they must change their marketing strategy in order to avoid failure.

PART II

CHARACTERISTICS OF SUCCESSFUL MARKETING STRATEGIES

2

Screening Condition I: Do You Have a Complete Marketing Strategy? Do the Elements of Your Marketing Strategy Create Synergy?

Marketing is a very old human activity. In the United States most grade school children are introduced to marketing in their early history classes. They do not recognize the activity as marketing because the schoolbooks and schoolteachers refer to it as *trade*. Prehistoric humans traded economic goods they had in surplus for other economic goods that they wanted or needed but did not have. Fortunately, some other humans had a surplus of the goods that the first group wanted, and those other humans also wanted what the first group had in surplus. Thus, they found it beneficial to trade. We know, for example, that before the time of Christ, Romans were trading with China for silk and other products. What we today call the Silk Road was the lengthy route those products had to travel to complete this trade.

The term *marketing* was not applied to this activity until the twentieth century, when economists and other scholars began studying it. At first those early social scientists focused on the very visible institutions that were active in marketing—wholesalers and retailers. Also, because it was so visible to any observer, the activity of advertising was a popular subject of study by scholars. Other frequently studied topics were buying and selling, shipping and storing, the use of financing and credit, and still other visible activities associated with marketing.

Regarding the study of marketing strategy, a notable breakthrough occurred in the late 1950s when the study of marketing shifted away from the study of marketing institutions and marketing functions and began to focus instead on the four topics of product, price, promotion and distribution. By referring to distribution as *place*, the study of marketing was consolidated into the study of "the four P's." By the early 1960s the topic of *market* was added to the four P's, and when that occurred, it brought more clearly into focus those things that constitute a complete marketing strategy.[1]

I described in Chapter 1 a framework that a person starting a new business can use when developing a successful marketing strategy for his or her business. That framework consists of four screening conditions, the first of which states that a marketing strategy must be a complete strategy that highly integrates all of the marketing elements that constitute the strategy. That is to say, the marketing strategy must be both complete and also synergistic. This is Condition I.

What Constitutes a Complete Marketing Strategy?

Since the 1960s, essentially every textbook on the principles of marketing and marketing management has treated marketing as consisting of these five topics, the four P's—product, price, promotion, place (distribution)— and a market. To be complete, a marketing strategy must address each of these five elements.

A complete marketing strategy must have a specific *product or service* to offer, and a specific *market* for which the product/service is intended. The market will not be aware that someone has designed a specific product/ service to satisfy its wants and needs unless that someone *promotes* that fact to the individual consumers in that market. The product/service must also be *priced* so as to be a good value to individual consumers when they compare it with the alternative products/services that are available on the market. Lastly, those individual consumers are not likely to purchase the product/ service unless it is *distributed* in a manner convenient to them. If any one of these elements is absent, a sale to an individual consumer is not likely to occur, and therefore the activity of marketing is not likely to occur.

The two examples below illustrate the difference between an incomplete marketing strategy (New Product Showcase) and a complete marketing strategy (Glacier Nursery). The owners of New Product Showcase did not identify a target market of buyers for their store. They did not have a product designed specifically for a target market. It fact, the store would display almost any product on its shelves for $350. It did no promoting, and it did not price to "create value." Its distribution—consisting of the store's location—was not based on the convenience of the target market, because it had no target market.

NEW PRODUCT SHOWCASE

Zane Causey and Robert Clark opened a store called the New Product Showcase in a low-rent shopping mall in Irving, Texas. For $350, New Product Showcase offered inventors an opportunity to display their inventions for 90 days on the store's shelves. This gave the inventors a retail outlet for their inventions, which, hopefully, the public would find and buy. Each invention's price was based on a large markup over the cost of producing the item. Causey and Clark did not have a clear vision of who they wanted to attract as customers to their store. The New Product Showcase did no consumer advertising. Visitors to the store tended to be older, lower-to-middle-income homeowners looking for gadgets.[2]

A sharp contrast to the above example is Glacier Nursery. This small new business used a complete marketing strategy from the very beginning. It had a very specific target market. Its products were specially developed for that target market and priced to be a good value. Because the retail garden center business was a close-knit one, the owner did all the promotion via personal selling and telephone calls and sending free samples to several garden centers each year. The owner used local trucking companies to deliver shipments to customers throughout the growing season.

GLACIER NURSERY

Brad Brown bought twenty acres of farmland in Montana's Flathead Valley to start a tree nursery on a part-time basis while working full-time as a foreman on a Christmas tree farm. At the time, there was not one tree nursery in all of Montana, so the 40–50 retail garden centers in the state had to order trees from out-of-state nurseries. Because of the great distances involved, those out-of-state nurseries found it unprofitable to provide Montana's retail garden centers with regular delivery service throughout the growing season. Brown hoped to attract those garden centers as regular customers by offering both better service and higher quality plants.

In his nursery, Brown hoped to grow "hardier" trees and shrubs than those grown in nurseries located in climates more temperate than Montana's. He expected his Montana-grown trees and shrubs would be in great demand by Montana's homeowners and, therefore, by Montana's retail garden centers. In addition to providing hardier and higher quality plants, Brown expected to offer regular and convenient delivery service throughout the Montana growing season by using three local trucking companies.

The nursery business was a close-knit one, so Brown himself did all the promotion via personal selling and telephone calls to the 40–50 retail garden centers located in Montana. Each year he sent free samples to a handful of those garden centers. To attract customers to his new business, his products were priced about 10 percent lower than competition, but he expected he could increase prices after his reputation for superior quality became established.[3]

The New Product Showcase made a weak attempt at marketing. Its efforts were not at all focused on any target market, and it did little or no promotion. Its products were not selected for a particular target market, and its pricing practices were not designed to "create good value" in the eyes of its potential customers. Consequently, the little marketing it undertook had no chance at all of being effective.

On the other hand, Glacier Nursery *had a complete marketing strategy* in which each of its five elements was well integrated with at least one of the other elements. It selected a target market that was not being well served by out-of-state nurseries. Its products were specifically developed for the Montana market. Personal contacts informed Montana garden centers of the advantages of Glacier Nursery's products. Lower initial prices offered value to those making a purchase. Glacier Nursery scheduled deliveries throughout the growing season.

These observations introduce the reader to the second important characteristic of a small new business's marketing strategy if it is to be successful: *the five elements of the marketing strategy should be highly integrated with one another so as to create synergy. Each marketing element must strongly support one or more of the other four elements, and each element must be strongly supported by one or more of the other four elements.*

Does the Marketing Strategy Create Synergy?

Marketing is expensive! In the absence of plentiful financial resources, individuals starting small new businesses will want their marketing to be both effective and efficient. Effective marketing is needed if the new business is to accomplish its marketing goals and create enough sales revenues to survive. Small business owners also want their marketing to be efficient, that is, to be able to accomplish those marketing goals *as inexpensively as possible.* After all, the more efficient the new business's marketing, the faster it will become profitable.

The best way to accomplish both effectiveness and efficiency is to create a marketing strategy in which each of the five elements supports or complements or reinforces one or more of the other four elements in the marketing strategy. If all the elements are supportive of one another, or are in some way highly interdependent, the strategy will be a synergistic one, it will be both effective and efficient, and *it will be able to achieve its marketing objectives quickly and with a relatively small marketing budget.* The presence or absence of these last two outcomes very often is the difference between success and failure for a small new business.

What can you do to create a synergistic marketing strategy for your small new business? You must first make certain that you are putting together a complete marketing strategy, as described in the previous section. Then, you must evaluate and refine that strategy to make certain that each element somehow supports or reinforces one or more of the other elements. What follows is a list of the five components that must be present if a marketing strategy is to achieve synergy. This list is very useful to anyone who is beginning to create a small new business. Your marketing strategy must

1. **Identify a target market whose needs your new business can satisfy more effectively than any competitor.**
2. **Design or differentiate your product/service so it is more appealing to the individuals in your target market than the products/services offered by competitors.**

3. **Promote your product/service to the individuals in your target market so that they understand and appreciate how it will satisfy their needs better than competitors' offerings.**

4. **Price your product/service is such a way that the individuals in your target market will find it to be a good value when comparing the benefits received from your product/service against those offered by competing products/services.**

5. **Distribute your product/service in a manner that is most convenient to the individuals in your target market.**

I have never seen a successful marketing strategy that did not display these five elements.

It is especially important to note how each of these five characteristics is integrated into a unified marketing strategy. The product/service is strongly linked to the target market and its wants and needs. Promotion brings together the target market and the product/service by making the former fully aware of the latter and all its desirable features and benefits. Price is an attraction or stimulus that brings the target market and product/service even more closely together than promotion alone can accomplish. Promotion primed the target market for a possible purchase of the product/service, but then price revealed to the target market that a purchase would be a good value. Finally, the product/service must be distributed so its availability is very convenient for the individuals in the target market. The more these five elements are strongly integrated with one another, the more synergistic the marketing strategy will be.

Glacier Nursery created a synergistic marketing strategy; the New Product Showcase did not.

Synergistic Marketing Strategies: Two Outstanding Examples

Every small new business owner should be fully knowledgeable about synergistic marketing strategies. Because they typically have far fewer resources than the average business owner, it is critically important for all small new business owners to understand the concept of synergy in marketing strategies and how to create synergy when developing the marketing strategies they will use for their small new businesses.

As reported in Chapter 1, I have been researching successful and unsuccessful marketing strategies for well over thirty years. Of the many marketing strategies I have studied, there are two that are by far the very best examples of how a business can go about creating synergy in its marketing strategy. If you are thinking of starting a small new business, you will want to employ synergy in the marketing strategy you use for your new business. To do so, you will want to fully understand the following two examples and use them to guide your efforts when developing your own marketing strategy.

Whenever young, male, college graduates gather to watch a sporting event on television these days, beer is the liquid refreshment of choice. But not just any beer! Most likely the beer of choice will be a *light* beer. But that would not have been possible in the early 1970s, because there were no light beers on the market at that time.

When Miller Lite beer was introduced in 1975, it caused a tremendous change in beer consumption preferences in the United States. Some 30 years later, in the early 2000s, *three of the top four beer brands in the United States were light beers*. Think of it: From no light beer brands at all, to three of the top four in approximately thirty years! This huge change in beer preference almost certainly occurred thanks to the successful introduction of Miller Lite. At least part of the reason for that success was that Miller Brewing Company used a very synergistic marketing strategy to introduce its light beer.

MILLER LITE BEER

In the early 1970s the Miller Brewing Company was a relatively small brewer, the number seven brewer in the U.S. beer industry. Their sales were flat while beer industry sales were growing at 5–7 percent a year. Their only product was Miller High Life, which was distributed nationally and was available in most taverns and liquor stores. But Miller High Life was consumed mostly by women, who typically did not drink much beer.

In 1975, to improve their position in the beer market, the Miller Brewing Company introduced Miller Lite, a low-calorie beer. It was not the first low-calorie beer to be introduced. However, all of the previously introduced low-calorie beers had either failed or barely survived. Miller Lite, on the other hand, proved to be an outstanding success, thanks to a very synergistic marketing strategy.

Miller's strategy targeted the heaviest of beer drinkers: males aged 21–30 who were college graduates or blue-collar workers. This group was very sports oriented. Many of them had played sports in their younger days and fantasized of gaining some kind of sports fame, either in high school or college or even professionally. Being heavy beer drinkers, almost all of them tended to be overweight and either wanted to lose weight or avoid putting on more weight.

Miller's market research showed that these beer drinkers thought their new beer, Miller Lite, tasted good and seemed less filling than other beers. Consequently, Miller Lite was differentiated from other beers with the theme of "Tastes Great! Less Filling." Although the beer had one-third fewer calories than other popular beers, that feature was not given the main emphasis in advertisements. This was because Miller Lite's managers believed their target market might not have considered it a "macho" thing to be drinking a low-calorie beer.

Miller Lite used television commercials that featured adult males in a friendly tavern scene that involved sports in some way. Two well-known sports personalities—easily recognized by the target market, and probably also admired by them—would be arguing in a friendly but competitive manner about why they liked Miller Lite. One personality liked Miller Lite because it "Tastes Great!"; the other liked it because it was "Less Filling." The arguing scene usually ended in a humorous manner.

Miller Lite's strategy clearly matched its product's characteristics to the needs of its target market. It used television commercials that employed several symbols (taverns, sports activities, sports personalities) familiar to and liked by its target market. Those television commercials clearly communicated the product's benefits to the beer drinkers Miller was trying to attract. The commercials themselves were heavily used during telecasts of sporting events the target market most certainly would be watching. Miller Lite was also well promoted in taverns. To create good value, it was priced comparable to the leading premium brands of beer.[4]

Miller Lite's marketing strategy was synergistic in a number of ways.

- This new brand of beer was developed for a specific market segment whose wants and needs were not being satisfied by current beer brands.
- Miller Lite's main message ("Tastes Great! Less Filling") was very short and very clear, easily understood and appealing to the target market.

- Television commercials used personalities and symbols that the target market recognized and looked upon most favorably.
- The bars and taverns used in the commercials echoed the favorite hangouts of the target market.
- To convey Miller Lite's main message, commercials employed both humor and a sense of competition, two characteristics greatly appreciated by the fun-loving target market.
- Commercials were aired primarily on telecasts of sporting events that the target market was very likely to be watching.
- Miller sales personnel promoted the new brand extensively in bars and taverns frequented by the target market.

Miller Lite created a new product category for the beer industry, and the brand essentially had a monopoly among adult males who began consuming a light beer. This monopoly continued for some six to eight years and helped the Miller Brewing Company become the second largest brewery in the United States. And, as noted above, the introduction of Miller Lite began the trend of American beer drinkers switching to light beers.

The second example of a very synergistic marketing strategy involved women's hosiery. In the 1960s and before, women could only purchase good-quality hosiery in department stores and women's specialty stores. Because hosiery was sold in many sizes and colors, a sales clerk, always a woman, would be behind the counter to help a customer select the style and color she wanted. Most such hosiery was moderately or high priced.

Today women can buy hosiery almost anywhere: in grocery stores, in supermarkets, in drug stores, in convenience stores, and in still other outlets. *In a relatively short period of time, a completely new and dominant channel of distribution was created for women's hosiery.* This revolution in the marketing of women's hosiery was brought about by the Hanes Company when it introduced the now famous L'eggs brand. And like the Miller Brewing Company, they did it using a very synergetic marketing strategy.

L'EGGS

In the 1950s and 1960s more and more women began working full-time, even after getting married and having children. Through their market research, the Hanes Company, the smallest of the three main suppliers of women's hosiery, found that some of these working women were able to buy store-brand hosiery in their supermarkets while shopping for groceries. This was much more convenient than making a special trip to a department store or a woman's specialty store, the only other places hosiery was typically sold. However, the Hanes Company noted that the women found the store-brand hosiery generally of poor quality, and perhaps even more upsetting, often unavailable in their supermarkets when they needed a new pair.

The Hanes Company believed the large and growing market of working women would welcome a reliable supply of reasonably priced, quality hosiery in their favorite supermarket or drugstore. In 1970 they introduced L'eggs, a line of good quality hosiery priced at $.99 a pair, which was noticeably cheaper than the hosiery sold in department stores and women's specialty stores. Offered in a number of colors, L'eggs was a one-size-fits-all type of hosiery (actually it fit about 70–80% of all women). A woman shopping for hosiery in a supermarket or drugstore would now have a very good chance of finding at least one pair of L'eggs to meet her needs.

The hosiery traditionally sold in department and women's specialty stores was attractively presented in see-through packaging. The L'eggs hosiery, on the other hand, had a very wrinkled, crinkly look when laid out on a flat surface. Its appearance could honestly be described as unattractive, even ugly! If seen in that manner, it was very unlikely that any woman would buy a pair of L'eggs. This meant that the product needed a package to hide its ugliness. It also needed a name. Hanes selected a name that suggested the product's usage, but they very creatively and synergistically spelled the name L'eggs. To add to that name-usage synergy, they packaged the unattractive-looking product in a plastic, egg-shaped container to create a name-usage-package synergy. Hanes used television commercials on programs viewed by working women to inform them that "Our L'eggs Fit Your Legs," and that the product was available in drugstores and supermarkets where they did their shopping. In a very short period of time, women throughout the United States became informed about this new product, its name, what it was, and the package it came in. And they bought it frequently.

Hanes's marketing strategy also included some incentives to get supermarkets and drugstores to display a product they had not carried before. The one-size-fits-all characteristic meant that retailers—and Hanes as well—would not have to carry inventories of each hosiery size. This smaller inventory requirement allowed Hanes to deliver L'eggs hosiery directly to retailers in Hanes trucks, thus assuring the retailers that they would always have a good supply for their women customers. Hanes also used a vertical, free-standing display that could be placed at end-of-aisle locations, or elsewhere. Again, thanks to the one-size-fits-all feature and the smaller inventory requirements, the free-standing display did not have to be very big. And because it did not take up much floor space, Hanes did not have to ask retailers to give up floor space or shelf space they were allocating to other profitable products. With L'eggs priced less expensively than hosiery sold in traditional stores, women found the product to be a good value. But Hanes also made certain that retailers found the product to be profitable. They did this by selling the product on consignment. This meant the retailers never owned, or paid for, the L'eggs products being sold in their stores. So they did not have any inventory costs associated with the product. When a woman paid for her L'eggs purchases at the checkout cashier, the retailer would subtract his margin from the price being paid and send the balance to Hanes. So, except for the floor space needed for the L'eggs free-standing display, retailers had no investment in the product. Yet L'eggs were well advertised and reasonably priced, and women bought them in large quantities. This strategy was very profitable for retailers, and it made them very happy to carry L'eggs.[5]

Like Miller Lite's marketing strategy, L'eggs's strategy was also one of the most outstanding examples of a synergistic marketing strategy. Look at how the elements fit together and supported one another:

- Working women were looking for a good quality product at a value price.
- Supermarkets and drugstores provided very convenient distribution for working women who were pressed for time.
- The marketing strategy created a synergy between the product, its name, what the product was used for, and the shape of the package.
- Hanes's promotion informed the target market of product usage characteristics and distribution availability.
- L'eggs's one-size-fits-all characteristic resulted in smaller inventories, which allowed for the direct distribution to stores, the use of the free-standing displays, and the use of consignment pricing for the retailers.
- The use of consignment pricing and free-standing displays resulted in retailers enjoying a very large return on investment for carrying L'eggs.

ACHIEVING SCREENING CONDITION I

If you want your small new business to have a reasonable chance of surviving its launch period, you must be certain that your marketing strategy is both complete and synergistic. To achieve those two qualities, it must include the five characteristics presented on pages 25–26. The remainder of this chapter addresses each of those characteristics.

1. Target Market Identification
2. Product Design or Differentiation
3. Persuasive Promotion
4. Price to Create Good Value
5. Convenient Distribution

In each of the following five discussions, I describe marketing strategies that achieved the characteristic being discussed. This will serve to illustrate *the kinds of things you must include in your marketing strategy if it is to be both complete and synergistic.*

In each of the following discussions I also present several examples of marketing strategies that did not achieve the particular characteristic being discussed. Those examples serve to demonstrate some of the problems, difficulties, and mistakes that people encountered or made when trying to create complete and synergistic marketing strategies for their small new businesses. You must be made aware of these kinds of problems, difficulties, and mistakes, and *you must avoid them when designing a marketing strategy for your new business.*

1. Identify a Target Market Whose Needs You Can Satisfy More Effectively Than Any Competitor

The foregoing descriptions of Miller Lite beer, L'eggs hosiery, and Glacier Nursery pointed out that each had a very clearly defined business or consumer segment that was being targeted. Furthermore, each one of those targeted segments was not being fully served by its current suppliers. In contrast, the New Products Showcase did not target anyone or anything in particular. Like the first three of these four examples, you must identify a target market whose needs you can satisfy more effectively than any competitor. This is the first of the five characteristics your marketing strategy must display if it is to be both complete and synergistic.

There are two parties of great importance in this characteristic: the members of the target market, and the competitor(s) pursuing them. Each deserves your most serious attention. If your small new business is to succeed, it must have a target market that has wants and needs that currently are not being fully satisfied by any competitor. You do not want to pick a target market that is very satisfied with its current supplier(s). It will be almost impossible to persuade the individuals in that market to abandon suppliers who are serving them well. Nor do you want a target market that is reasonably satisfied with its suppliers. Most individuals in such a market are unlikely to switch suppliers, and those that will switch may take their time making up their minds to do so. There is a good chance your new business will deplete all its financial resources long before they make such a switch.

On the other hand, you will greatly enhance your new business's chances of success by identifying a target market whose individuals are being poorly served by their current suppliers—or not being served at all. Think of the retail garden centers in Montana that could not get tree and shrub deliveries throughout the growing season, or the working women who could not find decent hosiery in the supermarkets where they did their shopping. Such target market individuals are dissatisfied and are likely to welcome with open arms any new supplier who can serve them better. If your new business can be that new supplier, this component of your marketing strategy will be making a solid contribution to your new business's potential success.

The second main player in the target market is the competition. When you have selected your target market, you will also have selected your competitors—those firms that are already active in your target market. You should avoid selecting a market segment if there are several strong companies already pursuing that segment. Rather, select as your target a market segment that is only being poorly served by one or two small firms, or that is not being served at all. If your small new business can avoid strong competitors, this component of your marketing strategy will give your business a much greater chance of surviving long enough to begin generating a self-sustaining sales revenue stream.

To repeat: (1) select a target market whose needs are currently being poorly served and which your new business can serve very well, and (2) select a target market in which your new business will encounter only small or weak competitors or, better still, no competitors at all.

Examples

You have already seen three examples of marketing strategies whose target market selection greatly contributed to the new business's good fortune: Miller Lite beer, Hanes's L'eggs hosiery, and Glacier Nursery.

The Miller Brewing Company discovered that heavy beer drinkers did not want to give up drinking beer, but they also did not want to put on more weight. This was a target market that was in some way not being satisfied by any of the beer brands then currently available. Moreover, Miller noticed that no competing brewer was making serious attempts to address the dissatisfaction of this heavy beer-drinking market segment.

As its target market, Hanes selected working women who wanted the convenience of buying good-quality hosiery in grocery and drug stores where they regularly shopped. This target market was not currently being served with the level of convenience and service it desired. Also, supermarkets and drugstores were not being pursued by any of Hanes's competitors, even though those retailers had a long history of welcoming profitable new products. Hanes saw the situation as an opportunity worth exploiting, and they did.

Glacier Nursery selected retail garden centers in Montana as its target market. Those garden centers were not receiving regular delivery service throughout the growing season from their suppliers, all of which were located out-of-state. This was an underserved target market, and Glacier Nursery had no direct competitors in its home state of Montana. Its only competitors were located out-of-state. Because of the great distances between themselves and Montana's garden centers, those competitors were not anxious to provide regular delivery services to them, especially for smaller-size orders after the peak spring selling season.

Miller Lite, L'eggs, and Glacier Nursery each identified a target market that was not being fully satisfied by its current supplier. An added attraction of each of those markets was that no established competitors were addressing its dissatisfactions.

Other Marketing Strategies That Successfully Achieved Characteristic 1

Now lets look at some other small new businesses that made target market selections that contributed very beneficially to their overall strategies. Wallace Leyshon started Appliance Control Technologies, Inc for the purpose of supplying electronic controls to U.S. manufacturers of mid-price kitchen and laundry appliances.[6] Those companies were still using the traditional electro-mechanical control buttons, knobs, and switches people turned or pushed when making their appliances work. However, the trend among appliance manufacturers was to replace their electro-mechanical controls with electronic controls when the latter became price competitive with the former. But no supplier was offering these manufacturers inexpensive electronic controls. There were fewer than one hundred such manufacturers, and Leyshon was in contact with many of them to determine their needs. Based on what he learned from those companies, he believed that Appliance Control Technologies, Inc. could be the first to manufacture electronic controls cheaply enough to successfully break into the mid-price appliance market.

Robert Bennett noticed that students living in college dormitories often used more electrical appliances than their room's electrical wiring could accommodate. Typically, the result was a fuse being blown or a circuit breaker being tripped. Bennett formed a company to design and market a miniaturized microwave oven-freezer-refrigerator combination that could run on a single electrical cord plugged into an ordinary electrical outlet, and not blow a fuse or trip a circuit breaker.[7] The product was named the MicroFridge. At the time there was no product on the market that offered the features of a combined microwave oven-freezer-refrigerator. College dormitories were chosen as the primary target market for MicroFridge because a vast majority of college students used hot plates in their rooms. Budget motels were another attractive market for the MicroFridge. Almost 80 percent of the guests at a nationwide budget motel chain said they would be willing to pay an extra $3 a night to have a MicroFridge in their rooms. Both target markets were very easy to identify and contact, and no competitor was actively pursuing them.

What You Should Do

There are four very useful guidelines to follow concerning target market selection when designing the marketing strategy for your small new business. (1) Identify a target market whose needs your new business can satisfy more effectively than any competitor. (2) Be absolutely certain that your marketing strategy has identified a target market that is being poorly served, or not being served at all. Glacier Nursery, Appliance Control Technologies, Inc., and MicroFridge, Inc. are good examples of these first two target market selection guidelines. (3) Your target market should be easy to identify and contact. Montana garden centers, manufacturers of mid-price appliances, and college dormitories and budget motels are all target markets that satisfy these conditions. (4) Select a target market where you will not encounter strong competitors. Wallace Leyshon and Robert Bennett did not face direct competitors when they started their new businesses.

Marketing Strategies That Did Not Achieve Characteristic 1

There are at least three mistakes that small new business owners often make regarding their selection of a target market.

(1) Their new business did not identify a target market it could serve.
(2) Their target market did not want or need the product they offered.
(3) Their target market was not easy to contact.

(1) Their New Business Did Not Identify a Target Market It Could Serve

Early in this chapter we saw that the New Products Showcase did not have a defined target market. Another very clear instance of poor target market identification comes from the beginnings of Neurogen Laboratories, Inc., created by Michael Kuperstein to design computer software that performed much like the human brain. Kuperstein tried to develop four or five different products before he eventually turned his attention to the problem of computer recognition of human handwriting. The company developed a product that could read handwritten digits if they were not touching one another. Kuperstein thought that the potential applications for the machine might include reading handwritten numbers on checks; miscellaneous business, medical, and government printed forms; addressed mail envelopes; and credit card slips. But which application should the company pursue? According to the company's vice president of sales: "We figured if I showed this to enough end users, we'd find out where the demand was. We wanted the market to tell us where to sell. Then we'd react."[8] The lack of a specific target market to pursue aggressively resulted in delays that noticeably extended Neurogen's launch period and put severe financial pressures on the company.

(2) Their Target Market Did Not Want or Need the Product They Offered

Entrepreneurs select target markets they believe will buy the products or services they are offer, but often this decision is based more on gut feeling than on accurate market knowledge. The vast majority of those new businesses end in failure.

For example, Alan Robbins started the Plastic Lumber Company to recycle used plastic into automobile speed bumps and parking lot car stops, mailbox posts, picnic tables, and still other products where recycled plastic might replace the traditional material used. He thought there was a huge market for such products because society was becoming more environmentally conscious. In Robbin's eyes, people were ready to accept the use of plastic lumber because doing so would help solve the problem of what to do with all the waste plastic the economy was generating. Robbins figured that the easiest place to sell plastic products would be universities, because they would probably take an enlightened approach to helping improve the environment. And he also thought it would be easy to sell to municipalities because of their concerns about easing the landfill shortage problem facing almost all communities. He believed these markets would appreciate plastic lumber's durability—lasting up to twice as long as wood—and be willing, therefore, to pay a little more for that benefit. Much to his disappointment, those markets proved to be more cost conscious than environment friendly. Robbins started out with the idea that he would "let his market tell him what his sales, positioning, and pricing strategy should be. Unfortunately, the market is speaking with about as much clarity as was heard from the tower of Babel."[9]

(3) Their Target Market Was Not Easy to Contact

Some new businesses are started with the hope that they will attract the attention of a target market of individuals who have a certain kind of attitude. Very often such individuals do exist, but they may not be easy to identify and contact. Under such circumstances, the new businesses are likely to encounter difficulties trying to promote their products or services to those target markets.

David Fokos started Icon Acoustics, Inc. to manufacture high-end audio speakers for people who "would rather buy a new set of speakers than eat."[10] Carolyne Greene founded F.R.O.Y.D., Inc. to market a different kind of doll that would have character and personality. The doll "would encourage children from ages 5 to 13 to achieve their dreams."[11] Quite likely there are individuals similar to those identified by Fokos and Greene, but it is not clear how many there are, who they are, where they are, and how to reach them. When a new business's target market is only vaguely defined, if at all, it becomes much more difficult to design a complete and synergistic marketing strategy. Each of the last four new businesses discussed in this section enjoyed no success at all as they were originally conceived. Three of them were unable to begin generating significant sales volumes, while the fourth was able to survive and to begin enjoying some success, but only after a serious retrenching led to a completely new strategic approach.

Mistakes You Should Avoid

Small new business owners often handicap themselves severely because of the target market selection mistakes they make. There are at least three such mistakes. (1) They do not carefully identify and analyze their target markets and the competition they will encounter in those markets. (2) They select target markets that really do not need or want their product or service offerings. (3) They select attitude-based target markets that are difficult and/or costly to contact. Your marketing strategy should avoid making these kinds of mistakes.

The following is a *summary of guidelines and warnings associated with target market identification*.

THE ONE GUIDELINE YOUR MARKETING STRATEGY MUST SATISFY

Guideline 1a. Identify a target market whose needs your new business can satisfy more effectively than any competitor.

VERY SUPPORTIVE GUIDELINES YOUR MARKETING STRATEGY SHOULD STRIVE TO SATISFY

Guideline 1b. Identify a target market that is being poorly served, or not being served at all.

Guideline 1c. Identify a target market that is easy to describe and contact.

Guideline 1d. Identify a target market where your new business will not encounter strong competitors.

WARNINGS OF THINGS YOUR MARKETING STRATEGY SHOULD AVOID

Warning 1a. Avoid not carefully identifying and analyzing your target market and the competition you will encounter in that target market.

Warning 1b. Avoid selecting a target market that really does not want or need your product/service offering.

Warning 1c. Avoid selecting an attitude-based target market that is difficult and/or costly to contact.

---

2. Design Your Product to Appeal to Your Target Market

If your marketing strategy achieves characteristic 1, your small new business will have identified a target market that is being underserved or poorly served. The individuals constituting that market are dissatisfied with current suppliers and are willing to switch if someone better comes along. They have the welcome mat out for you, and you must make it your business to deliver the satisfaction they are looking for. That is characteristic 2—making your offering more appealing to your target market than any competitor's.

Notice that just knowing the target market is dissatisfied is not enough to assure success. If you want your marketing strategy to satisfy characteristic 2, you must also be very knowledgeable about your competitors' offerings, their strengths and weaknesses, and the specific reasons for the target market's dissatisfaction. Then you and your small new business must find a way to transform that knowledge into a design that will make your product/service different from those of competitors' in ways that are very important to your target market. You want the individuals in your target market to look upon your product/service as unique, as something that was specially designed for their wants and needs, as something they can get from no one but you. In short, you have to offer them something so attractive that they have a very good reason to switch suppliers. This is what your small new business has to do if you hope to achieve characteristic 2.

A Note on "Product/Service"

For simplification in presentation, throughout the remainder of the book, instead of referring to "product/service" I will generally employ the simple term "product," but I will use that term to mean (1) a product only (e.g., a tube of toothpaste), or (2) a product which includes a service component with it (e.g., a fast food item), or (3) a pure service (e.g., a haircut).

Examples

So how did our three familiar examples of Miller Lite beer, L'eggs hosiery, and Glacier Nursery achieve characteristic 2 in their marketing strategies? When the Miller Brewing Company introduced Miller Lite beer, there was no competitor producing a low-calorie beer that "tasted great and was less filling," and this was a combination of beer benefits that the target market found very desirable. Before the introduction of L'eggs, when working women did find hosiery in their favorite supermarkets and drugstores, they greatly appreciated the convenience. But such hosiery was rarely available, and then typically of only rather poor quality. Hanes exploited this dissatisfaction by introducing L'eggs hosiery, which women found to be of good quality at a reasonable price, and always available in convenient locations—their favorite supermarkets and drug stores. Before Brad Brown started Glacier Nursery, the only trees and shrubs Montana garden centers could get were grown out of state. Brown's trees and shrubs were grown in Montana, and he cultivated them to be much hardier than those grown out of state. He believed Montana garden centers would prize his trees and shrubs for their hardiness, and greatly appreciate the all-season-long delivery service he would provide, which was not available from out-of-state nurseries. And he was right on both counts.

Other Marketing Strategies That Successfully Achieved Characteristic 2

Wallace Leyshon started Appliance Control Technologies, Inc. to sell electronic control devices to manufacturers of mid-price appliances.[12] Those manufacturers were still using electro-mechanical knobs, buttons, and switches to control their appliances, as they were cheaper than electronic controls. Because different appliances and different models of the same appliance used different controls, manufacturers had to maintain large and costly inventories of those controls. A key element in Leyshon's strategy to enter the market with electronic controls was to use the same basic parts for different models of the same appliance, and even for completely different appliances. Only the controlling software would be different from model to model and appliance to appliance. By using standardized parts, appliance manufacturers could significantly reduce overall manufacturing costs because the standardized parts would greatly reduce the inventory of controls they had to maintain. The electronic controls also allowed the manufacturers to offer their customers higher quality and more modern appliances. As a result, the manufacturers were very much attracted to Leyshon's product differentiation.

We saw that Robert Bennett designed his MicroFridge (a combined microwave oven-freezer-refrigerator) to operate with a single electrical cord plugged into an ordinary household electrical outlet without blowing a fuse or tripping a circuit breaker.[13] College students in their dormitories would find this appliance very convenient and useful. And guests in budget motels could economize even more by not having to eat all their meals in restaurants if a MicroFridge were available to them in their rooms.

The MicroFridge could satisfy the needs of both of these markets, and no other product like it was available at the time.

The above product differentiation examples were based on a different kind of beer, a different kind of hosiery, a different kind of appliance control, a different kind of combination electrical appliance, as well as hardier trees and shrubs. Each was designed to appeal to a specific target market's needs. As illustrated by those examples, the range of differentiated products that might become the basis of a successful new business can be very broad.

What You Should Do

The entrepreneurs noted above first made themselves very familiar with the wants and needs of their respective target markets. They then carefully analyzed the competitors' products to determine how those offerings were not serving their respective target markets as well as might be possible. Based on that knowledge, they differentiated their products to make them more appealing to the individuals in their target markets than the products offered by competitors. How did they do that? Compared with the competitors' products, their products offered better quality and/or important new features and benefits and/or greater convenience and/or better value. In the above examples, the improved offerings were based on one or more of the following: (1) better quality (hardier trees); (2) new features that provided important new benefits (Miller Lite, MicroFridge); (3) greater convenience (L'eggs, MicroFridge); or (4) better value (electronic appliance controls). When you are creating a marketing strategy for your new business and are attempting to satisfy characteristic 2, it is most important that the product improvements you are offering will be easily recognized and understood, and greatly appreciated by the target market.

Marketing Strategies That Did Not Achieve Characteristic 2

In my research I found that between one-fourth and one-half of all new businesses did not offer their target markets a product that was more appealing than what was already available. How can someone starting a new business make such a mistake? The answer, it seems, is that entrepreneurs usually become overly enthusiastic about their product offerings. Often this causes them to be quite unrealistic when they somehow arrive at their conclusions that their target markets will find their products to be wonderfully differentiated compared with established competitors' products. Whatever the reasons for their misguided enthusiasm, there are at least at least four types of product differentiation mistakes that small new business owners make.

(1) Offering a differentiated product for which there is little or no demand, or at least much less demand than was expected.

(2) Offering a product that is of average quality, or less.

(3) Offering a quality product that the target market does not feel is very differentiated.

(4) Offering a differentiated product that requires installation—a form of service—but not providing that installation service.

(1) The Product Had Less Demand Than Was Expected

Theis Rice and Frank Mitchell got the idea of radio broadcasting the ongoing events at a professional golf tournament to the spectators attending the tournament, and they started SportsBand Network.[14] The only action spectators at a golf tournament know about is what they see with their own eyes. SportsBand would rent them a small radio for five dollars a day, and with it they would hear a real-time broadcast of the action occurring throughout the golf course. While the concept of radio broadcasting the events of a golf tournament seemed very appealing in general, rentals of the radios to tournament spectators were much slower than expected. Even price reductions and price promotions did not result in the expected increases in rental revenues.

Thomas Manning started Buddy Systems, Inc. to market a computer-based system that could monitor the important health signs of patients who had been allowed to go home after having had major medical procedures in a hospital.[15] Recently released hospital patients could easily use the system to transmit via telephone their blood pressure, pulse rate, heartbeat, etc. to appropriate medical personnel, who would study the data to make an evaluation of the patient's improving health. Manning believed that the system would help to significantly reduce the costs of post-operative health care by allowing patients to leave the hospital early and by reducing the frequency with which visiting nurses would have to see them in their homes. Although the system performed very well technically, many doctors proved unwilling to make decisions regarding their patients' health without first seeing them in person. Without doctors' support for the system, home-care organizations were also reluctant to use the system to monitor the health signs of the patients under their care.

Clearly, both of these products were differentiated, but target market individuals did not find the differentiation appealing enough to make these two new businesses profitable.

(2) The Product Was of Average Quality, or Less

Barbara Lamont founded Crescent City Communications, Inc. to operate an independent television station in New Orleans, a city that was already being served by three network stations and two strong independent stations.[16] All were well established in the market. Lamont's programming selection was based on minimal cost, on what was available and cheap. It was not guided by any attempt to offer differentiated programming that would attract a specific segment of the New Orleans market that was not currently being well served by the five established stations. Consequently, the station's audience remained small and it was unable to attract enough advertisers to become profitable.

(3) The Product Was Not Sufficiently Differentiated

To have a reasonable chance of succeeding, a new business's product should be designed or differentiated to be more appealing than competitors' products. Unfortunately, a common error among people starting new businesses is believing their product is much more special than it actually is in the eyes of the intended market.

Carolyne Greene got the idea for a different kind of doll for children aged 5–13, so she started F.R.O.Y.D., Inc. to develop and market "FROYD," a large doll with character and personality. FROYD was short "for the reality of your dreams." Each child that received a FROYD doll would be encouraged to send in her or his dream on a post card to "Dream Team Headquarters." They would then receive a "Dream Come True" poster and some "Official Yellow Dream Stickers." Whenever a child accomplished another goal, she or he was to apply one of the stickers to the poster. Major toy makers showed no interest in Greene's doll, probably because fifty large dolls were already competing in the market. The editor of *Toy & Hobby World Magazine* did not see Greene's doll as being very differentiated.

> The best friend concept is not, in my estimation, unique. Almost every toy company has a best friend toy. So I don't think it's a good point of differentiation. The rest of the concept, the acronyms and the dream fulfillment also are not points of differentiation.[17]

David Fokos started Icon Acoustics, Inc. to manufacture high quality audio speakers for people who were passionate high-fidelity music fans.[18] Fokos's speakers were made with very high-quality components and constructed by hand to achieve a high level of craftsmanship. The speakers, sad to say, faced at least three factors complicating their entry into the market. Only about 10 percent of the audio market purchased such high priced equipment, so Fokos was pursuing a rather small segment of the total market. But to make matters worse, there were more than two hundred speaker companies already competing for that high-priced market. In addition, Fokos did not identify how his speakers would be more appealing to audiophiles than the other two hundred speakers going after the same market.

Neither of these two new businesses enjoyed any success, and there can be no doubt that their lack of a truly differentiated product was a major contribution to those outcomes.

(4) The Product Required Installation, but Installation Service Was Not Provided

From his chicken farming background, Randy Wise had learned that chickens wearing red contact lenses demonstrated three desirable characteristics: they were less cannibalistic; they ate less food; and they increased their egg production. These three changes in chicken behavior had the potential of helping egg farmers quadruple their profit margins. Believing that he was onto a very lucrative business opportunity, Wise incorporated Animalens, Inc. to manufacture red contact lenses for chickens and market them to large egg farmers in the United States. He promoted the lenses at large poultry trade shows, in advertisements in poultry magazines, and through a direct mail campaign to large egg farmers. The farmers did not respond favorably to the marketing efforts of Animalens because, among other things, they were skeptical about the costs and difficulties of installing the lenses into the eyes of their chickens. A poultry specialist noted:

> Wise will have to provide more detail about the installation. Two people installing 1,200 pairs a day may seem fast to him, but it sounds like a snail's pace to me, particularly when you're talking about chicken houses with 100,000 chickens. It means you need about twenty people doing nothing but putting in lenses for around eight days straight. Even if the labor cost only works out to $.10 a chicken, not every rancher has access to that kind of manpower.[19]

This new business had a very differentiated product to offer its target market. Unfortunately, it required an installation activity that the target market found too burdensome to undertake.

Mistakes You Should Avoid

The foregoing examples illustrate several product differentiation mistakes you want to avoid when starting your new business. The following suggestions will help you do so. (1) Make certain your target market wants and needs the differentiated product your business will be offering. Just because *you think* it is a good idea does not necessarily mean your target market will feel the same way. (2) Critically compare your product against established competitors' products to assure yourself that its quality is at least as good—but preferably noticeably better. (3) Do not just assume the target market will consider your product to be differentiated in an important way. Find a way to let them try your product so you can confirm your beliefs. (4) If your product requires installation that is not idiot proof, either provide that service yourself or arrange for a third party to do it.

The following is a *summary of guidelines and warnings associated with designing your product to appeal to your target market.*

YOUR MARKETING STRATEGY MUST SATISFY AT LEAST ONE OF THESE GUIDELINES

Guideline 2a. Design or differentiate your product so it is more appealing to the individuals in your target market than the products offered by competitors.

Guideline 2b. Your product should provide better quality and/or important new features and benefits and/or greater convenience and/or better value than your competitors' offerings.

WARNINGS OF THINGS YOU SHOULD AVOID

Warning 2a. Avoid supposing that your target market will want your differentiated product because you think it is a good idea.

Warning 2b. Avoid not making a critical comparison of the strengths/advantages and weaknesses/disadvantages of your product versus competitors' products.

Warning 2c. Avoid not confirming through testing and research that your target market actually believes that your product is different in an important way.

Warning 2d. Avoid thinking that the customer will install your product or arrange for someone else to install it.

---

3. Persuasively Promote to Your Target Market

If the marketing strategy you have created satisfies characteristics 1 and 2, you have made a good start on the road to a successful new business. You have selected a target market whose needs currently are not being fully satisfied by any competitor, and you are designing your new business to satisfy those needs more effectively than any competitor. You have also differentiated your product so as to make it more appealing to that target market than any competing product already available in the marketplace. As I say, you have made a good start, but you still have a long way to go.

Satisfying characteristics 1 and 2 is not going to result in a successful new business if you do not also persuade potential customers to buy your product. Do not lose sight of the fact that potential customers are already buying and using a competitor's product, and deriving at least some satisfaction from doing so. Also do not forget that your potential customers have never heard of you, your company, and your product. Even if they somehow have heard of your existence, they still would be taking a risk if they stop buying from their old supplier and instead start buying from you. People need a very good reason to switch suppliers, and your new business has to give them one. This means that you must promote your product in such a way that the individuals in your target market understand and appreciate how it will satisfy their needs better than competitors' offerings. That is characteristic 3, and your marketing strategy must achieve it if you want people to actually buy your product.

What does your new business have to do to achieve characteristic 3? In its communications with its potential customers, your marketing strategy must effectively address the following three questions.

What will your promotions say to the target market about your product?
How will your promotions say it?
What media will your promotions use to reach the individuals in your target market?

How you answer these three questions will determine how effectively and persuasively your new business will communicate your product's features, benefits, and advantages to potential customers.

Examples

It will be very helpful if we look carefully at how Miller Lite answered the above three questions. What did the Miller Lite promotions say to its target market? Commercials told heavy beer drinkers that Miller Lite "Tastes great, and is less filling," and that it "had a third less calories." This message is short and to the point, very clear, and simple to understand. These were benefits and advantages that target market individuals wanted and no other beer could claim to have. Consider question two. How did the promotions say what they had to say? In its commercials, Miller Lite used symbols with which the target market was very familiar— especially the warm friendly taverns and well-known former professional athletes, but also the competitive and humorous arguments that were part of most commercials. The use of these familiar and friendly symbols greatly contributed to the easy understanding and acceptance of the Miller Lite message by their target market. What media carried the promotions? Miller Lite's target market consisted of ardent sports enthusiasts who spent many hours watching sporting events on television. Miller made heavy use of those televised sporting events to bring their commercial messages to their target market.

When the Hanes company introduced its innovative L'eggs hosiery, its television commercials not only told women that there was now a new brand of hosiery available to them, but also that "Our L'eggs fit your legs." The selection and spelling (L'eggs) of the product's name effectively communicated how the product was used, and the combination of creative name spelling and the shape of the product's packaging was extremely attention-getting, which greatly contributed to working women quickly becoming well informed about the product's availability. Television commercials also informed viewers that L'eggs were value priced and conveniently available where they regularly shopped for most of their groceries and other household products. These were benefits that working women easily understood and appreciated. The commercials appeared on prime time network television programs heavily watched by working women. These were the same programs that showed commercials for many of the grocery, drug and household products working women regularly purchased in supermarkets and drugstores.

How did Glacier Nursery answer the three promotion questions? Brad Brown was in frequent personal contact with all of the 40–50 garden center operators in Montana, directly promoting the hardiness and superior quality of his Montana-grown plants as well as his value pricing. In support of this message, every spring he sent free samples of some of his plants to a number of Montana's garden centers. Glacier Nursery also provided delivery services throughout the growing season. These were very welcome benefits that were not available from out-of-state nurseries.

When designing your new business's promotional activities, it will be very helpful if you remember how these three new businesses answered the three promotional questions listed above. You must be certain that your promotional activities effectively address each of those questions.

Other Marketing Strategies That Successfully Achieved Characteristic 3

Wallace Leyshon of Appliance Control Technologies, Inc. was in personal contact with the several dozens of manufacturers of mid-price kitchen and laundry appliances.[20] He communicated three simple messages about his company's products: His company's electronic controls were less expensive than the electro-mechanical controls the manufacturers currently used; his electronic controls would result in an improved final product; and thanks to the use of standardized parts for different models of the same appliance and even for different appliances, the appliance manufacturers would realize cost savings through reduced inventory expense. Each of these ideas had attractive benefits in the eyes of the target market.

College dormitories and budget motels were Robert Bennett's target markets for the miniaturized microwave oven-freezer-refrigerator combination he called the MicroFridge.[21] He used direct personal selling with college authorities to make them aware of the MicroFridge's unique characteristics (i.e., it was specially designed for small living quarters). Direct mail campaigns were used to inform budget motel operators that they could raise their daily room rates if those rooms offered their guests the convenience and the savings associated with a MicroFridge. The mailings also informed the motel operators that they could add to their revenues by selling their guests packaged frozen foods and snacks that could be stored in and/or prepared by a MicroFridge. Bennett's communications clearly presented the MicroFridge's advantages to both of those target markets.

What You Should Do

It is absolutely essential that you inform your target market of your existence and your unique product offering. You have to give the individual members of your target market very good reasons to drop their current supplier and to become your customer. To do so, your communications with them must address three questions: (1) What should you say to your target market so they know your product offering will be more satisfying than any competitor's? Make it as short and simple as possible, but also very important and meaningful. (2) How should you say what you have to say; that is, what is the most effective way to present your message? Keep in mind how Miller Lite use symbols that their target market recognized and strongly embraced. (3) What is the most efficient and effective media to use to reach your target market? The foregoing examples—Miller Lite beer, L'eggs hosiery, Glacier Nursery, Appliance Control Technologies, and MicroFridge—are good illustrations of how successful marketing strategies can succeed in satisfying characteristic 3 with a variety of media. The key is to find the one(s) that will work best with your target market.

Marketing Strategies That Did Not Achieve Characteristic 3

My research findings suggest that more than half of all small new businesses use strategies that do not achieve characteristic 3. They tend to make three types of mistakes that you should be aware of.

(1) Not including any promotional element at all in their marketing strategy.
(2) Using an ineffective message in their promotion.
(3) Mounting promotions that do not reach all the important decision-making constituencies in their target markets.

(1) No Promotional Elements Included in the Marketing Strategy

You have already encountered several new businesses in this chapter that did not have any promotion elements in their marketing strategies. The New Product Showcase did not promote its retail store, probably because it did not have a clearly defined target market.[22] Michael Kuperstein founded Neurogen Labs, Inc. to design computer software that performed like the human brain, but his marketing strategy did not include promotion. He thought he would wait for the various potential markets to tell him where the demand would come from. Only then would he start promoting.[23] Theis Rice and Frank Mitchell started SportsBand Network to radio broadcast ongoing events to spectators attending professional golf tournaments.[24] They devoted much energy to gaining acceptance of their service by both the Professional Golf Association and individual golf tournament operators, but apparently they did not do enough to promote their service to its final customers—the golf spectators themselves.

(2) Using an Ineffective Message

If a new business does not have a persuasive message to send its target market, or if it has not found a creative and effective way to say what it wants to say to its target market, it will not be able to satisfy characteristic 3. Carolyne Greene designed her FROYD doll for kids and introduced it into the New York, Boston, and Philadelphia markets with a four-week television and public relations campaign using the message, "for the reality of your dreams." The introduction was not successful, and part of the reason may have been that FROYD's message was unclear to the target market and their parents. One investor in the toy market said: "Greene has to go out and educate the market about her concept, and that's tough to do . . . in the toy marketplace."[25]

(3) Promotions Not Reaching All the Important Constituencies in the Target Market

Thomas Manning started Buddy Systems, Inc. to manufacture and market a computer-based system that could monitor important health signs of patients who had been allowed to go home after having heart surgery or some other medical procedure in a hospital. Manning promoted his system to large home-care companies in the United States, but he did not directly promote to doctors, who, it turned out, were unwilling to make decisions regarding their patients' health without first seeing them in person. Lacking the support of doctors, the home-care companies were reluctant to adopt Manning's system. Manning did not promote to an important target market constituency that played a critical role in the acceptance of his new product. An interested observer noted: "I question Buddy's ability to market without a large direct sales force. I would say they are going to have to establish credibility and a reference base with doctors—and that's expensive and takes lots of time."[26]

Mistakes You Should Avoid

These examples highlight three things you should avoid. (1) Do not start a new business if you do not have a complete promotional activity to support it. (2) Do not start your new business without a clear, easy-to-understand, and persuasive message that will cause your target market to understand and appreciate how your offering will be more satisfying and more rewarding than your competitors'. (Remember, you must persuade them to switch from the supplier they have been using to a completely new and unfamiliar one.) (3) Your new business will encounter delays—and probably failure—if your promotional activities do not reach all the important target market constituencies who, one way or another, influence the decision to buy your product.

The following is a *summary of guidelines and warnings associated with persuasively promoting to your target market.*

YOUR MARKETING STRATEGY MUST SATISFY ALL THREE OF THESE GUIDELINES

Guideline 3a. Communicate with the individuals in your target market in a manner that will cause them to understand and appreciate how your product will satisfy their needs better than your competitors'.

Guideline 3b. In a short, clear, easy-to-understand persuasive message, tell your target market individuals why your product offering will be more satisfying to them than your competitors'.

Guideline 3c. Use an efficient and effective communications medium to deliver your message (see guideline 3b) to the individuals in your target market and to all other persons involved in the purchase decision.

WARNINGS OF THINGS YOU SHOULD AVOID

Warning 3a. Avoid thinking your new business can succeed without a promotional activity (and budget) to support it.

Warning 3b. Avoid thinking your target market individuals will, without strong communication from you, somehow (e.g., word of mouth) become aware of your product, learn all about it, and come to prefer it to the ones they have been using for years.

Warning 3c. Avoid not sending effective communications to all individuals who must be persuaded to approve your product before it can be purchased by your target market.

---

4. Price to Create Good Value

You are making good progress toward a synergistic marketing strategy if you satisfy each of characteristics 1, 2, and 3. You have strongly linked your product to the wants and needs of your target market, and your promotion will make the latter fully aware of the desirable features and benefits you are offering. But now your marketing strategy must convey to them the very important message that your offering is a better value than what is available from competitors. You must do this if you want target customers to stop buying the products they are currently using and switch to your brand. In other words, your marketing strategy must also satisfy characteristic 4.

Since your marketing strategy has already satisfied characteristic 2, your product is more appealing to your target market than your competitors'. Consequently, if you price your product *lower* than your competitor's, your offering would be a good value and would very likely attract the attention of potential customers. If the benefits of your product are clearly greater than those of your competitor, you can price your product to *match* your competitor's price and still have potential customers view your offering as a better value. In such a case, you must make certain that (i) you have significantly differentiated your product in a manner that is very meaningful to your target market and (ii) you persuasively communicate those benefits to potential customers. You cannot set your price higher than your competitor's unless the benefits of your offering far, far exceed those of your competitor.

Examples

How did Miller Lite beer go about satisfying characteristic 4? Miller Lite satisfied characteristics 2 and 3 with their "Tastes Great! Less Filling" product and promotional approach. Their target market found those benefits to be very desirable. By using the same price as the leading premium brands, Miller Lite created good value in the minds of their potential customers, who could find no other brand of beer that offered similar benefits.

When they introduced L'eggs hosiery, Hanes targeted working women who often found it inconvenient to shop for hosiery in a department store or women's specialty store. Their television commercials informed women that "Our L'eggs Fit Your Legs," and that the product was available in supermarkets and drugstores where they regularly shopped. Those locations were very convenient for working women. L'eggs, a line of good quality hosiery, was priced at $.99 a pair—noticeably cheaper than hosiery available in traditional outlets. The combination of good quality, convenient locations, and low price represented a very good value to working women, and they responded by making the product an outstanding success.

Brad Brown was trying to establish Glacier Nursery as Montana's only in-state tree nursery. At the time, all of the state's 40–50 retail garden centers were being supplied by out-of-state nurseries that did not offer regular delivery service. In order to break into the market, Brown used higher quality products, frequent personal contact, and all-season-long delivery service to gain a competitive advantage. But he also used 10 percent lower prices to create a greater value than what was available from the out-of-state nurseries.

Other Marketing Strategies That Successfully Achieved Characteristic 4

Mid-price appliance manufacturers were still using traditional electro-mechanical control devices when Wallace Leyshon founded Appliance Control Technologies, Inc. Leyshon thought he could manufacture electronic control devices cheaply enough to break into that market. While his electronic controls did prove to be less expensive than the electro-mechanical controls those manufacturers had been using, they also proved to be beneficial in two other ways. They helped the appliance manufacturers become more cost efficient, thanks to reduced inventory expense. In addition, the electronic controls made the final products more attractive to consumers. All three of these outcomes lead to greater value for the appliance manufacturers.[27]

A different example of a strategy that achieved characteristic 4 involved the miniaturized microwave oven-freezer-refrigerator combination called the MicroFridge. Robert Bennett designed the MicroFridge for the college dormitory and budget motel markets. While the product offered clear benefits to both markets, the really good news was that nothing like it was available from any appliance manufacturer. On the other hand, Bennett was uncertain about what price to charge for the MicroFridge since there was nothing on the market he could use for comparison. To play it safe, he avoided overpricing the MicroFridge. Initially, he priced it at $369, but a favorable market response quickly led him to increase the price by $20. Demand continued strong even with that price increase, so he soon raised the price again to $429.[28] When MicroFridge sales continued to grow, a further price hike came under consideration. Like Brad Brown at Glacier Nursery, Bennett felt it was more advantageous to start out with a lower price in order for the product to appear as a good value in the minds of buyers. But Bennett did not have competitive prices on which he could base a comparison, so initially he picked a price that was on the low side while still resulting in a profit.

What You Should Do

First and foremost, be absolutely certain that you are offering your target market a product that is more appealing than competitors' products. You must give your target market individuals a good reason to consider giving up the brands they are currently using and switching to your brand.

(1) If your product is better than—but not obviously superior to—the one offered by your main competitor, potential customers are not likely to break your door down to buy your product. But if your product *is priced noticeably lower* than the competitors', your target market is more likely to notice your product and consider the possibility that it may represent a better value than their current one. (2) On the other hand, if your product has a clear advantage or benefit compared with the competition, you should try to create value in the minds of your potential customers by using *a price slightly lower* than your competitor's. Like Brad Brown of Glacier Nursery, you can consider raising your price after your product's advantages have become established in the marketplace. (3) Lastly, if it is quite obvious that your product has a very significant advantage or benefit over your competitor's product, you can create good value for your product in the minds of potential customers by *setting your price essentially equal* to that of your competitor. Later, after buyers acknowledge your product's superiority through their purchases, you may choose to increase your price, as Robert Bennett did in the MicroFridge example described above.

Marketing Strategies That Did Not Achieve Characteristic 4

People starting small new businesses seem to make three types of mistakes related to the value of their product offerings.

(1) Pricing the product too high.
(2) Price is not a good value.
(3) Not taking into consideration other costs customers must incur if they buy your product.

(1) Pricing the Product Too High

One small new business that set its prices too high was the Plastic Lumber Company.[29] Founder Alan Robbins believed the best markets for his recycled plastic materials and products would be universities and municipalities, because they were more likely to be environmentally friendly than corporations. But the plastic products Robins planned on making were more costly than the wood or concrete items of his competitors. This had a most unfortunate effect, because universities and municipalities proved to be more cost conscious than environment friendly. Due to the higher prices, neither of those two types of institutions became a significant market for the Plastic Lumber Company.

(2) Price Is Not a Good Value

Theis Rice and Frank Mitchell started SportsBand Network to radio broadcast the events going on at professional golf tournaments to the attending spectators via a SportsBand radio available for a $5 rental charge. But the $5 fee for the radios proved unpopular with spectators. Rice and Mitchell began offering the radios at no charge on Fridays, and then only for $2 on Saturdays and Sundays. Still, radio rentals were well below forecast, and the two owners had to look for alternate ways to market their product.[30]

(3) Not Taking into Consideration Other Costs Customers Must Incur If They Buy Your Product

Animalens, Inc., a company founded by Randy Wise to manufacture and market red contact lenses for chickens, illustrates a quite different pricing example.[31] The lenses were to be marketed to large egg farmers in the United States at a cost to them of $.15 per chicken. According to Wise, the use of the contact lenses could result in cost savings of as much as $.80 per chicken, an amount that would result in greatly increased profits. While a savings of $.80 per chicken compared with a cost of $.15 per chicken mathematically represented a good value on paper, farmers recognized that the calculation did not represent the complete picture. The farmer still faced installing those lenses into the eyes of tens of thousands of chickens—and the unknown problems and costs associated with doing so. And there was also the question of whether the lenses would actually perform as claimed by Wise. So the lenses posed two uncertainties that could have great negative impact on their profitability if farmers adopted them. In the end, based on their poor response to Wise's product, it appears that farmers did not view a price of $.15 per chicken to be a good value.

Mistakes You Should Avoid

The essence of characteristic 4 is that your marketing strategy must provide good value to your potential customers. If your product does not have obvious and significant advantages over the competition, do not set your price equal to or greater than the competitor's. Clearly, plastic lumber and the SportsBand radio were unable to provide good value. These are straight-forward mistakes you must avoid.

But Animalens, Inc. illustrates another mistake you need to be aware of and avoid. If you market your product to other businesses, it will be very important for you to be well informed of the complexities of those businesses, how they operate, and how your product offering will affect those operations. You must be absolutely certain that your product fits smoothly into their operations and does not increase their costs or complicate their operations. If your product does the latter, your potential customers may not consider it to be a good value.

The following is a *summary of guidelines and warnings associated with pricing to create good value.*

The Guideline Your Marketing Strategy Must Satisfy

Guideline 4a. Price your product in such a way that the individuals in your target market will find it a good value when comparing the benefits received from your product against those offered by competing products.

Very Supportive Guidelines Your Marketing Strategy Should Strive to Satisfy

Guideline 4b. If your product is better than—but not obviously superior to—the competitor's, create good value by pricing your product notice-ably lower than the competitor's price.

Guideline 4c. If your product has clear advantages compared with the competitor's product, create good value by pricing your product slightly lower than the competitor's.

Guideline 4d. If your product has very significant advantages compared with the competitor's product, create good value by pricing your product equal to the price of the competitor's product.

Warnings of Things You Should Avoid

Warning 4a. Avoid setting the price of your product equal to or higher than the competitor's if your product does not have obvious and signifi-cant advantages over the competitor's.

Warning 4b. Avoid not thinking about all the other costs your potential customers must incur if they buy and use your product (e.g., installation and maintenance).

---

5. Offer Convenient Distribution to Your Target Market

If your marketing strategy achieves characteristics 1, 2, 3, and 4, you have a product that has been differentiated to meet the needs of a specific target market that currently is not being well served by any competitor, and you will be effectively communicating and promoting to the individuals in that target market in a manner that will make them fully understand and appreciate the benefits you are offering them. On top of that, you will be pricing your product so the individuals in your target market clearly see it to be a good value in comparison with competing products. Now all you have to do is distribute your product to make its availability most convenient to them. This means two things: (1) you have to know where and how your target market will find it most convenient to buy your product; and (2) your marketing strategy has to include whatever it takes to get your product delivered to and displayed in those locations. This is characteristic 5.

Characteristic 5 can be easily accomplished if you market your product or service directly to other business institutions that are quite visible and easily identified (e.g., banks, appliance manufacturers, universities, etc.). In such situations, your new business can arrange to ship its product directly to the individual business institutions that become your customers. On the other hand, this guideline can prove to be a very serious obstacle to overcome if your target market is, for example, consumer households in general, or working women, or parents of high school students, or retired persons, or any one of a number of other groups who are widely dispersed geographically. If one of those is your target market, more than likely it will be necessary to engage the services of certain wholesalers, distributors, dealers, and/or retailers who can place your product where the target market wants to buy it. *Do not lose sight of the fact that all such intermediaries are entrepreneurs like you, in business to make a profit.* What does this mean to you and your small new business? It means that your marketing strategy must include product and pricing elements they will find attractive, as well as sufficient rewards and monetary incentives. If you do not help them make a profit, you will not gain their cooperation.

There are two important observations you should make with respect to achieving characteristic 5. First, if an intermediary is already serving your target market with a good competitive product and making a good profit doing so, it is highly unlikely that your marketing strategy will be able to persuade him or her to drop their current supplier and switch their allegiance to you. You will probably be wasting your time and effort to pursue such a distributor. The second observation is that you should be looking for someone (a) who wants to be serving your target market but currently does not have a product that allows her or him to do so, or (b) who is currently serving your target market but is very dissatisfied with his supplier's product quality, pricing, or service. You are more likely to gain the cooperation of such distributors, and they will be more effective because they share common interests with your new business.

Examples

At the time they introduced Miller Lite beer, the Miller Brewing Company's bottlers were already distributing its only other product, Miller High Life beer, to taverns, liquor stores, and other beer outlets. That is, their bottlers already had a well-functioning beer delivery system, so securing distribution for Miller Lite in those established outlets was relatively easy to achieve. And, with the help of its highly successful television advertising campaign, and its incentive programs for bars and taverns, Miller Lite quickly became established as a draft beer in practically all bars and taverns heavily patronized by its target market of sports-minded adult males. The bottlers, liquor stores, bars and taverns all embraced the introduction of Miller Lite beer because of the increased sales and profitability it brought them.

The Hanes Company used company-owned trucks to deliver L'eggs hosiery directly into supermarkets and drugstores. That direct delivery ensured that adequate supplies of hosiery were always available to working women in locations that were very convenient to them. Inside the stores, Hanes's delivery persons placed free-standing displays at the end of aisles. Those types of displays meant that the retailers would not have to give up profitable shelf space for this new, and as yet unproven, product. The company also employed consignment pricing, so retailers did not have to pay for the inventory of L'eggs on display in their stores. Thanks to the distribution and pricing elements of L'eggs's marketing strategy, it cost retailers almost nothing to display and sell this new product. With its attractive price of $.99 for a pair of hosiery and its successful television advertising campaign, working women bought huge quantities of L'eggs hosiery. Because it provided retailers with a very profitable new product, L'eggs quickly gained distribution in practically all supermarkets and drugstores throughout the United States.

Montana's 40–50 retail garden centers were not receiving regular, season-long delivery services from the out-of-state nurseries they were using as suppliers. Glacier Nursery owner Brad Brown offered those retailers convenient delivery service throughout the growing season by using three local trucking companies. Thanks to this previously unavailable season-long delivery service, those garden centers could reorder plants and trees from Glacier Nursery throughout the growing season. This allowed the garden centers to provide better service to their customers, which resulted in increased sales for them, and for Glacier Nursery as well.

Other Marketing Strategies That Successfully Achieved Characteristic 5

A new business that markets directly to a relatively small number of easily identified customers can usually achieve characteristic 5 in a straightforward manner. You have already encountered one such new business. Appliance Control Technologies, Inc.[32] This manufacturer of electronic controls, shipped those devices directly to their customers, the manufacturers of mid-price household appliances. Appliance Control Technologies was able to achieve characteristic 5 without using any wholesalers or distributors because it sold directly to their relatively small number of easily identified customers.

On the other hand, MicroFridge, Inc., was a small new business that achieved characteristic 5 using distributors to market its miniaturized microwave oven-freezer-refrigerator combination to budget motels and college dormitories.[33] The company found that traditional appliance distributors wanted to carry the MicroFridge because it opened up to them two new markets they had previously not served. In addition, those distributors realized a higher profit margin on MicroFridge sales because they were selling appliances to end users rather than to dealers or retailers, who required their usual discounts. The traditional appliance distributors welcomed the opportunity to cooperate with MicroFridge, Inc. because of the benefits they received from doing so.

R. W. Frookies, Inc. is an interesting example of a new business that absolutely had to distribute its products through supermarkets in order to survive. When Richard Worth noted that almost every food category in grocery stores—except cookies—included all natural products, he believed he had discovered an opportunity for a new business. As a result, he started R. W. Frookies, Inc. to create and market "all-natural" cookies. Instead of sugar for the sweetener, he used natural fruit juices. He called his product "Frookies."

Worth's new company faced formidable obstacles because the cookie aisle in grocery stores was dominated by industry giants Nabisco,

Keebler, and Pepperidge Farm. Two things helped Worth gain the distribution he needed for his cookies. First of all, he had created a very tasty cookie made of all-natural ingredients, and his was the first company to do so. The Kroger supermarket chain, very impressed with the taste of Worth's creations, believed their customers would welcome the new Frookies, so they created permanent shelves for them. Second, to help assure good distribution for Frookies, Worth offered an ownership interest in R. W. Frookies, Inc. to his distributors. Accord to Worth: "A distributor may handle 500 to 1,000 products, but if he is a shareholder, you become one of the products he really devotes his time to."[34] Worth was able to gain distribution in the very competitive cookie aisle because he offered distributors significant incentives that strongly encouraged their cooperation, and he offered supermarkets a product their customers wanted but could not get from any other supplier.

What You Should Do

(1) If your target market consists of *a relatively small number* of easily identified businesses, your marketing strategy should include direct distribution to your customers, as exemplified by Appliance Control Technologies and Glacier Nursery. (2) If your target market consists of *a large number* of easily identified businesses, you will have to use intermediaries to distribute your product. Do not try to use anyone who is already serving your target market with a competitive product and making a nice profit doing so. They are satisfied with their current suppliers, and are not likely to pay much attention to an unproven newcomer. Rather, select as your distributor someone who does not have an acceptable supplier and is therefore currently unable to serve your target market, or who is dissatisfied with his or her current supplier and looking for a better one. To gain the cooperation of any distributors, your marketing strategy must include (a) a new and appealing product they will want to distribute and/or one or more new markets they will want to serve, and (b) sufficiently attractive rewards and incentives. Recall the example of MicroFridge, Inc. (3) If you target *the large consumer market*, or a sizable portion of it, your marketing strategy must include, first, a unique product your target market strongly desires but can not get and, second, sufficient incentives to make it well worthwhile for intermediaries to participate in the marketing of your product. Frookies is a good example of such a scenario. If your marketing strategy excludes either of these two elements, your new business will not achieve characteristic 5.

Marketing Strategies That Did Not Achieve Characteristic 5

There are at least four things small new business owners do wrong that prevent them from achieving good distribution for their products.

(1) Their product offering does not attract important distribution participants.

(2) They use the wrong distribution channel.

(3) They select a distribution channel that is not available to their product.

(4) Their customers need or want installation services, but their distribution system does not provide it.

(1) Product Offering Does Not Attract Important Distribution Participants

In some marketing situations there are important participants who, while not being intermediaries in a strict sense, can make or break a company's distribution efforts. An example of this occurred with Keener-Blodee, Inc, a company that began with a limited product line consisting only of two types of wooden office chairs. This new business used a dozen manufacturers' representatives to promote the chairs to interior designers, who typically specify the type and brand of furniture to be purchased for new or remodeled business offices. When promoting to those interior designers, Keener-Blodee's manufacturers' representatives faced at least three or four established competitors, all of which had broader product lines than Keener-Blodee. When designing furnishings for a new or remodeled business office, interior designers prefer to use a small number of furniture suppliers with broad product lines, rather than a large number of suppliers with narrow product lines. Doing so just makes their work much easier. This put Keener-Blodee at a disadvantage. Referring to Keener-Blodee's situation, one specialist in the business furniture industry said:

> Consolidation [in the office furniture industry] resulted in the loss of lots of independent distribution avenues, making it much tougher to start up in this business today. ... Distribution is going to be much more of a key, much more important to the success of their company than they appear to believe. It'll be the single most difficult issue they'll face.[35]

You have already encountered another example where a small new business's product did not attract important distribution participants. Buddy Systems, Inc. manufactured a computer-based system for in-home use that could monitor the health signs of patients recently released from hospitals.[36]

The company hoped to market the system to large home-health-care organizations responsible for looking after the well-being of patients just released from hospitals. However, those organizations were reluctant to use the system because doctors were unwilling to make decisions about their patients' health without first seeing them in person. Buddy Systems' managers had failed to convince doctors of the safety and effectiveness of their system.

(2) Using the Wrong Distribution Channel

Carolyne Greene tried marketing her large character and personality doll called FROYD through major toy retailers. In doing so, she chose to compete in the general large-doll market, which was already being pursued by some fifty competing dolls. Two experienced toy industry executives thought that her concept was not a good match for people purchasing gifts from major toy retailers. Rather, they said, she should have tried distributing her doll through gift shops and department stores. According to one of the executives:

> Going the gift-market route makes a lot of sense because F.R.O.Y.D. is such a specialized product. I think the mass market is made up of people going into Toys R Us knowing what they're going to buy for a child. Whereas in a gift situation, you don't really know what you're going to walk out of the store with.[37]

(3) Selecting a Distribution Channel That Is Not Available to Their Product

Just because you start a new business, you should not assume that the best channels of distribution—or even any channel of distribution—will be available to you. In the United States, more than half of all products and services are marketed through corporate-owned distribution systems or large franchise chains. For example, about two-thirds of the distribution of soft drinks, bottled water, and fruit juices are controlled by the two cola giants. Probably some 70–80 percent of the fast food products sold in the United States are controlled by the top 10 fast food chains. Any small business that hopes to distribute its products through these "closed" channels of distribution will be severely disappointed. If the success of the business is contingent upon gaining such distribution, the business will certainly fail.

Rick Cardin started the O! Deli Corporation with the hope of growing it into a nationwide chain of franchised shops offering high quality sandwiches.[38] O! Deli intended to distinguish itself from other fast food competitors by locating their shops in office buildings. Cardin believed employees in the building would be a captive market and patronize the sandwich shop about three times a week. Perhaps the idea looked very attractive in theory. But it turned out that those potential locations often did not want any kind of food service in their buildings, or specifically did not want a sandwich shop. Those distribution locations were an extremely critical aspect of the O! Deli marketing strategy, but they simply were not available to the extent Cardin imagined. Small new businesses should be aware of the fact that many channels of distribution are not available to them. Individuals starting such small new businesses must take that into consideration when designing their marketing strategies.

(4) Customers Need or Want Installation Services, but Their Distribution System Does Not Provide It

You already saw, in the above discussion on pricing, that Animalens, Inc. was marketing a product that required installation. However, installation of the product was very labor intensive, and the company's marketing system did not provide the needed installation services.

Keith Burnett thought he had the basis for a successful new business, Waste Energy, Inc., when he designed a machine (the Goldfire) that could convert trash, dirty motor oil, and other combustible waste material into electricity.[39] Potential customer firms could use the machine both to get rid of their waste materials and to create electricity they could use to run their operations. If more electricity was created than their businesses could use, they could sell the excess to local electric companies. Their businesses would save money by not having to pay someone to haul away those waste materials and by not having to buy as much electricity. However, several difficulties emerged that caused Burnett's machine to be somewhat unattractive to the businesses being targeted. First, in converting waste to electricity, the machine could create hazardous emissions, which meant it would first require approval by local and state environmental authorities. Second, the burden of selling the surplus electricity to the local electric company fell on the customer, and it turned out to be more complicated than it appeared at first glance, with varying conditions and arrangements for different locations and for different electric companies. Although potential buyers of the Goldfire were greatly interested in its benefits, they clearly did not like the hassle of obtaining the required environmental permits or negotiating the necessary arrangement with local electric companies. They would have been very interested in an installed and approved system that only had to be turned on and off, but Burnett's distribution system was not prepared to provide such installation services.

Mistakes You Should Avoid

A key element in achieving characteristic 5 is *convenience*. Your distribution channel must make it very convenient for your potential customers to find, buy, and use your product. Distribution mistakes small new businesses make, and which you should avoid, are the following. (1) Do not start your new business if you are not absolutely certain that your product will attract the important intermediaries and/or other distribution participants you will need to achieve characteristic 5. If your product will not do that, redesign it so it will. (2) Do not just assume that a given channel will be effective in reaching your target market. Distributors who are already profitably serving the target market with a competitive product and are satisfied doing so are not likely to become effective distribution partners. (3) Just because an optimum channel of distribution exists for your product, do not assume that it will be available to you and your product. (4) Do not lose sight of the fact that some products require installation and/or maintenance services that your target market individuals cannot or will not provide for themselves. If you are offering such a product, you must find a distribution channel that will provide those services, or you must provide them yourself.

The following is a *summary of guidelines and warnings associated with offering convenient distribution to your target market.*

THE GUIDELINE YOUR MARKETING STRATEGY MUST SATISFY

Guideline 5a. Distribute your product in a manner that is most convenient for the individuals in your target market.

VERY SUPPORTIVE GUIDELINES YOUR MARKETING STRATEGY SHOULD STRIVE TO SATISFY

Guideline 5b. Select intermediaries who will be able to place your product in all locations where potential consumers go when looking to buy a product like yours.

Guideline 5c. Select distributors who currently are unable to serve your target market because they do not have an acceptable supplier, or who are dissatisfied with their current supplier and looking for a better one.

Guideline 5d. If you are targeting the large consumer market, you must have a unique product that the target market strongly desires but cannot get, and you must offer intermediaries sufficient incentives to make it worthwhile for them to participate in the marketing of your product.

WARNINGS OF THINGS YOU SHOULD AVOID

Warning 5a. Avoid starting a new business if your product will not attract the intermediaries and/or the other distribution participants needed to reach your target market.

Warning 5b. Avoid assuming that a given channel of distribution will be effective in reaching your target market. Distributors who are already profitably serving the target market with a competitive product and are satisfied doing so are not likely to become effective distribution partners.

Warning 5c. Avoid assuming that the optimum distribution channel for your product will be available to your new business.

Warning 5d. Avoid assuming that target market individuals will be able to install and maintain your product, if your product requires those services.

Summary

If your small new business is to have a reasonable chance of being successful, it must have a complete and synergistic marketing strategy. Such a strategy will display the following five characteristics.

1. Identify a target market whose needs your business can satisfy more effectively than any competitor.
2. Design or differentiate your product/service so it is more appealing to the individuals in your target market than are the products/services offered by competitors.
3. Promote your product/service to the individuals in your target market so they understand and appreciate how it will satisfy their needs better than competitors' offerings.
4. Price your product/service is such a way that the individuals in your target market will find it to be a good value when comparing the benefits received from your product/service against those offered by competing products/services.
5. Distribute your product/service in a manner that is most convenient to the individuals in your target market.

Of the many small new business startups that I have studied, I estimate that fewer than one in five were able to design marketing strategies that satisfied all five of the above characteristics. The other 80 percent of new businesses did not even have complete marketing strategies, let alone synergistic ones. In effect, those new businesses already had one foot in the grave even before they entered their launch periods. This poor showing clearly indicates that achieving a complete and synergistic marketing strategy is not a simple task.

Regarding the selection of a target market for your new business, it is imperative that you identify a segment of a market that currently is being poorly served or not being served at all. That market segment must consist of individuals who are dissatisfied with the business or businesses currently trying to serve them. Those individuals will be actively searching for a better supplier, and you want to be that better supplier.

If you want to be a better supplier, your product must be designed to offer your target market the features and benefits they strongly desire but do not find in currently available products. You want your product's features and benefits to be so unique and desirable to your potential customers that they will no longer consider buying a competitor's product. In effect, by so designing your product you will be creating a monopoly for your new business among the individuals in your selected target market.

But those individuals do not yet know that your new business even exists. You have to change that. In your communications and promotions you have to say things about your product, its features, and its benefits that are easily understood and greatly appreciated by your target market. Not only must these communications/promotions tell your target market the most important things they want to hear about your product, those things have to be communicated in the most effective way possible, and they have to be communicated using the most efficient and economical media.

Next, your product must be priced to be an obviously good value in the eyes of your target market. A good value can be achieved by selecting a price below that of your product's main competitor. If your product's features and benefits noticeably exceed those of your main competitor, your product's price can equal that of your competitor and still be considered a good value by your target market.

Last but not least, you must find a way to distribute your product in a manner that is most convenient to your target market. In some cases you might do so directly to individual customers. If you cannot do that, you must determine where your target market wants to buy your product.

Then, you have to find distributors who want to serve your target market but are unable to do so because they do not currently have a good supplier. And your new business has to offer those intermediaries a product that they can use to successfully serve their—and your—target market, and you must also offer them sufficient financial rewards and other incentives in order to secure their cooperation.

3

Screening Condition II: Do You Use Marketing Elements That Can Cause Significant Time Delays in the Execution of Your Marketing Strategy?

If the marketing strategy you have designed conforms to all five guidelines discussed in Chapter 2, your small new business has identified a target market not currently being fully satisfied by any competitor and is now ready to offer that target market a product that will satisfy its needs. The promotion element of the strategy will cause individuals in your target market to easily understand—and welcome—the benefits of your differentiated product, and they will be pleased to learn that a supplier who knows how to satisfy their needs has finally come along. Furthermore, when they learn that the price of your product makes it a very attractive value, your marketing strategy will have created a great deal of synergy because it has highly integrated the four elements of target market, product differentiation, promotional communications, and price. Lastly, you created a complete marketing strategy when you arranged for your product to be distributed in a manner that is most convenient for the individuals in your target market. Because your marketing strategy has highly integrated all five of these elements, it should prove to be both very effective and very efficient. The end result will be that your marketing strategy will provide a solid foundation upon which your new business can build as it starts out on the road headed toward your desired destination—success.

But do not rest on your laurels yet. You still have lots of work to do. If you want your new business to have a reasonably good chance of succeeding, you still have to make certain that your marketing strategy will also achieve Screening Conditions II, III, and IV.

Recall from Chapter 1 that there are two time periods critical to the survival of every new business—the prelaunch period and the launch period. The *prelaunch period* begins with the conception of the new business idea and lasts until the new business opens its doors to potential customers. At that point the new business enters its *launch period*, during which it hopes to quickly achieve a self-sustaining cash flow from its sales. Without such a cash flow, the new business will fail. If your new business is to achieve its cash flow goal, it must have its marketing strategy in place and ready to "hit the ground running" on the day the business enters its launch period. If it is to survive, your new business must begin to generate sales revenues immediately.

In this chapter, I will describe several factors that can prevent you from putting your marketing strategy into action in a timely manner. That is to say, these factors can prevent your new business from entering its launch period, and thereby prevent it from beginning to realize the sales revenues it needs to succeed. These delaying factors are the heart of Screening Condition II, and you must be certain that you have designed your marketing strategy to avoid such critical delays.

During my research on successful marketing strategies for small new businesses, I discovered that certain undesirable factors might be present in a marketing strategy, even if that strategy has satisfied Screening Condition I. Any one of those factors can delay or even prevent a new business from executing its marketing strategy in an effective and timely manner. There are four of them:

1. The new business encounters difficulties in identifying and measuring its target market.
2. Competitors create barriers that the new business cannot easily circumvent.
3. Distribution channels are not available to the new business, or are not as cooperative as expected.
4. Legal and/or environmental regulations cause unanticipated barriers and delays for the new business.

I refer to these as *marketing strategy execution delaying factors*, and each is explained in the remainder of this chapter.

1. Delays Caused by Target Market Issues

In Chapter 2 you saw how a synergistic marketing strategy closely tied its product differentiation, promotional communications, and channel of distribution to a target market that the new business could serve better that any competitor. That synergistic marketing strategy would also price its product so the target market would find it to be of greater value than any competitor's offering. It should be very clear from those Chapter 2 discussions that a successful small new business owner must be very well informed about his new business's target market and the competitors who are already pursing that target market.

To be well informed about your new business's target market, you should have asked and answered the following questions:

- Has the target market been clearly defined and identified?
- Do you truly understand the target market's wants and needs, and why target market individuals are not satisfied with their current suppliers?
- Are you absolutely certain that your product offering will be looked upon very favorably by target market individuals?
- Have you accurately estimated the size of the target market? Is it large enough to be profitable?
- How much of the target market's purchases will your business be able to capture from already well-established competitors?

If you want to be successful in your small new business, you must know how many people, households, or organizations in the target market are dissatisfied with their current suppliers. You must also know *why* those customers are dissatisfied and whether your product offering will overcome those dissatisfactions. In order to promote your product effectively, you must know in what ways potential customers find your product's features and benefits attractive. You must also know where the target market will find it most convenient to purchase your product, and the price at which they will consider it to be a good value. These are the kinds of information you must know about your target market. If you do not have this information when your new business enters into its launch period, very likely your marketing strategy will be ineffective and your launch period will necessarily be delayed until you gather the needed information.

Clearly, the acquisition of such target market information represents a formidable challenge for any small new business owner. But, without such information the new business owner will not be able to design a synergistic marketing strategy.

Marketing Strategies That Avoided Delays Caused by Target Market Issues

Let us look again at three of the successful examples of marketing strategies discussed throughout Chapter 2. Appliance Control Technologies, Inc. targeted U.S. manufacturers of mid-price kitchen and laundry appliances.[1] There were only a relatively small number of such manufacturers, which made it quite easy for founder Wallace Leyshon to be in personal or telephone contact with most of them. Given that the target market was likely to be very interested in Appliance Control Technologies' cost-saving product offering, Leyshon was able to gather most of the information specified in the above five question through his personal contacts.

Robert Bennett targeted budget motels and college dormitory rooms for his product, the microwave oven-freezer-refrigerator combination called the MicroFridge.[2] Budget motels and colleges and universities are quite easy to identify and contact. Estimates regarding the number of budget motel rooms and dormitory rooms in the United States could be gathered from a number of sources. Since the MicroFridge was unique (no competitive product existed at the time) and fulfilled a latent need not being satisfied in budget motels and only poorly satisfied in dormitory rooms, Bennett strongly believed that the MicroFridge was quite capable of meeting the target market's unsatisfied needs. And in the end, it turned out he had been able to inform himself well and fully about his target markets when the MicroFridge was ready to be marketed.

When he started his Glacier Nursery, Brad Brown already had several years of experience working as a foreman on a Christmas tree farm.[3] The target market for his nursery was the 40–50 retail garden centers in the state of Montana, and he already knew every one of them. He also knew that the only suppliers to those garden centers offered trees and plants grown out-of-state, which were less hardy than plants grown in Montana, and that those out-of-state suppliers did not offer regular delivery service in Montana throughout the growing season. Like Wallace Leyshon and Robert Bennett, Brad Brown was very knowledgeable about his target market, his competitors, and about the share of the target market's purchases his new business might gain.

What You Should Do

If you are starting a small new business, there are three things you must be certain to do. (1) Clearly define your target market and the sales potential it represents for the product offered by your new business. You must know who your potential customers are and how to reach them. (2) Know exactly why target market individuals are dissatisfied with current suppliers, and be certain that they will strongly approve of the new product your new business is going to offer them. (3) Make a critical evaluation of your product offering *vis-à-vis* the competitor's, and make a realistic estimate of how large a share of the target market's purchases your new business is likely to capture.

Marketing Strategies That Experienced Delays Caused by Target Market Issues

There are three different ways that a small new business can encounter strategy execution delays caused by their target market selection:

(1) The new business owner has not identified a target market, or has made a poor target market selection.

(2) The new business has multiple target markets and/or several constituencies that must somehow participate in the new business's marketing effort if it is to succeed.

(3) The new business has a target market that is solely or predominantly based on an attitude.

(1) The New Business Owner Has Not Identified a Target Market, or Has Made a Poor Target Market Selection

If a new business has not clearly identified the target market it will pursue, it cannot execute an effective marketing strategy when it enters into its launch period. Without a good target market selection, properly identified, a new business cannot know how it should differentiate its product offering, or how it should be promoted or priced or distributed. Without all this knowledge a new business owner cannot possibly design a synergistic marketing strategy. Without such a strategy, there is little chance that it will begin to generate the sales revenue stream it needs quickly enough for survival.

Zane Causey and Robert Clark opened a retail store in a low-rent shopping mall in Texas. They called it the New Product Showcase. For a fee of

$350 they would display anyone's invention in their store for three months. The New Product Showcase did not identify a target market, so it did no consumer advertising. Individuals who visited the store were primarily people doing business elsewhere in the mall:

> Causey and Clark had only the dimmest vision of who their retail customer might be. As it turns out, [New Product Showcase] tends to attract older customers, mostly low- to middle-income homeowners browsing for gadgets. . . . Causey and Clark see more curiosity seekers than serious buyers.[4]

Alan Robbins founded The Plastic Lumber Company to make speed bumps and parking lot car-stops, picnic tables, and similar products using recycled plastic. Robbins believed that universities were motivated to improve the environment and, therefore, would buy his environment-friendly recycled plastic products. He also thought municipalities would do so as well, because of their concern about excessive trash caused by plastic packaging. Unfortunately, both of those markets turned out to be far more cost conscious than environmentally friendly. Regarding Robbins' selection of target markets, one expert financier said:

> One of the common mistakes is to think people are going to buy products just because they're environmentally correct. You can't rely on that kind of altruism.[5]

If a small new business does not have a specific target market that will quickly be attracted to its product offering, it will almost certainly experience lengthy delays in creating the sales revenue stream it badly needs to survive.

(2) The New Business Has Multiple Target Markets and/or Several Constituencies That Must Be Persuaded to Support the New Business's Marketing Efforts

When a small new business appears to have more than one promising target market, the entrepreneur may believe that the demand for his product is so large that it essentially guarantees the success of his new business. He may believe that it is not necessary to identify the individual target markets or to attempt to measure what their demand will be. Or he may think it is too demanding of his time to make it worthwhile. Whatever the reasons, the presence of multiple target markets seems to be a cause of marketing strategy execution delays for some small new businesses.

Michael Kuperstein's Neurogen, Inc. was developing a computer product that would read human handwriting. There seemed to be seven potential markets for Kuperstein's product: insurance companies: the Internal Revenue Service, banks, the U.S. Postal Service, all sorts of sales ordering forms, mutual funds, and credit card companies. But which one should be the company's target market? The company's sales vice-president reported:

> We figured that if I showed this to enough end users we'd find out where the demand was. We wanted to let the market tell us where the demand was. Then we'd react.[6]

This lack of direction, due to the absence of a clearly specified target market, contributed to the company's inability to initiate a badly needed sales revenue stream. Regarding the company's lack of target market identification, a managing partner of Price Waterhouse's Entrepreneurial Services said:

> They've let two years slip by, and they still don't know what their market is. They need to focus. Instead of trying to do six different things, they need to stop and say, "this is the one place where we think we can make a dent in the market" and go for it. If they don't, the lack of funds, given what they are trying to do, will kill this company.[7]

Sometimes a new business targets a market in which one or more external constituencies has a role to play in the marketing of a new product offering. Such constituencies are not themselves the actual target markets, but they can be important participants in a new product's success, or they can contribute to its failure.

Thomas Manning started Buddy Systems, Inc. to manufacture and market a computer-based system that could monitor the important health signs of a patient who had gone home from the hospital after having had a serious medical procedure. Manning believed his machine—called Buddy for its friendliness—would help minimize health care costs by allowing patients to leave the hospital sooner and by reducing the frequency of visiting nurse calls during the patient's recuperation at home. Manning hoped to sell his Buddy system to large home-health-care organizations, but first he had to get explicit or implicit approval of his machine from three constituencies. The Food and Drug Administration required lengthy clinical trials before they would approve the Buddy system for general use.

Doctors were a second constituency essential to Buddy's marketing success. Unfortunately, many doctors proved reluctant to make decisions about their patients' health without first seeing them in person. One director of medicine at a large urban hospital said:

> Physicians are conservative in that they make decisions based on judgment, and they may feel judgment is interfered with by having just a few pieces of paper and bits of information to make decisions on. We need clinical information, whether the patient is short of breath or looks ashen, whether the lungs are clear. Doctors need to feel they know what the patient looks like.[8]

Insurance companies constituted a third group. They would have to cover some of the costs of Buddy in order for it to achieve market success, and to do that, they needed to be convinced that it would result in overall health care cost savings. But because Buddy did not have much support from doctors, home-health-care companies were slow to adopt it and insurance companies saw no great need to support if financially. This complex web of a target market and three very important external constituencies caused marketing strategy execution delays that were very harmful to Manning and his new business.

Sometimes an entrepreneur wants to start a new business that she or he believes can be developed into a franchise system. Such a new business can encounter strategy execution delays because it faces two sets of serious obstacles, rather than only one: trying to make the small new business a success in and of itself, and trying to transform the successful small new business into a successful regional or national franchise system. These represent two different objectives, and each needs its own marketing strategy and marketing plan. However, the entrepreneur's first priority has to be success for the small new business. Only after that has been accomplished should developing the small new business into a successful franchise be attempted. Unfortunately, some people starting such new businesses try to achieve these two very different objectives simultaneously. In doing so, they are likely to encounter strategy execution delays and other serious difficulties.

(3) The New Business Has a Target Market That Is Solely or Predominantly Based on an Attitude

Some people start a new business with a target market consisting of individuals who possess a certain attitude. In almost all such cases—perhaps in all of them—it is safe to say that such a target market actually exists. That is, there are people with the attitude the new business's entrepreneur has identified, and those people constitute a market segment that can be targeted by the new business.

Consider, for example, the Miller Lite Beer example discussed in Chapter 2. The Miller Brewery selected an attitude-based target market—enthusiastic sports fans who also happened to be heavy beer drinkers. This proved to be a very good target market selection because marketing research had shown that those young men were heavy beer drinkers who would welcome a less filling, lower calorie beer that still had great taste. Miller also knew that these people were almost exclusively male, in their early twenties to mid-thirties, blue-collar workers or recent college graduates, and best of all, that there were literally millions of them. Furthermore, because those enthusiastic sports fans were also ardent viewers of televised sporting events, the channel of communications Miller should use to reach this target market was obvious. Miller Brewery knew an awful lot about the target market when it introduced Miller Lite Beer.

On the other hand, there are numerous examples of new businesses with attitude-based target markets where the owners appear to know very little about their target market, except that the individuals in it possess a certain attitude. The entrepreneurs do not know how many such persons there are or where they are located, they usually do not know very much about their demographics, and often they may not know which media are best for communicating with them. If a new business's target market is based solely on an attitude, and little more, it will be almost impossible for the new business owner to highly integrate the target market with the new business's product offering, its promotions, its price, and its distribution. In other words, the new business owner will not be able to create a complete and synergistic marketing strategy. Without such a strategy, the new business has almost no chance of succeeding.

David Fokos was an audio engineer who designed loudspeakers for a company that manufactured quality audio equipment. He felt he could design higher quality loudspeakers than his employer wanted to sell, so he started Icon Acoustics, Inc. with that goal in mind. Fokos defined his target market as:

> people who love to listen to music, equipment junkies, the audio-addicted. They tend to be educated, affluent and obsessed. These people would rather buy a new set of speakers than eat.[9]

More than likely there were people that fit Fokos's description, but he did not seem to have much other information about them. If a new business is to have a synergistic marketing strategy, its product differentiation, promotional communications, and distribution method must all be closely tied to its target market. This means that the new business owner must go beyond that attitude component and have reliable information about the size of the target market, their demographics, their wants and needs and current dissatisfactions, how to communicate with them, and what distribution outlets they would find convenient.

Mistakes You Should Avoid

There are four. (1) Do not be like Zane Causey and Robert Clark, who started their new business without first having clearly identified and described their target market. And do not be like Alan Robbins and assume your target market will buy your product because you think they should do so. Remember, to be successful, a new business must have a clearly identified target market it can serve better than any competitor. (2) If you believe your new business has several target markets, do not be like Michael Kuperstein and assume that the markets will search out your new business and hand you success on a platter. Every target market is already being pursued by at least one competitor, so if you hope to gain its patronage, you too will have to pursue it. If your new business has more than one target market, select the best one to pursue and pursue it as if your new business's survival depended on it. It does! (3) Unless your new business has huge financial resources, avoid selecting a target market that requires the support of any independent constituencies. Remember the delays that Thomas Manning his company Buddy Systems, Inc. encountered when he selected a target market that was reluctant to respond to his product offering without the endorsement of several independent constituencies. (4) Do not select a target market based solely or predominantly on an attitude. Remember the lack of success and the delays that David Fokos and Icon Acoustics, Inc. experienced when he identified a target market based almost exclusively on attitudes.

The following is *a summary of guidelines and warnings associated with avoiding marketing strategy execution delays caused by target market issues.*

YOUR MARKETING STRATEGY MUST SATISFY THESE TWO GUIDELINES

Guideline 1a. Clearly define your target market and estimate the sales potential it represents for the type of product your new business is offering. You must know who your potential customers are and how to reach them.

Guideline 1b. Know exactly why target market individuals are dissatisfied with their current suppliers, and be certain that they will strongly approve of your new business's product.

VERY SUPPORTIVE GUIDELINES YOUR MARKETING STRATEGY SHOULD STRIVE TO SATISFY

Guideline 1c. Make a realistic estimate of how large a market share your new business is likely to realize.

WARNINGS OF THINGS YOU SHOULD AVOID

Warning 1a. Avoid not making a clear identification and description of your target market.

Warning 1b. Avoid focusing on several target markets. If there are several target markets for your product, identify the single most attractive one and pursue it. Pursue the second most attractive target market only after you have conquered the first.

Warning 1c. Avoid target markets where your new business's sales success will require the support and cooperation of independent constituencies.

Warning 1d. Avoid selecting a target market based solely or predominantly on an attitude.

2. Delays Caused by Competitive Barriers

The vast, vast majority of small new businesses enter a marketplace where competitors have been active for quite some time. Depending upon the specific product or service being offered, a small new business may face only a handful of established competitors, or it may face dozens of them, or, in some cases, hundreds. Whether there are only a few established competitors, or dozens, their mere presence represents a significant obstacle that a small new business will have to overcome if it is to survive.

Individuals starting small new businesses often give the impression that they expect the established competitors to roll over and play dead, or just go away. Even when those entrepreneurs do acknowledge the presence of well-established competitors, they very often seem to act as though those competitors will not have anything to say about the success or failure of their new businesses. Both attitudes are completely foolhardy.

If your small new business is to have a reasonable chance of overcoming the strong barriers put in place by established competitors, you must be very realistic about your competitors, how strong they are, and what responses they might have when they see a small new business entering their marketplace. To be fully prepared for the competitive obstacles your new business is likely to encounter, you should ask and realistically answer the following types of questions:

- Who are the competitors my new business will face in the marketplace? How many are there? How strong or weak are they?
- Will my new business face only strong competitors? Only weak competitors?
- Are my product's advantages so apparent that customers of competitors' products will quickly switch to my product?
- What proportion of my new business's sales will be taken from strong competitors? What proportion from weak competitors?
- What kinds of competitive responses can I expect from strong competitors who are losing sales to my new business? What kinds of responses can I expect from weak competitors?

People starting new businesses are always very optimistic about them, often to the extent that they lose sight of two critical questions involving competitors. First, what must a new business do to persuade competitors' customers to purchase the new product instead of the one they have been purchasing all along? Second, if and when competitors' customers make such a purchasing switch, what retaliatory actions will the competitors take?

Consider the case where a small new business enters a marketplace being served by 10 or more established competitors. Although most of those competitors will be small, they will be experienced in their ability to compete and survive, and this includes having the skills and know-how to prevent other competitors from stealing their customers. They have developed good relationships with their customers and those customers find it convenient, and even rewarding, to continue doing business with their current suppliers. Those established relationships represent huge obstacles the small new business must overcome if it is to have any chance of surviving.

Even if the established competitors take no special competitive action against the small new business, it will take a Herculean effort by the latter to overcome the built-in inertia of customers with long-established relationships with competitors. Owners of small new businesses must ask themselves if their marketing strategy has what it takes to cause competitors' customers to switch allegiances to their new business. If the new business's marketing strategy is not certain to cause such switching, more than likely customers will take a long time before they change, if they ever do so. And if the switching process takes a long time, the survival of the small new business will be doubtful. It is in this way that established competitors represent a significant barrier for the small new business to overcome. If it cannot overcome those obstacles, the small new business will experience very critical time delays in its attempts to generate the sales revenue stream it needs to survive.

Now consider the case where a small new business enters a marketplace being served by only a handful of competitors, all medium sized or larger, and all long established in the marketplace. Surviving years of competition, they have proved themselves to be strong, very savvy, and strongly aggressive. They will not take the matter lightly when they see a new business trying to encroach upon what they consider to be their marketplace. To put such young upstarts in their place and to teach them a big lesson, they will take action to create obstacles and roadblocks to make market entry difficult, if not impossible.

The owner of a small new business must anticipate the very likely probability that one or more of the larger established competitors will take strong actions to impede any upstart rival from being able to execute his or her marketing strategy in a timely manner, or in the manner originally intended. If a small new business does not have a marketing strategy able to prevent, resist or get around any strong preemptive measures against it from established competitors, those measures can doom the small new business. The following illustrates the kinds of actions a strong competitor can take to disrupt the plans of a small new business.

AMERICAN AIRLINES AND LEGEND AIRLINES AT LOVE FIELD IN DALLAS[10]

In 2000, American Airlines was one of the world's largest airlines, and it controlled 70 percent of the air traffic at the Dallas-Fort Worth International Airport. A new start-up airline, Legend Airlines, planned to begin offering first-class-only flights from Dallas to Los Angeles and Washington, D.C. with gourmet meals and other luxuries. Their flights would originate out of Love Field in Dallas, a small, older airport that was limited to airplanes with no more than fifty-six seats—a restriction established by the federal government to enable the Dallas-Fort Worth International Airport to gain dominance in the region. Legend's aim was to attract the most desirable type of air traveler—frequent business fliers who pay full fare. But this was a direct attempt to steal American Airlines' best customers, something that American Airlines would not take sitting down.

> In its efforts to ground a tiny start-up, American Airlines sued the city of Dallas, the federal government and the new airlines itself. It also lobbied Congress, beseeched its frequent fliers, posted billboards around the city and secretly paid for radio advertising from a "concerned citizens" group protesting expanded use of Dallas's close-in airport, Love Field.[11]

The lawsuits cost Legend Airlines some two million dollars and had a negative effect on its fund-raising activities. American Airlines also quickly and quietly leased the abandoned terminal at Love Field that Legend had been trying to secure for its own use. The loss of that space forced Legend to spend $21 million to build its own terminal and garage, money that had been intended for other purposes. American Airlines also quickly geared up to initiate its own flights out of Love Field, offering the same services as Legend. When Legend started their marketing campaign by calling on local big businesses, they found that American Airlines had already been there to offer them incentives for remaining loyal to American Airlines. Eventually, Legend Airlines was able to start flying, but the obstacles and barriers American Airlines had set up were too many and too large for the new airline to overcome and survive.

Whether a new business faces many small competitors, or a lesser number of large competitors, all of them will have served the market for quite some time. As established competitors, their mere presence will tend to cause delays when a small new business attempts to persuade customers to switch allegiances. The owner of a small new business must be aware of such likely delays and make every attempt to avoid them.

Marketing Strategies That Avoided Delays Caused by Competitive Barriers

So how did the three successful examples of marketing strategies discussed in Chapter 2 deal with the issue of competitive barriers?

When Robert Bennett introduced his microwave oven-freezer-refrigerator combination (the MicroFridge) to the budget motel and college dormitory markets, no other firm was offering a similar product, or anything even close to it.[12] The MicroFridge was a new and unique product, so it had no established competitors and there were no buyers of competitive products who had to be persuaded to switch suppliers. Consequently, MicroFridge experienced no strategy execution delays caused by the presence of established competitors.

Wallace Leyshon founded Appliance Control Technology, Inc. (ACT) to market electronic controls to U.S. manufacturers of medium-priced kitchen and laundry appliances.[13] Those manufacturers were still using electro-mechanical controls for their appliances because they were less expensive than electronic controls. But ACT offered its target market standardized controls that were of higher quality than electro-mechanical controls. Furthermore, being located domestically, ACT was able to help appliance manufacturers shorten their lead times on new model development, and the standardized parts significantly reduced the manufacturers' overall inventory carrying costs. ACT's only U.S.-based competitor used overseas manufacturing facilities, and only manufactured proprietary controls for specific appliances, and even for different models of the same appliance. Overseas manufacturing resulted in longer delivery schedules, and proprietary controls resulted in appliance manufacturers needing larger inventories. Both of those factors led to higher inventory costs for the appliance manufacturers. In effect, ACT faced only one direct competitor in its target market, but, because of its strategy, it had the advantage of offering higher quality, lower prices and costs, and better service. Customers were willing, even eager, to give the small new business a chance. ACT experienced no strategy execution delays because it marketing strategy prevented the competitor from being able to establish barriers and obstacles that could cause such delays.

Glacier Nursery was the only tree and plant nursery located in Montana, and its owner, Brad Brown, already knew every retail garden center in the state.[14] As the only in-state nursery, Brown expected his trees and plants to be hardier than those grown in more temperate, out-of-state climates. Further, Montana being a relatively small retail market, out-of-state nurseries showed little interest in regularly supplying Montana's retail garden centers throughout the growing season. Brown's nursery took advantage of this competitive weakness by providing the state's garden centers with season-long delivery service. Because Brown could offer a better product—hardier trees and plants—and better, all-season delivery, Montana's retail garden centers were quite willing to give Glacier Nursery a chance at becoming a regular supplier. And its out-of-state competitors were either unable or unwilling to create the kinds of barriers and obstacles that could cause the small new business to fail.

What You Should Do

Two things should be obvious from the above examples. (1) You should be absolutely certain that your new business can serve its target market better than any competitor. (2) To do so, you must be very knowledgeable about your competitor's strengths and weaknesses. You should know the important weaknesses of your competitors' offerings, and your new business should offer a product that obviously does not possess those weaknesses. You must be certain that your target market clearly sees and appreciates that your new business's offering is superior to your competitor's offering. Robert Bennett's MicroFridge offered far more benefits to the budget motel and college dormitory markets than any of the substitute products that were available at the time. Wallace Leyshon's Appliance Control Technologies, Inc had one competitor, but Leyshon so designed his strategy for the mid-price appliance manufacturers' market that his offering had attractive advantages over that competitor. In effect, his strategy eliminated any delaying factor that could be caused by the competitor. Brad Brown looked at his competitors through the eyes of Montana's retail garden center operators. He took his competitors' weaknesses (i.e., less hardy plants and infrequent delivery) and turned them into competitive advantages for Glacier Nursery. These are the kinds of things you should do for your small new business if you wish to avoid critical delays caused by the well-established competitors in your marketplace.

Marketing Strategies That Experienced Delays Caused by Competitive Barriers

Competitors have two things they can call upon to impose a strategy execution delay on a new business entering their markets.

- Over the years they have been establishing solid relationships with their customers, and those relationships represent a serious obstacle for a small new business to overcome in order to survive. Established competitors know how to use those relationships to their own advantage, often with the result of imposing a strategy execution delay on the new competitor trying to break into the market.
- Owners of a small new business must convince customers of established competitors to switch allegiances to the new business. This huge task represents a significant barrier the small new business must overcome if it is to survive.

These are two very critical delaying factors, yet many small new business owners seem to ignore their existence. Why?

In studying the difficulties and delays small new businesses experienced due to their competitors, I observed that new business owners typically did not know very much about their new business's advantages and disadvantages relative to the competitors they would face in their target market. As a result, they frequently seem to make one or more of the following mistakes:

(1) They are not even aware of the existence of competitors.

(2) They have selected a target market with many established competitors. Perhaps because the numbers of competitors is so large, the task of dealing with them may appear to be overwhelming. Often the result is that they seem to ignore their existence.

(3) They believe their product offerings are so superior to competitors' offerings that potential customers will quickly abandon their past suppliers and begin buying from them.

Each of these mistakes is discussed below.

(1) The Entrepreneur Is Not Even Aware of the Existence of Any Competitors

Michael Kuperstein founded Neurogen, Inc. to design computer software that could perform certain tasks similar to those performed by the human brain. He developed a computer product that could read handwritten digits on a piece of paper. The banking industry, which processes millions of handwritten checks daily, was one market that had a great need for his product, Kuperstein believed. But banks were already working with large system integrators to handle their basic data processing needs—and to develop solutions to such tasks as computer reading of handwritten checks.[15] Neurogen, a small three-person new business, thus found itself in the uncomfortable position of learning from the banks (one of its potential target markets) that it would be competing against some of the very largest suppliers to the banking industry. This revelation forced the small new business to refocus its efforts elsewhere, and significantly delayed Neurogen from achieving the sales revenue stream it badly needed.

(2) The Small New Business Has Many Established Competitors, Yet Its Owner Seems to Ignore Their Presence or Underestimate Their Strengths

This strange behavior is displayed by some small new business owners. On the one hand, why would a person start a small new business if he knew that a large number of competitors were already active in that business's marketplace? It should be very obvious that the competition will be fierce under such circumstances. On the other hand, it just does not make sense for a small new business owner to enter into such a marketplace without having a specific plan for dealing with the competition. Yet, there are quite a few examples of such small new businesses, and the results are never pretty.

Recall that David Fokos started Icon Acoustics, Inc. to manufacture very high quality, top-of-the-line audio speakers.[16] Only about 10 percent of the audio equipment market purchased top-of-the-line, higher-priced equipment and accessories, and more than 200 audio-speaker companies were already competing for that business. Two hundred competitors! Can you believe it? A very small business with almost no marketing budget enters the smallest segment of a market where it faces more than 200 competitors. It simply makes no good sense to do something like that.

But this is not an isolated example. It is not uncommon to come across small new businesses where the owners either ignore competitors or pay little attention to how their presence can affect their new businesses.

(3) The Small New Business Owner Believes His Product Offering Is So Superior to Competitors' Offerings That Potential Customers Will Quickly Drop Their Current Suppliers and Switch to His New Business

Small new business owners usually attribute greater benefits and advantages to their product than do their potential customers. Entrepreneurs often see their products' advantages as huge when compared with their competitors' offerings. Unfortunately, potential customers do not always share the entrepreneur's enthusiasm for the new product. The typical result is that the new business does not achieve a growing sales revenue stream as quickly as its owner had hoped. Very often the projected sales revenue growth is never achieved.

Dick Keener and Lief Blodee started Keener-Blodee, Inc. to manufacture and sell stylish wood office chairs characterized by high quality, excellent craftsmanship, and European styling. When they started their new business, sales of wooden office furniture were flat, the office furniture industry was consolidating into fewer but larger firms, and the surviving companies were offering much broader product lines. Due to Keener and Blodee's limited resources, the new company initially could afford to manufacture only two different chair models. The founders felt that the design and construction of their chairs made them unique, but one consultant to the contract furniture industry did not see it that way:

> Keener-Blodee's competitors will be tough. . . . Probably 8 or 10 other manufacturers produce chairs that are very similar, have similar construction systems, and carry about the same price.[17]

Not only might the new company be neutralized in the marketplace by the 8–10 competitors noted in the above quote, it might also display a weakness due to its very narrow product line. In a no-growth market, the only way a new business can survive is to take market share from an established competitor. However, according to the same consultant quoted above:

> If you don't have a broad offering within your product line you greatly reduce your ability to take market share from someone else.[18]

It's clear that this industry observer saw Keener-Blodee, Inc. facing much stiffer competition than Dick Keener and Lief Blodee imagined, and worse, that the company displayed a weakness in the marketplace because of its very narrow product line.

Small new business owners seem to make this type of mistake fairly often. I firmly believe that such owners harbor two untested assumptions. One is that they think their products will be better received by their target markets than is reasonably justifiable. The second is that they believe their competition is much weaker that even a casual observer might suppose. These two types of mistakes almost always result in delaying or eliminating the sales revenue stream a small new business needs in order to survive.

Mistakes You Should Avoid

Here it is most useful to reflect on how Robert Bennett and his MicroFridge, Wallace Leyshon and his electronic appliance controls, and Brad Brown and his Glacier Nursery eliminated or minimized the level of competitive intensity their new businesses would face in their selected marketplaces. Recall that MicroFridge had no direct competitors, Appliance Control Technology, Inc. used a strategy that minimized the competitiveness of its lone rival, and Glacier Nursery turned its competitors' disadvantages into its own advantages. Those new businesses represent good examples of how a small new business should deal with the competition—namely, eliminate it, or reduce it to a very manageable level.

There are three mistakes you should avoid when starting your new business. (1) You should avoid being uninformed or misinformed about the competition you will face in your target market. Remember Michael Kuperstein and Neurogen, Inc. Kuperstein had did not take the time to really learn about the competition he was facing, and it cost him and his new business lost time and money. (2) Avoid markets where there are many established competitors, especially if your small new business has no clear advantages over them. David Fokos elected to enter a very competitive marketplace where it would take a tremendous effort to pry a single customer away from his or her regular supplier. Furthermore, he entered that highly competitive marketplace with no obvious advantage distinguishing his offering from the competition. (3) Avoid thinking your product offering is so superior to competitors' that you will have no difficulty attracting their customers. Look at Dick Keener and Lief Blodee. They started a new business in a mature market where sales were not growing, competition was already strong and on the increase, and prices were declining because of competitive pressures.

You want to avoid marketing strategy execution delays caused by competition, such as that experienced by Kuperstein, Fokos, and Keener and Blodee. You do want to design your marketing strategy in such a way that you will not encounter serious delays due to obstacles and barriers raised by competitors. To do so, remember what Bennett, Leyshon, and Brown did.

The following is a *summary of guidelines and warnings associated with avoiding marketing strategy execution delays caused by competitive barriers.*

THE GUIDELINE YOUR MARKETING STRATEGY MUST SATISFY

Guideline 2a. Be certain that your new business can serve its target market better than any competitor.

VERY SUPPORTIVE GUIDELINE YOUR MARKETING STRATEGY SHOULD STRIVE TO SATISFY

Guideline 2b. Be very knowledgeable about your competitor's strengths and weaknesses. You should know the important weaknesses of your competitor's offering and you should offer a product that obviously overcomes those weaknesses. You must be certain that your target market clearly sees and appreciates that your new business's offering is superior to your competitor's.

WARNINGS OF THINGS YOU SHOULD AVOID

Warning 2a. Avoid being uninformed—or even misinformed—about the competitors you will face in your target market.

Warning 2b. Avoid mature markets or markets approaching maturity where there are many established competitors, especially if your new business has no clear advantage over them.

Warning 2c. Avoid thinking your product offering is so superior to competitor's offerings that your new business will have no difficulty attracting competitors' customers.

3. Delays Caused by Distribution Barriers

If it is to have any chance of being successful, a small new business must be able to distribute its products in a manner that is most convenient for its target market. Without such convenient distribution, the small new business is likely to fail. It is therefore imperative that such distribution be designed as an integral part of the new business's marketing strategy. *It is also most imperative that the distribution design be completed during the prelaunch period.* If a small new business enters its launch period without its distribution channel already established and ready to go, the product's launch will be delayed. Precious resources will continue to be expended during the delay, but no sales revenues will be forthcoming.

Some new businesses choose to distribute directly to their customers. For them, the distribution function may only involve arranging for appropriate transportation. But even that requires careful planning and management. Many new businesses, however, will require the services of independent intermediaries to perform the distribution function. For those new businesses, designing and managing their distribution channel is a much more demanding task.

There is a tendency for owners of small new business to pay less attention to the distribution aspects of their new business than they do to the other tasks that must be accomplished. Such behavior reflects the erroneous attitude that distribution facilities are ready and waiting for the small new business to come along and, when it does, the distribution task will somehow be taken care of in a timely and inexpensive manner. That is a most unfortunate attitude! Small new business owners must never lose sight of the fact that *all distributors and intermediaries are independent entrepreneurs who are in business to make a profit.* If a small new business does not help independent channel middlemen make a profit, those middlemen are not going to cooperate with the small new business, and it will have difficulty achieving effective distribution.

Entrepreneurs must be very realistic about the distribution delays their small new businesses might experience. They should make every effort to avoid mistakes that can prevent their new businesses from achieving the distribution needed in order to succeed. Unfortunately, my research identified four assumptions owners of small new businesses make with some frequency that can lead to lengthy strategy execution delays.

(1) They assume that whatever distribution facilities their small new business will need to reach its target market will be ready and waiting when the business enters its launch period.

(2) They presume to know what channel of distribution will be effective for their small new business, without doing any research into the matter.

(3) Some new businesses pursue a target market that currently is not being served by an already existing channel of distribution. And yet sometimes, those new business owners assume that the matter of channel of distribution will not be a problem. Eventually, they learn they will have to design a new channel of distribution to reach their intended target market—a task that requires time and money they do not have.

(4) Even when their product is somewhat complex, entrepreneurs starting small new business too often assume they are not responsible for its installation and/or service.

Marketing Strategies That Avoided Delays Caused by Distribution Barriers

Appliance Control Technology, Inc. manufactured electronic controls that were sold to manufacturers of mid-price kitchen and laundry appliances.[19] Appliance Control Technologies did not encounter any marketing strategy execution delays due to distribution because they shipped the electronic controls directly to the appliance manufacturers who had ordered them. No intermediaries were involved.

When Robert Bennett introduced the MicroFridge, his combination microwave oven-freezer-refrigerator, he found that established appliance distributors were very pleased to add the MicroFridge to their roster.[20] Not only did it represent an addition to their product lines, it added two new types of institutions—college dormitories and budget motels—to their lists of clients. Because MicroFridge broadened both their product line and their customer base, those distributors enjoyed added profits as a result of their association with Bennett's small new business.

Brad Brown designed Glacier Nursery's marketing strategy to give it an advantage over his out-of-state competitors, who found it unprofitable to provide season-long delivery services to Montana's retail garden centers.[21] They did make shipments during the spring buying surge, but then cut back sharply after that. Brown wanted to take advantage of the competitors' disadvantages by offering regular delivery services to Montana's retail garden centers. Due to his shortage of capital, he had no delivery trucks of his own. So, to make his deliveries, he used three local trucking firms who were happy to add other products to transport when making shipments around the state and elsewhere.

What You Should Do

Chapter 2 strongly argued that a small new business needs a synergistic marketing strategy if it is to succeed, and such a strategy must include a distribution element that compliments the new business's target market, and its product, price, and promotion. There are two things you should do to achieve this. (1) You must make certain that your marketing strategy includes an effective means of distribution that makes it very convenient for your potential customers to buy your new business's product. This means that you must make your product readily available to them and/or that your product must be available in all outlets where individuals in your target market expect to find it. (2) You must also make certain that your product is displayed in all appropriate locations within those outlets.

Such a channel of distribution should be completely designed, in place, and ready-to-go when your new business enters the launch period. None of the three small new businesses described above encountered any marketing strategy execution delays due to distribution because their owners had carefully planned the distribution channels their new businesses needed prior to entering their launch periods.

Marketing Strategies That Experienced Delays Caused by Distribution Barriers

A small new business can experience distribution delays if its owner makes any of the four assumptions listed above.

(1) Owners Assume That Distribution Facilities Will Be Available for Their New Business When It Enters Its Launch Period

Unfortunately, often this is not a valid assumption.

Rick Cardin was a senior manager in a reputable management consultant firm, but he really wanted to run a business of his own. So he started a chain of franchised sandwich shops he called O! Deli. These shops would be located in office buildings, and only operate weekdays from 7:00 AM to 5:00 PM. Cardin thought office buildings would be good locations for his franchisees, but many property managers were not looking to add a food retailer in their high-rise buildings. Of those that were, not all were looking for a sandwich shop. And if they were, they could choose from a number of already-established chains with solid financial credentials. Regarding the difficult task of finding locations, the founder of the Subway Sandwiches chain said:

> O! Deli may also have underestimated how tough it is to get sites in the first place. It's the most difficult task of franchising.[22]

It is clear that Rick Cardin did not carefully plan the distribution element of his marketing strategy during his new business's prelaunch period. Rather, he seems to have assumed that appropriate distribution facilities would simply be available when the time came to launch his new business. In the event, that wasn't true, and O! Deli encountered marketing strategy execution delays because of a problem with its distribution.

(2) The Owner Presumes to Know What Channel of Distribution Is Best
for His New Business Without Investigation

Some small new business owners select a target market with which they
have had no previous marketing experience. Yet some of them presume to
know which channel of distribution will be most effective in reaching this
new target market. That is, they select a channel of distribution for their
new business without making a reasonable research effort to determine
the right choice.

Carolyne Greene was a women's apparel designer who created a doll "for
the reality of your dreams," called FROYD for short. Greene believed the
doll would help children learn how to achieve their dreams. She tried—
unsuccessfully—to market her doll through three large toy retailers.
A former senior vice-president for toy-marketing giant, Mattel, Inc.,
believed that Greene had not selected the best channel of distribution for
her doll:

> I think Greene was incorrect in trying to sell FROYD to children and
> through the mass market. . . . I don't think children can relate to dreams.
> That's too abstract a concept. Its more young-adult oriented.[23]

After having failed in the large toy retailer channel of distribution,
Greene tried selling her doll through gift stores and department stores.
About her shift to the new channel, the former Mattel vice-president said:

> she should have gone that way first. . . . Gift shops and department stores
> tend to deal with an older market than toy stores do.[24]

The director of licensing for Jim Henson Productions agreed with the
above assessment.

> Going the gift-market route makes a lot of sense because FROYD is such a
> specialized product. I think the mass market is made up of people going
> into Toys-R-Us knowing what they're going to buy for a child. Whereas,
> in a gift situation, you don't really know what you're going to walk out of
> the store with.[25]

You already know that David Fokos was an experienced engineer who
designed high fidelity audio speakers for his employer. Because he
believed he could manufacture and sell higher-quality speakers than those

his employer produced, he started his own company, Icon Acoustics, Inc.[26] Fokos chose to sell his speakers direct to the public via an 800 telephone number. He did so to enable customers to get his high quality speakers for about half the price they would cost if they were marketed through a dealer. However, Fokos's choice of distribution method did not take into account how consumers actually shopped for audio equipment. Most people buying expensive audio speakers want to hear how they sound in comparison with other speakers they might consider buying. That is probably the main justification for the existence of audio dealers—to provide a retail outlet where potential customers can go to listen to different brands of audio equipment before deciding on which brand they will purchase. By selecting a distribution channel that did not match consumers shopping habits, Fokos created a situation that caused his new business to experience lengthy marketing strategy execution delays.

Greene and Fokos selected distribution channels that were not well matched with the products they were offering or the target markets they were pursuing. The wrong choices they made caused their new businesses to experience lengthy strategy execution delays.

(3) No Existing Channel of Distribution Currently Serves the New Business's Target Market, So Owners Must Design a New Distribution System for Their New Business

Some new businesses have a very basic channel of distribution—they ship their products directly to their customers. Many other small new businesses are forced to use existing intermediaries to distribute their products to their target markets. A third and different kind of situation occurs when an entrepreneur organizes a small new business to serve a target market that is not being served by any appropriate, existing channel of distribution. In such cases, the small new business owner finds himself in the very difficult position of having to design a new channel of distribution. This task will almost certainly cause his new business to experience lengthy marketing strategy execution delays.

Christopher Nolan started Landmark Legal Plans, Inc. to sell legal services to individuals and small businesses for a modest annual fee. To operate the new business, Nolan had to recruit lawyers who would do the actual legal work. Lawyers were attracted to Nolan's new business concept, but they wanted assurances that the legal plan would be marketed in a manner that would bring them large numbers of clients. Since no established channel of distribution existed for marketing legal plans to consumers and small businesses, Nolan had to find his own solution to the problem. Eventually he signed an agreement with an insurance marketing company to sell his legal plans through their nationwide force of 1,700 insurance agents. But Nolan knew that his contrived distribution system was far from perfect:

> I'm betting very, very heavily on brokerage community acceptance. I am putting all my eggs in one basket.[27]

There were two potential problems associated with using insurance brokers: (1) that the brokers were not trained to sell legal plans to consumers and small businesses, and they much preferred to sell high commission items like group health insurance, and (2) if legal plans were slow to catch on, the brokers would concentrate on what was easiest to sell—insurance. The managing editor of an insurance broker magazine said the following of Nolan's use of insurance brokers.

> His problem, though, is depending on the broker as a means of marketing. He plans on getting a substantial number of his clients from group sales, but I don't think the market's there. Employers aren't ready to put money into it. They have to provide medical and life insurance because everyone else does, but there's no pressure to offer a group legal plan. And with recent increases of up to 40% for medical plans, they've been cutting back on benefits, not adding new ones. Brokers are already struggling to put together reasonable packages of basic insurance for their clients. Convincing those clients to do anything else now is tremendously difficult.[28]

When a friend asked Paul Gruenberg if he would like to invest in a business that would market video yearbooks to high school seniors, he found the idea attractive. In fact, he liked the idea so much that he started VideOvation for that very purpose. But there was no readily available channel of distribution that Gruenberg could use to sell his video yearbooks to high-school students. At first he used three field producers to market VideOvation, but they were unable to even talk with high school principals about video yearbooks, and faculty yearbook advisors showed little interest in the concept. Gruenberg's next move was to partner with an established yearbook company to have their sales representatives promote video yearbooks in the high schools they called on. That was unsuccessful because, reportedly, those sales representatives also did not have any contact with high school principals. Then Gruenberg signed an agreement with a company that helped high school principals design fund-raising programs for special student projects. Even this third attempt at developing a viable channel of distribution for video yearbooks had skeptics. A venture capitalist who formerly had worked with yearbook companies said:

> Whenever you rely on an outside group whose business is different from yours to do the sales, you have to worry about whether the partner will give it the attention it requires—and whether its interest will be diverted to something else next year. We see it all the time in the high-tech field: something looks like a natural add-on product for a third party selling organization, but it doesn't always pan out.[29]

The owners of these small new businesses did not have established channels of distribution in place and/or waiting for them when they entered their launch periods. Both of them had to contrive or patch together some kind of distribution system for their products as best they could during the launch period. The resulting distribution systems proved to be ineffective, and they caused those new businesses to experience long marketing strategy execution delays.

(4) The New Business's Product Is Somewhat Complex, but Owners Assume They Are Not Responsible for Its Installation and/or Service

Some small new businesses sell relatively simple products that do not require installation and/or service. But other new businesses sell more complex products that sometimes do require installation or service, or both. If the installation and service are too complicated for customers to perform by themselves, the responsibility for those two important activities must fall on the new business itself, or on the channel system the new business uses to distribute the product. Without adequate installation and service, complex products will have no success in any market.

An interesting new business that involved product installation was Animalens, Inc. Randy Wise started the company to sell red contact lenses to chicken farmers. Reportedly, chickens fitted with red contact lenses would lay more eggs, eat less feed, and be less cannibalistic toward other chickens, all very desirable traits for increasing a chicken farmer's profits. How could they not want to buy these lenses for their chickens, Wise thought. But he soon encountered a problem he had not fully foreseen: the matter of who would install the lenses in the eyes of the chickens. Wise had calculated the additional cost to the farmer of installing the lenses at 10¢ per bird, and did not believe that would significantly deter farmers from buying the contact lenses. But a poultry specialist raised a different problem with installation that Wise had not anticipated:

> Wise will also have to provide more details about the installation. Two people installing 1,200 pairs a day may seem fast to him, but it sounds like a snail's pace to me, particularly when you're talking about chicken houses with 100,000 birds. It means you'd need about 20 people doing nothing but putting in lenses for around eight days straight. Even if the labor cost only works out to $.10 a chicken, not every rancher has access to that kind of manpower.[30]

This small new business encountered marketing strategy execution delays because it entered its launch period without being prepared to provide the installation and service required by potential customers. This new business either had to provide such installation and service, or it needed a channel of distribution that could do so. But Rick Wise had not thought to include installation as part of his product, and since he had chosen to distribute his lenses to the farmers directly, there was no channel of distribution he could turn to—he was it.

Mistakes You Should Avoid

(1) Small new business owners often seem to ignore the critical importance of distribution to the success of their new ventures, or they seem to assume that somehow appropriate distribution will just happen. Such attitudes can be disastrous! Do not make the same kind of mistake Rick Cardin of O! Deli made. (2) If you are starting a small new business whose target market is one with which you have had no previous experience, do not just assume you know which channel of distribution will be best for your new business. Do some research to help you identify which distribution system is most effective at reaching your target market. Avoid the kinds of mistakes made by David Fokos of Icon Acoustics, Inc. and Carolyne Greene with her FROYD doll. (3) Be very careful of starting a new business whose target market is not easily reached by using direct selling or through existing channels of distribution. Under those circumstances, you will probably have to create a new channel of distribution, and that can cause lengthy strategy execution delays. Remember, and avoid, the difficulties encountered by Christopher Nolan of Landmark Legal Plans, Inc. and Paul Gruenberg of VideOvation. (4) If you start a new business with a product requiring installation and/or service that cannot be performed by the customers themselves, you must have a channel of distribution that will

provide the needed installation and service, or you must include installation and service capability as part of your product marketing plan. Avoid the kind of mistake made by Randy Wise of Animalens, Inc.

The following is a *summary of guidelines and warnings associated with avoiding marketing strategy execution delays caused by channel of distribution barriers.*

YOUR MARKETING STRATEGY MUST SATISFY THESE TWO GUIDELINES

Guideline 3a. Develop a distribution system that makes it very convenient for target market individuals to buy your product. Your product must be readily available to all potential customers and/or be available in all outlets where potential customers expect to find it.

Guideline 3b. Your product must be displayed in all appropriate location within those outlets.

WARNINGS OF THINGS YOU SHOULD AVOID

Warning 3a. Avoid assuming that distribution facilities will be available to your new business when it enters its launch period.

Warning 3b. Avoid assuming you know what channel of distribution is best for your new business, especially if its target market is one with which you have had no previous experience.

Warning 3c. If you cannot sell directly to potential customers, avoid target markets that currently are not being served by an existing channel of distribution that is appropriate for your new business.

Warning 3d. If your product requires installation and/or service, do not select a distribution channel that cannot or will not provide those two important functions.

---

4. Delays Caused by Environmental or Legal Barriers

Some small new businesses can encounter environmental or legal regulations that must be satisfied before they will be allowed to begin operating as on-going enterprises. These can be federal, state, or local regulations, or a combination thereof. Compliance with some of these regulations might be easily accomplished, but compliance with others can prove to be quite costly and time consuming. Owners of a small new business will serve themselves very well by becoming knowledgeable about all the regulations that can affect their business. This familiarization should occur early in the business's prelaunch period, to give the owner sufficient time to design the business in a manner that satisfies all of the appropriate regulations. If the owner does not take such precautions, and instead waits to learn about applicable regulations as the new business tries to enter its launch period, one or more regulatory agencies may prevent it from doing so. When that happens, very likely the new business will experience costly and time-consuming strategy execution delays.

Marketing Strategies That Experienced Delays Caused by Environmental, Legal, or Federal Regulations

Environmental Regulations

Many businesses are affected by environmental regulations. In the past, for example, environmental regulations required that landfill operators use soil every day to cover the trash that came into their landfills that day. Paul Kittle started Rusmar, Inc. to make and sell foam that landfill operators could use instead of soil to cover trash. The advantage of foam was that it would collapse after 36 hours and take up less space than would soil. This meant that the landfill operators could use more of their capacity for storing revenue-generating trash. When viewed in this light, foam appeared to be a very attractive alternative to soil. But the presence of environmental regulations and regulators proved to have a delaying effect on the quick adoption of foam by landfill operators:

> It wasn't as if [Kittle's assistant] could win blanket permission from the Environmental Protection Agency to begin selling foam. The EPA sets the macro standards for landfills but leaves micro regulations to the states. And some state regulatory agencies, mostly byzantine bureaucracies, issue permits for the use of such products as foam on a case-by-case basis. They'd have nothing to gain by issuing permits to landfills and everything to lose if, once approved, the foam had an unforeseen downside.
> Landfill operators could easily grasp the value of the product. But would they go to the mat with the state agencies? Not likely. . . . landfill operators were now facing new national regulations requiring the installation of pumping systems and liners to protect the groundwater, a tremendous burden. They didn't need a fight for foam permits.[31]

According to one landfill operator:

> I'd be using Rusmar's foam right now if it weren't for the regulatory nightmare. We have a severe capacity crunch. But any time you file a major

operational change here—and foam would fit into that category—you need new permits from three separate agencies. It would cost us more than $1 million just to apply for them, given all the monitoring and documentation they require.[32]

Another new business that encountered environmental regulations was Waste Energy, Inc. Keith Burnett founded the company to manufacture and market a machine (Goldfire) that could convert trash, waste oil, and other combustible waste materials into electricity. Buyers of the Goldfire machine could use the generated electricity to run their businesses, or they could sell the electricity to their local power company. Not only would Goldfire buyers save the cost of having their trash hauled away, they would also reduce their electricity costs. But several potential environmental issues could cause problems either for Waste Energy, Inc. or for the buyers of Goldfire. According to a venture capitalist who invested in environmental companies, three potential problems could arise:

how reasonable is it to ask these small operators to tackle the complex task of securing environmental permits for this kind of facility (Goldfire), as well as to monitor and comply with the ever changing body of regulations? If Waste Energy wants to assist in the permit process and offer it as a customer service, it will have to become expert in air quality and other regulations of all 50 states.

It is also quite possible that mandated air-emission controls would make these units uneconomical:

there is the question of what the residuals from these units (Goldfire) will be. In the worst case, you could be turning non-hazardous waste into hazardous waste by converting waste oil into small quantities of ash or other residuals that are considered hazardous.[33]

Both of these new businesses encountered environmental regulations that caused serious strategy execution delays when the respective companies entered their launch periods.

Legal Regulations

Some new businesses encounter legal issues and regulations that can cause delays when they attempt to execute their marketing strategies. Christopher Nolan started Landmark Legal Plans, Inc. because he wanted to offer average consumers a better prepaid legal plan than those available at the time. He believed that the market for such plans was huge—approximately 70 percent of the U.S. population. Although Nolan's new business appeared attractive to both potential customers and the lawyers who would service them, Landmark Legal Plans faced serious legal regulatory barriers. A consultant to the legal plan industry pointed out that:

> Nolan needs to analyze the regulatory impact on his plan. In a large number of states, they won't allow him to operate this closed-panel approach—where he is referring customers to individual law firms—on a for-profit basis. The disciplinary rules that govern the bar in many states simply won't permit for-profit legal plans. A majority of states will require underwriting on Nolan's plan to be a licensed insurer.
>
> Maybe he'll be able to turn decent profits in the limited number of states he's able to operate in without regulation. But in the long run, he might well need to get an underwriter. Without any regulatory problems, he's probably got only five or six states to sell in. What happens after that? It's really an oversight.[34]

Federal Regulations

When a new business involves a product or service related to a person's health and well-being, there is a very good chance that it will have to be approved by the Food and Drug Administration. Historically, such approvals take time and are likely to delay a company's entry into its launch period. Very often, the length of the delay will be highly uncertain. That was true for Buddy Systems, Inc., a company that marketed a computer-based system called Buddy that could monitor the important health signs of a person who had returned home after having had a serious medical procedure in a hospital. Those important health signs could be transmitted by telephone to medical personnel who could monitor from a distance the medical condition of the patient recuperating at home. Thomas Manning, the founder of the company, believed that his Buddy system could help reduce the cost of caring for patients after they had left the hospital. As well intentioned as he was with respect to reducing medical costs, Manning learned also that he was

> in a business that demands more patience than most. Any new medical device must first win approval from the Food and Drug Administration before it can be sold. With equipment such as Buddy, gaining that crucial green light could take at least a couple of years of testing, paperwork, and clinical trials, all while operating costs are mounting and before a single sale is made.[35]

A small new business can be seriously affected by a change in the rules governing the industry to which it belongs. A small new financial institution found this out the hard way. Ann Hartman and Daniel Dart started a low overhead bank in a section of Boston that was poorly served by the banking community. Nine months after it opened for business the Blackstone Bank and Trust Company was breaking even on deposits of $25 million. Six months after that the bank was enjoying profits on deposits of $40 million. But then the Federal Deposit Insurance Corporation (FDIC), which regulates some aspects of the banking industry, introduced a rule change that had a significant negative impact on the bank:

> Blackstone's main problem hasn't been competition, but shifting federal banking requirements. When the start-up opened, the FDIC expected it to keep a 6% capital-to-asset ratio; six months later the policy changed, requiring a 10% ratio for a bank's first three years. As a result, Dart and Hartman had to raise $1.1 million more in capital, and cap deposits at $56 million instead of nearly $100 million they had expected to carry.[36]

Dart estimated that the FDIC rule change deprived the bank of more than $1 million in additional net revenue that it could have earned had not the FDIC changed its rules. Blackstone Bank went out of business two years later. According to Dart:

> the bank received a fatal blow when the FDIC refused to allow it to raise additional capital through a form of subordinated debt securities . . . then turned around and demanded it do so a year later. By then New England's banking situation had deteriorated so much that Blackstone hadn't a prayer of finding $2 million in new equity.[37]

The failures of Buddy Systems and Blackstone Bank must be attributed, at least in part, to the interruptive actions and the resulting delays arising from the regulatory oversight of the two federal agencies mentioned.

The first four of the above five examples illustrate how various governmental regulations can cause new businesses to experience strategy execution delays that prevent them from generating the sales revenue streams they need for survival. Such delays can be a harsh reality for any new business that needs approvals from one or more regulatory bodies. The fifth example showed how a change in regulations can cause the death of a new business that showed promise of succeeding.

What You Should Do

Practically all new businesses must satisfy some federal, state, or local regulations, even if it is no more that obtaining from local governments the permits and licenses required by law. When starting your new business, there are two things you must do. (1) In addition to securing basic permits and licenses, you must be completely aware of all serious regulations that apply to your industry and business, and since there is nothing your small new business can do to change those regulations, you must also take the necessary steps to comply with them. (2) You need to incorporate into your planning process all of activities associated with such regulations, and complete them during your new business's prelaunch period so that you are in full compliance with all appropriate regulations prior to the launch of your new business.

Mistakes You Should Avoid

The five examples discussed above illustrate that environmental and/or legal regulations can seriously delay a new business from entering its launch period and beginning to enjoy sales revenues. When planning your new business during the prelaunch period, you will make a very serious mistake if you assume that it will not be affected by any regulations and/or if you do not fully address all of the appropriate environmental, legal, and other regulatory matters that are required of your new business. To fail to take into full consideration all appropriate regulatory matters can be fatal.

The following is a *summary of guidelines and warnings associated with avoiding marketing strategy execution delays caused by environmental or legal barriers.*

YOUR MARKETING STRATEGY MUST SATISFY THESE TWO GUIDELINES

Guideline 4a. Be very knowledgeable about, and comply with, all environmental and legal regulations (federal, state, and local) affecting your new business.

Guideline 4b. During your new business's prelaunch period, fully incorporate all appropriate regulations into your planning process.

WARNINGS OF THINGS YOU SHOULD AVOID

Warning 4a. Avoid assuming your new business will not be affected by any federal, state, or local environmental or legal regulations.

Be Alert for Other Sources of Delays

Based on my study of many small new businesses over the years, I have concluded that small new business owners often experience serious marketing strategy execution delays because they did not adequately analyze and understand their target markets, their competitors, their distribution channels, and/or the regulations affecting their new businesses. If the hundreds of thousands of new businesses started each year in the United States could be studied in great detail, we would more than likely find a few more factors that cause strategy execution delays besides those discussed in this chapter. What this means for entrepreneurs starting a new business is (1) they should be very aware that still other factors might cause delays, (2) they should be on the lookout for possible delaying factors that can affect their new business, and (3) they should try to respond as quickly as possible by taking appropriate action that will shorten the delay or eliminate it altogether.

Summary

If a small new business has a marketing strategy that satisfies Screening Condition I, it will have a complete and synergistic marketing strategy. With such a strategy in hand, the new business has much potential for success and is poised to exit the prelaunch period. A new business's *prelaunch period* is characterized by the expenditure of precious resources in getting the business organized while having absolutely no sales revenues. The new business enters its *launch period* when it first opens its doors to potential customers, expecting to begin enjoying a sales revenue stream that is the direct result of effectively executing its synergistic marketing strategy. To achieve that sales revenue stream, the small new business owner must make certain that his marketing strategy will not encounter any serious marketing strategy execution delays, which—if they last long enough—can lead to its failure. This chapter identified four categories of marketing strategy characteristics that can cause strategy execution delays. The purpose of Screening Condition II is to help owners of small new businesses avoid such strategy execution delays.

Based on my research, I estimate that about 80 percent of small new businesses experience serious delays caused by the presence of one or more factors in their marketing strategies. That means marketing strategy delaying factors can make a significant contribution to small new business failures. Small business owners should be fully aware of the possible existence of these delaying factors and make certain that none of them is included in their new business's marketing strategy. There are four categories of delaying factors, each consisting of three or more subcategories.

A new business can encounter delays caused by the following *target market issues*.

- Its owner has not carefully defined its target market.
- The new business has multiple target markets and/or constituencies.
- The new business targets a market based solely on attitudes.

Each of these factors can result in a marketing strategy that is not sharply focused on a specific and reachable target market, and the resulting lack of focus is likely to cause the marketing strategy to be ineffective and slow in execution. Such delay may very well last until the small new business owner makes the necessary change in the target market element of the marketing strategy.

Many small new businesses experience delays because their owners have not adequately evaluated the *strength of competition*. Three categories of competition-based delays are the following:

- Owners are unaware of their new business's competition.
- Owners choose to ignore, or not take seriously, the many competitors their new business faces.
- Owners unrealistically overvalue their product's superiority over their competitors'.

When any of these factors is present, a new business will experience delays and will likely not achieve the sales revenues the owner had been expecting. Delays caused by these factors will last until the owner adjusts the marketing strategy to somehow make the new product offering more attractive to people currently buying from the competitors.

Channels of distribution can be a source of marketing strategy execution delays in four different ways.

1. The owner assumes that appropriate channels of distribution will be available when the new business enters its launch period.
2. The owner presumes to know what channel of distribution is most appropriate for the new business.
3. No channel of distribution is available to serve the new business's target market.
4. The new business's product needs installation and/or servicing, but neither the new business nor its channel of distribution provides those services.

If any of these factors is present, a new business will experience delays because the channel of distribution element in its marketing strategy is faulty or incomplete. These types of delays will persist until the owner establishes an effective channel of distribution for the new business.

If a new business does not comply with all appropriate federal, state, and local environmental, legal, and other *regulations*, the new business will experience strategy execution delays. Those delays will remain in place until the new business satisfies all applicable regulations.

4

Screening Condition III: Is Your Marketing Strategy Compatible with a Small Marketing Budget?

If you've designed your new business's marketing strategy to satisfy the five characteristics discussed in Chapter 2, it will be both a complete and a synergistic marketing strategy, and it will have successfully achieved Screening Condition I. With such a strategy, your small new business will have taken a very important first step toward becoming successful. If your marketing strategy *does not include any* of the four undesirable factors discussed in Chapter 3, it will also have satisfied Screening Condition II, and your new business should not encounter any serious strategy execution delays caused by those undesirable factors.

You must be absolutely certain that your marketing strategy will achieve both Screening Conditions I and II before you proceed further. Why? Because research findings indicate that very few small new business owners design marketing strategies that achieve both of those two conditions. For example, one study of 30 small new businesses revealed that only 4 of them used marketing strategies that achieved all five of the characteristics associated with Screening Condition I.[1] But of those four new businesses, only two successfully avoided all four of the undesirable factors constituting Screening Condition II. A third new business used a marketing strategy that encountered one of those undesirable factors, but it was able to quickly overcome the resulting strategy execution delay. The fourth new business used a marketing strategy that did not avoid all four of Screening Condition II's undesirable factors, and it soon encountered very serious strategy execution delays that caused it to fail. If only 3 of 30 new businesses came close to achieving both Screening Conditions I and II, then doing so must be something that is not easily accomplished. You want to make certain that your marketing strategy achieves both of those conditions before proceeding further.

This chapter focuses on another screening condition that your marketing strategy must satisfy in order for your small new business to make further progress toward becoming successful. That screening condition addresses the issue of whether your new business's marketing strategy can be executed with a small marketing budget. This is very important because most small new businesses have very meager marketing budgets. Often there is no marketing budget at all!

Even if your marketing strategy has successfully achieved both Screening Condition I and Screening Condition II, your new business can encounter very serious difficulties if its marketing strategy includes one or more elements that require a large marketing budget. If a large budget is not available, your marketing strategy cannot be executed effectively, and your new business will probably fail. You, and every other small new business owner, are therefore strongly advised to ask the question: *Does my marketing strategy require a larger budget than what is available?*

How can you determine if all of the elements in your marketing strategy are executable with a small marketing budget? This is essentially Screening Condition III, and its purpose is to help you and other small new business owners arrive at a good answer to that question.

Introduction to Small Budget Compatibility

How might an entrepreneur evaluate a proposed marketing strategy to determine if it is compatible with a small marketing budget? I addressed this question on two occasions several years ago.[2] In those exploratory studies, a number of well-established marketing and economic concepts were evaluated for the purpose of identifying intuitively whether those concepts could be compatible with a small budget. Each concept represented a situation that could apply to a small new business and its marketing strategy as it was just prior to the launch period. There were a total of 23 such concepts, all falling into five general topic areas:

1. Target market and market segmentation
2. Type of market competition
3. Stage of the product life cycle
4. Channels of distribution
5. Business and consumer product classifications

Based on an exhaustive search, these 23 concepts were believed to represent a complete list of all such concepts applicable to the issue of small budget compatibility. Each of the concepts was first evaluated and then classified into one of four categories—good match, fair match, poor match, or mismatch—based on the extent to which it was judged to be compatible with a small budget marketing strategy.

Eleven of the conceptual situations were judged to be good or fair matches with low-budget marketing strategies. There was at least one conceptual situation in each of the five topic areas identified above. Those 11 conceptual situations are shown in Table 4.1. The remaining

Table 4.1 Summary of Conceptual Situations Which Are Good and Fair Matches with a Low-Budget Marketing Strategy

Conceptual Situation	Evaluation of Match	Comments
Many Geographically Concentrated Buyers	Good	Select underserved segment in one geographic area
Few Geographically Concentrated Buyers	Fair	Need a significant product difference and must gain distribution
Monopolistic Competition	Good	Select small, well-defined target market
Introductory Stage of the Product Life Cycle	Good	Product needs fast acceptance in a well-defined market
Exclusive, Selective Distribution	Fair	Need good relationships with dealers
Short Channel of Distribution	Fair	If only a small number of retailers are needed
Open Channel of Distribution	Good	If independent middlemen want/need the product
Fabricating Parts & Materials	Fair	Need a significant product difference
Installations	Fair	For selected small installations
Accessory Equipment	Fair	Offer unique features for selected target market
Consumer Shopping Good	Fair	If selective distribution gains retailer support

Table 4.2   **Summary of Conceptual Situations Which Are Poor Matches or Mismatches with a Low-Budget Marketing Strategy**

Conceptual Situation	Evaluation of Match
Few Geographically Dispersed Buyers	Poor
Many Geographically Dispersed Buyers	Mismatch
Pure Competition	Mismatch
Oligopoly	Mismatch
Growth Stage of the Product Life Cycle	Mismatch
Mature, Decline Stage of Product Life Cycle	Mismatch
Extensive Distribution	Mismatch
Long Channel of Distribution	Poor
Closed Channel of Distribution	Mismatch
Raw Materials & Operating Supplies	Poor
Consumer Convenience Good	Mismatch
Consumer Specialty Good	Mismatch

12 conceptual situations were evaluated to be either poor matches or mismatches with a small marketing budget. They are listed in Table 4.2.

Tables 4.1 and 4.2 can help owners of small new businesses evaluate whether their proposed marketing strategy is compatible with a small budget. They should *avoid* marketing strategies that utilize any of the 12 conceptual situation listed in Table 4.2, because all of them require large marketing budgets. Instead, the new business owner should look for a marketing strategy *that only utilizes* the concepts presented in Table 4.1, because all of them can be compatible with small marketing budgets. If new business owners design a strategy that adheres to those two suggestions, they will very likely be able to execute it with a small marketing budget. This is the essence of Screening Condition III.

The 23 conceptual situations listed in Tables 4.1 and 4.2 are discussed below.

1. Target Market and Market Segmentation Concepts

You already saw in Chapter 2 that the target market element is crucial to the task of designing a complete and synergistic marketing strategy. And Chapter 3 described how a poorly identified target market might cause a small new business to experience strategy execution delays. The fact that this chapter begins with the target market concept is a further indication of how important that topic is to the success of a small new business.

The cardinal rule is that owners of small new businesses should avoid selecting a target market that is not compatible with a small marketing budget.

Although market segments can be defined in many ways using different bases, the dimensions which most impact the size of the marketing budget are (a) geographically concentrated versus geographically dispersed buyers, and (b) many versus fewer buyers.

If a small new business targets buyers in a relatively small geographic area, it will have a geographically concentrated target market, and such markets are more compatible with small marketing budgets than are geographically dispersed markets. There are three reasons why this is so: it is more economical to communicate with a relatively small number of geographically concentrated buyers; it is easier to achieve efficient distribution to them; and fewer competitors are likely to be encountered in a geographically concentrated market than a geographically dispersed one.

A market of many geographically dispersed buyers tends to be less compatible with a small marketing budget than a concentrated market of fewer buyers for two reasons. More competitors are likely to be actively pursuing large markets, and they will be more aggressive and competitive in their efforts to carve out their share of the market. A small new business without a large marketing budget will find it more difficult to communicate with potential customers in such a market than in a more geographically concentrated one.

Small new business owners should understand the realities of dimensions (a) and (b) above and select target markets and market segments that are compatible with the size of their marketing budgets.

Marketing Strategies That Are Compatible with Small Budgets

There are two target market/market segmentation situations that appear to be quite compatible with small marketing budgets.

(1) In a geographically concentrated market with many buyers, target a segment that is being poorly served, or not being served at all.

(2) Offer a significantly better product to a few geographically concentrated buyers.

(1) In a Market with Many Geographically Concentrated Buyers, Target a Segment That Is Being Poorly Served, or Not Being Served at All

The Blackstone Bank and Trust Company selected as its target market the low-income sections of Roxbury and the South End in Boston, both of which were being ignored by the Boston banking community.[3] Those geographic sections of Boston represented many underserved households and small businesses in a relatively confined geographical area. It was very easy for Blackstone Bank and Trust to communicate with individuals and small businesses in those neighborhoods, and those potential customers welcomed the service.

A second new business venture worth noting here is the MicroFridge, the combination microwave oven-refrigerator-freezer developed by Robert Bennett.[4] Until the MicroFridge came along, no such product was available for students living in college dormitory rooms. They were a market segment that was not being served, and no competitors gave evidence of being interested in serving it. Yet, each medium-sized and large college and university represented many geographically concentrated potential users of the MicroFridge. College and universities were easy to identify, and communication with each was relatively easily achieved. In these circumstances, only a relatively small marketing budget would be needed for each college and university.

(2) Offer a Significantly Better Product to a Few Geographically Concentrated Buyers

If a market consists of only a few buyers, those buyers are likely to receive a lot of attention from suppliers who have long-established relationships with them. A small new business would have much difficulty trying to take the place of those established suppliers unless it could offer a product with a significant difference that buyers considered important. If a small new business has a significantly better product to offer consumers than what is available from the established suppliers, its marketing strategy can be a fair match with a small marketing budget.

One company that successfully used this target market concept in its marketing strategy was Appliance Control Technology, Inc. (ACT).[5] This small new business offered kitchen and laundry appliance manufacturers electronic control devices to replace the electro-mechanical controls they had been using. Because those manufacturers were relatively few in number, it was not greatly time consuming or expensive to be in touch with all of them. And since ACT's electronic controls promised lower production costs, improved appliances, and faster introduction of new models, a number of appliance manufacturers viewed ACT's electronic controls as a significantly better product than what they had been using and were eager to learn as much as possible about what ACT had to offer.

What You Should Do

All three of these small new businesses were able to begin generating sales revenue streams early in their launch periods because they had selected target markets and market segments that were easily reached and quite compatible with small marketing budgets. Because not all target markets display such desirable characteristics, you should look for target markets that do. (1) Always look for potential customers that are being poorly served by their current suppliers. (2) Make certain those potential customers constitute as geographically concentrated a market as possible. Remember, the more geographically dispersed the market, the larger the marketing budget needed to address it. (3) If your small new business is going to target certain businesses as its potential customers, it can have a good chance of being successful if it offers them a significantly better product than what is available to them from current suppliers. Your new business will be able to manage with only a small marketing budget if your potential customers are relatively few and geographically concentrated.

Marketing Strategies That Are Not Compatible with Small Budgets

There are two target market/market segmentation concepts that are not likely to be compatible with a small budget: large target markets, and many geographically dispersed buyers.

In situations where a small new business targets a *large market* or a *market consisting of geographically dispersed buyers*, the new business will theoretically have more potential customers, but it will also encounter more competitors and it will have to develop a more widespread distribution system. Both the increased competition and the larger distribution system will lead to greater expenses, which translates into a need for a larger marketing budget. Such situations are at best a poor match with small budget compatibility, and very often will be a mismatch. Yet, at least half—and perhaps as many as two-thirds—of all small new businesses pursue target markets consisting of geographically dispersed buyers. Only a very small percentage of them will show some signs of being able to survive for more than a year or two. The rest of them will suffer very difficult times because their marketing budgets were not large enough to pursue such markets.

You've already encountered two such small new businesses. When Carolyne Greene introduced her dream-oriented F.R.O.Y.D. doll, she targeted all five-to-thirteen-year-old children.[6] David Fokos started Icon

Acoustics, Inc. to sell his top-quality audio speakers to high-fidelity music lovers throughout the United States.[7] Clearly, both of these small new businesses targeted large, geographically dispersed markets and needed large marketing budgets if they were to communicate effectively with their target markets.

Mistakes You Should Avoid

Small new businesses that target large and/or geographically dispersed markets almost always encounter serious difficulties or fail because they do not have a large marketing budget. You never want your small new business to target such a market unless you are certain that you can afford the large promotional program and the widespread distribution system you will need in order to have any chance of succeeding.

The following is a *summary of guidelines and warnings associated with target market/market segmentation concepts that are compatible with a small budget.*

YOUR MARKETING STRATEGY MUST SATISFY AT LEAST ONE OF THESE GUIDELINES

Guideline 1a. Target an underserved segment in a market with many geographically concentrated buyers.

Guideline 1b. Offer a significantly better product to a few geographically concentrated buyers.

WARNINGS OF THINGS YOU SHOULD AVOID

Warning 1a. Avoid pursuing a large target market unless you have a very large marketing budget.

Warning 1b. Avoid pursuing a target market consisting of many geographically dispersed buyers.

---

2. Type of Market Competition Concepts

Most businesses are engaged in one of three types of market competition: pure competition, oligopolistic competition, or monopolistic competition. When a person starts a small new business, more than likely it will enter into one of these three types of market competition. For reasons discussed below, both pure competition and oligopolistic competition are incompatible with starting a small new business with only a small marketing budget. That leaves monopolistic competition as the only one of the three in which a small new business might have a reasonable chance of succeeding.

Pure Competition

This type of competition is characterized by many buyers and many sellers of commodities or commodity-like products. Fruits and grains are commodity products, as are gasoline and most raw materials. Firms selling their products in pure competition have little or no control over price. All competitors sell their products at or near a market price that is determined by supply and demand. Some manufactured products, like office supplies, hardware store products, basic breakfast cereals, household paper products, and others can become commodity-like products if there are many sellers of the product and if there is little to distinguish one supplier's product from another's. Such a competitive situation can be characterized as nearly pure competition.

If a small new business enters into such market competition, it will not be able to gain a significant product advantage because there are already many competitors selling the same or very similar products. Without a clear product advantage, the small new business would have to do a great deal of advertising and promoting to persuade consumers to switch to its product. Such a new business is also likely to have difficulty gaining adequate distribution because wholesalers and retailers will have little reason to drop their current suppliers and take on the new business's product. A small new business with only a small marketing budget and no product advantage to attract consumers or distributors will be headed for certain failure. Its only chance of survival would be with a large marketing budget, one that could support a very effective promotional campaign directed at both consumers and intermediaries. Consequently, if a new business enters into a pure competition or nearly pure competition market, such a situation would be a mismatch with the successful use of a small marketing budget.

Oligopolistic Competition

In an oligopoly there are fewer competitors than in pure competition—often less than 10, sometimes only 3 or 4—but all the competitors offer identical products or very similar products. The products are similar in the sense that buyers tend to be equally satisfied with their purchases regardless of which brand they've selected. An important characteristic of oligopolistic competition is that most competitors charge quite similar prices. Typically, one of the competitors is the industry leader who decides if, when, and how much to change prices. The other competitors ("followers") take their cue from the industry leader and set prices at or slightly below the leader's price, but not so low as to start a price war. Often there is a "pecking order" among the followers, where those of lesser reputation must set a lower price in order to attract buyers. In oligopoly, price (i.e., low price) is often the dominant factor taken into account when many customers make purchase decisions.

Because the products offered by all competitors tend to be identical or very similar, a small new business entering this type of market competition would have to offer a lower price than most or all of the established competitors. If it does so and begins to threaten established competitors, they will quickly lower their prices, causing sales revenues for the small new business to fall. And when that happens, the small new business will not be able to survive for very long. Alternatively, a small new business entering oligopolistic competition could try to use heavy promotion to gain entry into the market. But if it pursues such a course, it will soon face strong retaliation from established competitors, quite likely in the form of deep price reductions, and once again, the end result will be failure for the small new business. For these reasons, oligopolistic competition is quite incompatible for a small new business unless it has a significant product advantage *and* a large marketing budget to promote that advantage.

Monopolistic Competition

In a monopolistic competition market, competitors offer differentiated products designed to be very appealing to a specific market segment. Owners of small new businesses entering a monopolistic competition market can enhance their chances of success by offering a truly differentiated product that the target market will find more attractive than ones offered by competitors. If the target market is small and well defined, and if the market does in fact find the new business's product offering more attractive than competitors', the small new business may be able to distribute and promote its product relatively efficiently and economically—that is, with a small marketing budget. Thus, of the three main types of market competition, monopolistic competition is the only one compatible with a small marketing budget.

Marketing Strategies That Are Compatible with Small Budgets

You are already well acquainted with three small new businesses that successfully practiced monopolistic competition with their marketing strategies. Wallace Leyshon launched Appliance Control Technology, Inc. to offer a differentiated product—electronic controls—to the underserved target market of manufacturers of mid-price kitchen and laundry appliances.[8] Leyshon's electronic controls offered those manufacturers significant advantages when compared with the electro-mechanical controls they had been using. Furthermore, since the number of mid-price kitchen and laundry appliance manufacturers was relatively small and easily identified, Appliance Control Technology was able to promote and distribute to them effectively with a small marketing budget.

Robert Bennett's MicroFridge, Inc. is another example of a small new business that entered a monopolistic competition market.[9] Many college students used electric hot plates, microwave ovens, small refrigerators, and still other devices to prepare meals in their dorm rooms. Such devices were, at best, marginally satisfactory, but there was nothing better available. Bennett's combination microwave oven-freezer-refrigerator was a differentiated product that many students found very appealing. Since colleges and universities constituted a well-defined market, it was not difficult for MicroFridge, Inc. to communicate with, and distribute to, that market, and that, in turn, allowed the new business to operate with a relatively small marketing budget.

Even Brad Brown's Glacier Nursery used a marketing strategy that enabled it to behave like a monopolistic competitor.[10] His small, well-defined target market comprised the retail garden centers located in Montana. To his potential customers, Brown offered a differentiated product—namely hardier trees and shrubs grown in Montana—and he also offered them differentiated service in the form of product delivery throughout the entire growing season. With such a differentiated product and service offering, and a small and well-defined target market, Brown was able to execute his marketing strategy with a rather small marketing budget.

What You Should Do

As a potential small new business owner you would be well advised to look for a monopolistic competition market to enter. To do so successfully, you must differentiate your product offering from those of other competitors in that market. You must also identify a small, well-defined target market that is not being well served by those competitors, and you must make certain that your differentiated product offering has distinguishing features that the target market will find very appealing. In these circumstances, your marketing strategy may requires only a relatively small marketing budget.

Marketing Strategies That Are Not Compatible with Small Budgets

Because both pure competition and oligopolistic competition are not compatible with a small budget, small new businesses should avoid entering into such market competition.

Avoid Entering into a Market That Can Be Characterized as Pure Competition or Nearly Pure Competition

To enter into such types of market competition, new business owners need a large marketing budget to help the new business somehow stand out from its competitors, either through effective promotion and/or through the creation of some kind of distribution advantage. But even with a large marketing budget, that can be difficult to accomplish in a pure or nearly pure competition market. Yet, some small new businesses do try to enter into such markets with little or no marketing budgets.

Tom Silverman's Sanctuary Recordings, Inc. was one new business that entered into a nearly pure competition market.[11] The recording studio business offers musicians a facility to rent when they wanted to make a record. There were dozens of competing recording studios within a short distance from the location Silverman chose for Sanctuary Recordings, and hundreds of them within a half-hour's drive. With so many competitors located nearby, market competition looked very much like nearly pure competition. But Silverman thought most recording studios were "cruddy," and he intended to attract customers by offering musicians more amenities than were available in most studios. On the other hand, his recording equipment was not all the latest technology. Silverman didn't have a large budget to promote his studio, and there was no way he could create a distribution advantage. So overall, it was unclear how much he was able to differentiate his recording studio from the hundreds of others available in the area.

David Fokos' Icon Acoustics, Inc. manufactured and sold high quality audio speakers to high-fidelity music enthusiasts.[12] Although Fokos' speakers were priced at the high end, there were over 200 competitors going after the same market segment. With that many competitors selling high quality speakers, it was difficult for consumers to distinguish between them. Thus, the market displayed characteristics of being in nearly pure competition. Fokos sold his speakers directly to consumers via an 800 telephone number, so he did not have a distribution or retail advantage. He was unable to create much demand for his speakers because he had very little money for promoting them.

Tom Silverman tried to distinguish his new business from competitors' through more amenities even though he lacked top of the line technology. David Fokos thought he had a higher quality speaker at a competitive price. But potential customers of these two new businesses had many competitive alternatives to choose from. Both of these new businesses entered into nearly pure competition markets, apparently with very little to distinguish themselves from the competition. Given the number of established competitors each faced in his market, and the fact that both businesses had little differentiation to offer, neither of them had much chance of successfully breaking into his respective market without a large marketing budget.

Avoid Entering a Market That Displays Oligopolistic Characteristics

After growing bored of retirement, Dick Keener and Lief Blodee started Keener-Blodee, Inc. to manufacture and sell stylish wooden office chairs. They did not have a large marketing budget, but they believed they had a highly differentiated chair that interior designers would appreciate. According to Keener:

> The uniqueness of design and construction give us a product with integrity that designers will respect.[13]

But they were entering a market that was becoming oligopolistic in character: fewer but larger competitors, flat demand, and the price competition that usually follows a stagnant market. Justin Thompson, a consultant to the industry, believed Keener-Blodee was facing 8–10 established manufacturers that offered similar chairs at similar prices. Of their optimism about selling many chairs during their first year in the face of such competition, Thompson said:

> This is not a growing market segment. For them to expect they're going to be able to whack 7,100 units out of somebody else's hide is a gross miscalculation. Not minor; gross.[14]

This small new business was facing well-established competitors in a mature market that displayed oligopolistic characteristics, yet it did not have a marketing budget that was large enough to effectively compete with those large competitors.

Mistakes You Should Avoid

The three new businesses discussed above tried to compete in types of market competition that are not receptive to small new businesses in general, and not forgiving of small new businesses with small marketing budgets. In those circumstances, such new businesses are very likely to fail. If you don't want to make the kinds of mistakes those new businesses made, (1) avoid entering into a market that can be characterized as pure or nearly pure competition, and (2) avoid entering a market that displays oligopolistic characteristics.

The following is a *summary of guidelines and warnings associated with types of market competition concepts that are compatible with a small budget.*

THE GUIDELINE YOUR MARKETING STRATEGY MUST SATISFY

Guideline 2a. Enter a monopolistic competition market by offering a differentiated product with distinguishing features that will appeal to a small, well-defined target market.

WARNINGS OF THINGS YOU SHOULD AVOID

Warning 2a. Avoid entering a market that can be characterized as pure or nearly pure competition.

Warning 2b. Avoid entering a market that displays oligopolistic characteristics.

---

3. Product Life Cycle Concepts

Every truly new product goes through a life cycle of its own. Someone invents or designs an innovative new product and introduces it to its intended market. If the market wants or needs the new product, some customers will start buying it. When that occurs the product enters the introductory stage of its life cycle, *during which it probably will not have any competitors.* As time passes and broader market acceptance begins to take hold, demand for the new product increases, and it then enters the growth stage of its life cycle. A second entrepreneur—or an established firm—will notice the growth of that new product, see it as a profit-making opportunity, and soon begin to offer a product similar to the one already available. If the demand for those two products continues to expand, one or more additional firms will enter the market, also hoping to gain a share of its profits. But these later entries into the market must take on the earlier entries, who by now may have become well-established competitors. To do so, the later entries must have a large promotional budget to announce their entry into the market and to overcome the disadvantages of being "johnny-come-latelies." Often the increased competition of more firms entering the market will trigger price decreases and that cause a decline in profit growth for all competitors. Eventually the market for these products will approach saturation, sales growth slows down and then disappears, the market matures, price competition becomes more severe, and most competitors begin to experience a decline in profitability. When that occurs, the product will have entered the maturity stage of its life cycle. Time passes and eventually sales go into decline as fewer and fewer potential customers remain in the marketplace. Taken together, this phenomenon of growth and decline is called the *product life cycle*.[15]

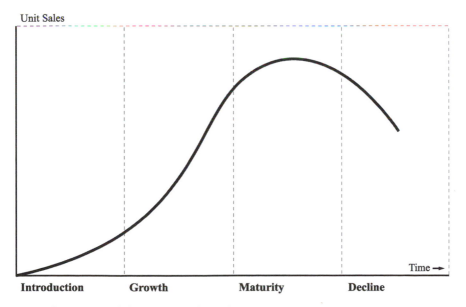

Figure 4.1   **Stages of the Product Life Cycle**

Familiar examples of products that have progressed all the way through their respective life cycles include steam-powered railroad locomotives, manual and electric typewriters, propeller-driven commercial aircraft, pocket pagers, videocassettes, analog television and others. These products have all died or are in decline, superseded by newer products. In the United States, even the desktop personal computer is about to enter the mature stage of its product life cycle, if it has not already done so.

Individuals thinking of starting a small new business should be very aware of, and use, the product life cycle concept when they first begin planning their new businesses. For example, if a person starts a small new business with a product that's in the introductory stage of its life cycle, that new business may be able to succeed with just a small marketing budget. On the other hand, if someone starts a new business with a product that is already well into its growth stage, that new business will have difficulty succeeding without a large marketing budget because of the more intense competition in that stage of the product's life cycle. It is obvious then, that this information about the product life cycle concept will be very important for entrepreneurs to know and use when they first begin planning a new small business.

Small Budgets and the Introductory Stage of the Product Life Cycle

Only the introductory stage of the product life cycle can be compatible with a small market budget.

If a person pioneers a truly new product, his or her new business should not encounter any direct competitors when it enters into the launch period. This represents a tremendous advantage in four ways. (1) If the product is well designed to satisfy the needs of a market segment that is not currently being well served by any competitor, that segment will quickly begin purchasing the new product. (2) Because it has no direct competitors, the new business will not need a large marketing budget to overcome competitors' promotions. (3) Since there is no equivalent product already on the market, many wholesalers and retailers that serve the new business's target market will very much want to carry the new business's product offering. (4) With no competitors' prices already established in the minds of potential consumers, the new business owner has some freedom in pricing his product so as to "create good value" in the eyes of the intended consumers. These are tremendous advantages.

If a small new business owner introduces a truly new product to a target market that is not being well served, two considerations will determine if such a marketing strategy can be successful with a small marketing budget.

One of those considerations has to do with the new business's target market being both (a) well defined and (b) underserved. These issues have been discussed in depth at the beginning of Chapter 3 and again at the beginning of this chapter. A well-defined and underserved target market is both more economical to reach and more receptive to informative communications. The second consideration that is critical to a successful marketing strategy is discussed in detail below.

Small Budgets Need Fast Adoption and High Acceptance

This second consideration has to do with how quickly the new product will be adopted by the target market and what proportion of the target market will eventually adopt it. These are called the rate of adoption and the level of acceptance, respectively. A new product has a good chance of achieving both a fast rate of adoption and a high level of acceptance if it possesses the characteristics discussed in the following four paragraphs.

When a business first introduces a truly new product, its launch period will coincide with the initial segment of the introductory life cycle stage of the new product. Consequently, the small new business will not encounter any competition when it does so. Even without any competition, however, there is no guarantee that the new product's target market will quickly adopt the new product.

So how can the owner of a small new business with a truly new product evaluate whether or not it will achieve both a fast adoption and a high level of acceptance by its target market? To make such an evaluation, the entrepreneur must turn to *diffusion of innovation theory*. This theory states that to achieve a fast rate of adoption and a high level of acceptance by its target market, a new product should

1. have important advantages over products currently being used by the target market.
2. be compatible with the target market's current life styles and values. That is, potential buyers should not have to change the manner in which they act, behave, or do things if they purchase and use the new product.
3. be easy to understand and use.
4. be capable of being sampled or used on a trial basis by the target market.
5. have advantages and benefits that can be easily communicated and/or demonstrated.[16]

According to this theory, if a new product possesses all five of these characteristics, the target market should enthusiastically embrace it, and it should enjoy both a fast rate of adoption and a high level of acceptance. In turn, that kind of market receptivity will cause distributors and dealers to want to carry the product. If the target market is well defined and easy to reach, promotional efforts will be both economical and relatively easy to achieve. The launch of a truly new product that possesses these characteristics should be very compatible with a small marketing budget.

Conversely, the fewer of these five characteristics a new product possesses, the more likely the product will encounter a slow rate of adoption and a low level of acceptance. A slow rate of adoption means the new product will not quickly begin to generate a sales revenue stream once it enters the launch period, and a low level of acceptance means less sales revenue potential for the new product in the long run. Because both of these outcomes are very incompatible with a small budget, an entrepreneur would be well advised not to start a small new business based on a product likely to experience a slow rate of adoption and/or a low level of acceptance.

Marketing Strategies That Are Compatible with Small Budgets

Let's look again at the three new businesses that achieved Screening Conditions I and II, and examine how they were able to incorporate this product life cycle concept into their marketing strategies.

Wallace Leyshon's Appliance Control Technology, Inc. (ACT) selected manufacturers of mid-price kitchen and laundry appliances as the target market for its electronic control devices.[17] Because prices of electronic controls had been too high until then, those manufacturers were still using electro-mechanical controls on their appliances. In effect, they were not being well served by the established suppliers of electronic controls. When Leyshon approached those appliance manufacturers with ACT's electronic controls, those controls appeared as a truly innovative product to them. Furthermore, with respect to the five diffusion of innovation characteristics associated with fast adoption, ACT's electronic controls had important advantages over the established competitors' products, they were compatible with the appliance manufacturer's current products and processes, they were easy to understand and use, their effectiveness could be demonstrated and their advantages easily communicated. These evaluations support the conclusion that ACT's electronic controls could be designed and promoted in a manner that would achieve fast adoption and high acceptance among the well-defined target market. These factors enabled Leyshon to accomplish ACT's marketing strategy with only a small budget.

Robert Bennett marketed his combination microwave oven-freezer-refrigerator, the MicroFridge, to the well-defined target market of students living in college dormitory rooms.[18] That market was not being served by any competitor, because there were no direct competitors to the MicroFridge. Evaluating the MicroFridge with respect to the above-described five diffusion of innovation characteristics shows that it had significant advantages over everything students had available in their dormitory rooms, it was easy to understand and use, it was very compatible with current college student life styles, and its effectiveness could be easily demonstrated and its advantages easily communicated. Bennett's design of the MicroFridge and his selected target market of college students living in dormitories favored both a fast rate of adoption and a high level of acceptance. That, in turn, allowed Bennett to get by with a reasonably small marketing budget.

Even Brad Brown's Glacier Nursery utilized the product life cycle concept in its marketing strategy, but his new product also included a service component.[19] Brown's well-defined target market consisted of Montana's 40–50 retail garden centers who were not being well served throughout the gardening season by out-of-state nurseries. Brown capitalized on that weakness of his competitors by offering all-season-long deliveries to the target market. And that service supplemented the superior product—hardier, Montana-grown trees and shrubs—that his competitors could not match. Even so, Brown found that adoption of his hardier trees and shrubs was not as fast as he would have liked. The slow rate of adoption was caused—at least in part—by the difficulty of demonstrating their superior hardiness. To offset that difficulty, every year Brown sent some free samples of his plants to a number of Montana retail garden centers.

What You Should Do

From the above discussion you can see that successful small new businesses identify a well-defined target market that is not being well served by current suppliers. The owners of those new businesses then offer a truly new product that will enjoy fast diffusion among the members of their target market. You should keep the examples of Wallace Leyshon, Robert Bennett, and Brad Brown in mind when you first start planning your new business if you want it to be successful with only a small marketing budget.

Marketing Strategies That Are Not Compatible with Small Budgets

There are three product life cycle situations that are not compatible with a small marketing budget.

(1) A new business based on a truly new product whose characteristics will not result in a fast rate of adoption and a high level of target market acceptance.

(2) A new business based on a product that is already in the growth stage of its product life cycle.

(3) A new business based on a product that is already in the maturity or decline stage of its product life cycle.

(1) A New Business Based on a Truly New Product Whose Characteristics Will Not Result in a Fast Rate of Adoption and a High Level of Acceptance

Some new businesses are based on truly new products that do not enjoy fast rates of adoption. Randy Wise's Animalens, Inc. offered large chicken farmers red contact lenses for their chickens, reportedly causing them to lay more eggs, eat less feed, and be less cannibalistic toward one another.[20] Chicken farmers showed very little interest in the lenses, probably because their advantages were not easily demonstrated and installing the lenses required a change in the farmers' operating procedures. Thomas Manning started Buddy Systems, Inc. to sell his remote patient-monitoring computer system to large home-health-care companies.[21] Manning believed his system could help reduce healthcare costs because patients could be sent home from the hospital earlier and visiting nurses could make fewer calls on patients recuperating in their homes. Despite what seemed like very attractive advantages, the adoption rate for Buddy was poor because the system was not compatible with doctors' established practice of wanting to see their patients face to face before making decisions regarding their health. If a new product will not enjoy a fast rate of adoption and a high level of acceptance, that product will be a mismatch with a small marketing budget.

(2) A New Business Based on a Product That Is Already Well into the Growth Stage of Its Product Life Cycle

When an innovative new product has been introduced to a market and begins to show significant growth in sales, potential competitors begin to enter the market because they are attracted by the profits they hope to realize. Their appearance marks the new product's entry into the growth stage of its product life cycle. As the market grows and the competition increases, most sellers will be trying to achieve broad distribution and create brand preference for their offerings. To do so, those competitors will be spending large amounts on marketing. As the product moves still further into the growth stage of its life cycle, even more competitors may be entering the market with even more differentiated products. The overall result is that the growth stage represents a period of strong and increasing competition, well into the latter portion of the stage. There the competitive situation becomes even more unpleasant because the rate of market growth declines, causing some competitors to begin reducing prices. At this point maximum profits for all competitors will already have been achieved. If a small new business tries to enter a market with a product that is already in the growth stage of its product life cycle, it will find itself facing a number of established competitors who are very actively spending their marketing budgets.

If you are thinking of starting a small new business in such a market, you should recognize that there is little or no chance of succeeding unless you have a huge product advantage *and* a large marketing budget. Without a large budget, your small new business will have great difficulty attracting customers away from competitors who already have become established in the market. With more competitors offering more differentiated products, your small new business will have difficulty gaining a significant product difference in the eyes of consumers. The appropriate channels of distribution have been besieged—and continue to be besieged—by all competitors, making it difficult for your small new business to gain the distribution advantage it would need to succeed. Overall, it is clear that your small new business would encounter intense competition if it enters a market with a product that is already in the growth stage of its product life cycle. To have even some small chance of success in such a market, it would need a very large marketing budget.

(3) A New Business Based on a Product That Is Already in the Maturity or Decline Stage of Its Product Life Cycle

When a product enters its maturity stage, total market sales for the product are growing only slightly, if at all. The product is already available in all of the distribution outlets where it is expected to be sold. One or more competitors may still enter the market, further intensifying competition.

More firms will pursue further product differentiation and/or price reductions in the hope of gaining—or at least not losing—market share. Firms that have the resources may increase their promotional spending.

Eventually total sales by all competitors begin to decrease, signaling that the product has entered into its decline stage. Supplies of the product from all competitors will exceed total market sales, causing a downward pressure on prices. Because of the numerous competitors, effective product differentiation will be difficult to maintain. Profitability will decline for all competitors, and completely disappear for some. The weakest competitor will abandon the market, and sooner or later others will follow suit.

Anyone thinking of starting a small new business should be aware of, and fully appreciate, the characteristics associated with products in the maturity and decline stages of their life cycle. Those characteristics are very grave and unforgiving, and they certainly should not instill optimism in the heart of anyone thinking of starting a small new business with such a product.

The above descriptions make it very clear that a small new business with little or no marketing budget will be well advised not to enter markets that are in the maturity or decline stages of their product life cycles. To do so will almost certainly invite failure. Yet, I believe that somewhere between one-third and one-half of all small new businesses enter such markets.

Consider Carolyne Greene and her F.R.O.Y.D. doll.[22] There were already 50 or more competing dolls on the market when she started her new business. David Fokos started his Icon Acoustics, Inc. when there were already some 200 high-quality audio speakers that potential customers could chose from.[23] When Dick Keener and Lief Blodee founded Keener-Blodee, Inc. to manufacture European-style wooden office chairs, the market for such chairs was already flat, and industry observers noted that there were probably 8–10 well-established competitors already in the market.[24] Each of these three small new businesses was unsuccessful in its attempt to enter a mature market.

Mistakes You Should Avoid

Do not base your new business on a truly new product if it will not enjoy a fast rate of adoption and a high level of acceptance in your target market. A new product that requires significant time and money to gain acceptance in its market is not compatible with a small marketing budget. When you first start planning your small new business, make certain you accurately identify the life cycle stage your product offering will be in. If your product offering is already in the growth, maturity, or decline stage of its product life cycle, it will be very much in your best interests to consider a different product as the basis of your small new business. If you insist on starting a small new business with a product already in its growth stage, you must have a very large marketing budget if you hope to have any chance of succeeding. A much, much better option, however, is to look for a product offering that is in the introductory stage of its product life cycle.

The following is a *summary of guidelines and warnings associated with product life cycle concepts that are compatible with a small budget.*

YOUR MARKETING STRATEGY MUST SATISFY AT LEAST ONE OF THESE GUIDELINES

Guideline 3a. Offer a truly new product that will enjoy fast adoption and a high level of acceptance by a well-defined target market that is not being served at all by any competitor—or only being poorly served.

Guideline 3b. If your new business will not be offering a truly new product, design or differentiate your product offering so that it will be more appealing to the individuals in your target market than the products offered by competitors. *(This is guideline 2a from Chapter 2.)*

Guideline 3c. If your new business will not be offering a truly new product, your product should offer better quality and/or important new features and benefits and/or greater convenience and/or better value compared to your competitors' offerings. *(This is guideline 2b from Chapter 2.)*

WARNINGS OF THINGS YOU SHOULD AVOID

Warning 3a. Avoid offering a truly new product that will not enjoy a fast rate of adoption and a high level of acceptance by the target market.

Warning 3b. Avoid entering a market where your offering will be competing against products that are already in their growth (especially late growth), maturity or decline stages.

---

4. Channels of Distribution Concepts

To have any chance of success, a new business must be capable of economically distributing its products and services to its customers.

Distribution can be accomplished in a number of ways, some of which can be very expensive, some less expensive. When planning a new business, the owner must select a distribution system that is compatible with the available budget. If there is a mismatch between the cost of distribution and the available budget, the new business will encounter serious difficulties that may cause it to fail.

There are three distribution channel concepts that small new business owners should be aware of when planning their small new businesses.

- Exclusive, selective, or extensive distribution
- Short or long channels of distribution
- Open or closed channels of distribution

Exclusive, Selective, or Extensive Distribution

A new business uses *exclusive* distribution if it sells its products through only one retailer or dealer in a given geographical market. If the new business sells its products through only a few retailers or dealers in a given market, it is using *selective* distribution. If a small new business's target market is geographically concentrated, the choice of either exclusive or selective distribution is appropriate for its target market and compatible with a limited marketing budget. Perhaps more importantly, exclusive or selective distribution can also help the new business owner establish solid relationships with a relatively small number of dealers and distributors without spending a lot of money.

Extensive distribution occurs when a new business sells its products through many retailers and dealers in a market. When a new business targets many geographically dispersed potential customers, it will have to use extensive distribution because its product must be available in many retail outlets. To achieve such distribution, the new business owner will have to commit the resources needed to build a large network of wholesalers and distributors to carry the product. The new business's marketing budget will probably also require a large promotional element to provide retailers with financial incentives to secure their cooperation. Typically, these kinds of activities require more than a small marketing budget.

Most products sold through grocery stores, drug stores, and convenience stores are targeting many geographically dispersed buyers. All new businesses based on such products will probably need extensive distribution to succeed, and establishing such distribution can be quite costly and/or difficult. Many retailers charge new suppliers a fee just to place their products on the retailers' shelves. These are referred to as "slotting fees." So if the small new business wants to use extensive distribution but does not have a large marketing budget, it will be in trouble even before it starts.

Short or Long Channels of Distribution

A firm uses a "short" channel of distribution if it sells directly to end users or if it sells to a retailer who resells to end users. A "long" channel is one where a firm uses two or more intermediaries to reach end users. For example, some firms sell to wholesalers, who in turn sell to retailers. Other firms use agents or brokers to sell to wholesalers, who then sell to retailers. In such channels, a firm has no contact with end users, and very little contact with retailers. To initiate and maintain some communications with these retailers and end users—and to motivate them—would require the establishment of an organization to do so, and that will likely be impossible with a small marketing budget. In general, the shorter the channel and/or the fewer the retailers or final end users, the greater the chance that a small new business can establish good relations with those parties. For example, a small new business could get by with a small marketing budget if it had to contact and maintain good relationships with only 50 end users, or with only 50 retailers who serve hundreds or perhaps thousands of end users. On this basis, short channels can be a fair match with a small marketing budget, while long channels are likely to be a poor match or a mismatch.

Long channels of distribution utilizing two or more intermediaries are typically employed when a firm is trying to target many geographically dispersed consumers being served by a large number of retailers. When a small new business needs the cooperation of many wholesalers, retailers, and consumers for its success, it will almost certainly need a large marketing budget to offer wholesalers and retailers incentives to gain their cooperation. Quite likely, promotional activities will have to be directed at the consumers as well. Without the cooperation of all three parties, there is little chance that the new business will succeed. For obvious reasons, long channels of distribution, typically, are not compatible with small marketing budgets.

Open or Closed Channels of Distribution

Well over half the goods and services marketed in the United States flow through what are called vertical marketing systems. A vertical marketing system is a channel of distribution that is closed to all suppliers and distributors except those specifically invited to be members of the channel. Some vertical marketing systems are corporate-owned. Goodyear sells some of its tires through its own retail stores, and Sherman-Williams sells its paints through its own retail stores. These channels of distribution are not open to a small new business except by permission of the corporate owners. Other vertical marketing systems are based on contractual arrangements. We know them as franchises, and they are found in fast foods, soft drinks, new automobiles, automotive repairs, and in other product and services markets. These vertical marketing systems, too, are closed to any firm without the permission of the franchising organization. If its target market is being well served by one or more existing vertical marketing systems, a small new business will have little chance of distributing its product through that channel unless specifically invited to do so.

On the other hand, an open channel consisting of independent distributors can help a small new business gain distribution for its product if those intermediaries have not yet been able to obtain a similar product from some other supplier. In this case, the open channel may welcome the small new business with open arms. Such collaboration can help a small new business gain a competitive advantage in that channel. When that occurs, when a small new business is welcomed by an open channel of distribution, the new business may very well be able to achieve a distribution advantage with a small marketing budget.

Marketing Strategies That Are Compatible with a Small Budget

There are three distribution channel concepts that can be compatible with small marketing budgets.

(1) Exclusive or selective distribution can reach geographically concentrated target markets.
(2) A short channel of distribution can reach a relatively small number of geographically dispersed customers.
(3) An open channel of distribution that wants to distribute your product will welcome your arrival on the scene.

(1) Exclusive or Selective Distribution Can Reach Geographically Concentrated Target Markets

Robert Bennett used appliance distributors to distribute his Micro-Fridge.[25] Those distributors welcomed the opportunity to carry his new appliance for three reasons: it was a new product line they were not carrying; the product opened up two new markets—colleges and budget motels—that the distributors were not already serving; and the distributors were given exclusive rights to distribute the MicroFridge in the areas they historically served. For these reasons, appliance distributors welcomed Bennett with open arms when he called upon them.

(2) Use a Short Channel of Distribution to Reach a Relatively Small Number of Geographically Dispersed Customers

A short channel involves either selling directly to end users, or selling to dealers and retailers who sell to end users.

Wallace Leyshon's Appliance Control Technology, Inc. had a target market consisting of several dozens of appliance manufacturers located in the United States.[26] Although the manufacturers were not geographically concentrated, they were relatively few in number, a fact that made it easy enough for Leyshon to be in personal contact with each. Since each manufacturer ordered in large quantities, the most efficient and the least expensive approach was for ACT to ship its controls directly to the individual manufacturers who had ordered them.

Brad Brown's Glacier Nursery also used a short channel to distribute his trees, shrubs, and plants in Montana.[27] It would have been quite impractical to try to sell directly to homeowners. Instead, he used local trucking companies to ship his plants to his target market—Montana's 40–50 retail garden centers—who then sold them to homeowners. His system was a good match for his small marketing budget, and it was relatively easy to maintain personal contact with those 40–50 retail garden centers.

(3) An Open Channel of Distribution That Wants to Distribute Your Product Will Welcome Your Arrival on the Scene

Earl Bentz was successful in starting a new business to build small boats for people who liked to fish for bass, walleye, pike, muskie, and other game fish. Much of his success was due to the fact that boat dealers were unhappy with the established boat manufacturers because the latter had shown no interest in providing them with new, up-to-date models of fishing boats. The dealers' customers were also very unhappy with the boat manufacturers for the same reason. Here then was a channel of distribution waiting and hoping for someone to supply it with the kinds of new boat models they wanted, but couldn't get. In short, it was a very open channel of distribution! Bentz recognized the situation for what it was and started a new boat-manufacturing business that successfully exploited that very dissatisfied channel of distribution.[28]

When Michael Stecyk noticed that millions of small business owners—just like all U.S. citizens—had to go to the post office to buy stamps, he got the idea for a postage meter machine designed especially for small businesses. Such a machine would not only weigh a piece of mail and apply the appropriate amount of postage, it could also print the return address on the envelope, as well as print other promotional messages on the front or back of the envelope. Most important, however, was that a new inventory of postage could be downloaded into the machine via a telephone connection, so the small business owner would not have to take the machine to the post office. Stecyk's employer asked him to start a small new business to design, manufacture, and market the new postage meter. Potential customers soon found the new postage meter to be very helpful, almost indispensable. But its success in the marketplace was also due to the existence of a very open channel of distribution that quickly embraced the postage meter when it became available. That open channel consisted of Staples, Office Depot, Office Max, and other retail chains that targeted small businesses. Before Stecyk's postage meter came along, those retailers had nothing to offer small business owners for their postage and mailing activities. The fact that those large retailers were ready and waiting when Stecyk's meter became available contributed greatly to its success in the marketplace.[29]

These two examples demonstrate that an open channel of distribution can quickly welcome a small new business's product with open arms, and then deliver that product to eagerly awaiting buyers. Very often, because of the speed at which channel acceptance can occur and the large sales volumes that such a channel can deliver, open channels of distribution can be very compatible with small marketing budgets.

What You Should Do

When planning your small new business, do not lose sight of the fact that there are three channel of distribution characteristics that are most compatible with a small budget. If you have a unique product offering for a well-defined and geographically concentrated target market, give serious thought to using exclusive or selective distribution in your marketing strategy. If you are serving a relatively small number of potential customers that are geographically dispersed, direct distribution or a short channel of distribution can be very compatible with a small budget.

If you can find an open and welcoming channel of distribution that serves your target market, such a channel will very likely be quite compatible with a small budget.

Marketing Strategies That Are Not Compatible with Small Budgets

Three distribution channel concepts that are not compatible with small budgets are (1) extensive distribution, (2) long channels of distribution, and (3) closed channels of distribution.

(1) Extensive Distribution

When a small new business tries to sell its products through many retailers and dealers in a market, it is using extensive distribution.

While on a Caribbean vacation, Octavia Randolph discovered some native food products she liked very much. She started Oualie, Ltd. to make those products and market them in the United States.[30] She was hoping to distribute her products through supermarkets, but was unable to gain such distribution. As noted earlier, large retail food chains often require new products to pay a "slotting fee," and usually expect the new product to be well advertised and promoted. Either one of these demands calls for more than a small budget, but when combined, they require a marketing budget well beyond the means of the typical small new business. Randolph's failed attempt to gain extensive supermarket distribution is not uncommon for small new businesses trying to sell products to the large consumer market.

Richard Worth, on the other hand, was much luckier. He founded Frookies, Inc. to market his fruit-sweetened cookies, the first cookies to be made from all natural ingredients. Worth was able to gain extensive distribution because the buyer of a large grocery chain was very impressed with the "great taste" of his cookies.[31] Even so, Worth had to utilize some very creative—and perhaps quite expensive—trade promotions in order to attract the attention of buyers. So, overall, it's not clear whether he was able to gain extensive distribution with only a small marketing budget. It is very possible that the overall cost of his distribution proved to be not so small in the long run.

Evidence suggests that a sizeable proportion of small new businesses must achieve extensive distribution in order to have some chance of succeeding. Yet, attempts to gain extensive distribution with only a small budget appear to have very little chance of succeeding.

(2) Long Channels of Distribution

A long channel of distribution uses two or more middlemen to reach final consumers. As noted above, when a small new business uses two or more intermediaries in its channel of distribution, it will be necessary to motivate and communicate with them on a regular basis, and that is very difficult to do with a small budget.

Landmark Legal Plans, Inc. tried using a long channel of distribution.[32] Landmark Legal Plans (LLP) hoped to sell inexpensive legal plans to individuals (for wills, leases, etc.) and to small businesses (for various contracts, leases, etc.). LLP planned to use independent lawyers to do the actual legal work involved in the plans, and it signed an agreement with an insurance marketing company with a nationwide network of 1,700 insurance agents. Those salespeople would be paid a commission for each legal plan sold. In effect, using only a small marketing budget, LLP tried to establish a long channel of distribution consisting of two different types of intermediaries. To shape it into an effective channel of distribution, however, LLP would first have to train those agents in the best ways to sell the plans and motivate them to find buyers for the plans. LLP would also have to coordinate each successful transaction with the lawyer component of the channel of distribution and make certain that the appropriate legal plan was returned to the prospect through the salesperson who made the sale. Such a multilayered channel of distribution is far too complex to be achieved with only a small budget.

(3) Closed Channels of Distribution

As noted earlier, this type of channel is closed to all suppliers and intermediaries who have not specifically been invited to be members of the channel. But a channel might also be closed for other reasons.

For example, at one time all cable television operators in the United States were required to carry all local, over-the-air broadcast programming on their systems. After a Supreme Court decision declared that requirement illegal, cable operators did not have to carry a local station's programming unless they felt it was in their best interests to do so. With that ruling, cable television was transformed from a completely open channel of distribution for all television programming to an arbitrarily closed system. When Barbara Lamont founded Crescent City Communications Co., she encountered that arbitrarily closed system, and it prevented her programming from reaching a part of the target market that relied on cable for their television reception.[33]

Some of the market she had hoped to reach with her programming turned out to be unreachable because of this closed distribution channel.

A small new business, O! Deli, wanted to locate its sandwich shops in office buildings.[34] Unfortunately, many of the managers of those buildings did not want any food service at all, many specifically did not want a sandwich shop food service, and, of those that did, some preferred competing sandwich shops over O! Deli. In effect, much of the envisioned channel of distribution was closed to this small new business.

Mistakes You Should Avoid

Given the examples presented above, if you are starting a small new business and do not have a large marketing budget, you very much want to avoid trying to use extensive distribution or long channels of distribution or closed channels of distribution. Each of these three types of distribution makes a poor match with a small marketing budget.

The following is a *summary of guidelines and warnings associated with channel of distribution concepts that are compatible with a small budget.*

YOUR MARKETING STRATEGY MUST SATISFY AT LEAST ONE OF THESE GUIDELINES

Guideline 4a. Use exclusive or selective distribution to reach well-defined, geographically concentrated target markets.

Guideline 4b. Use a short channel of distribution to reach a relatively small number of geographically dispersed customers.

Guideline 4c. Use an open channel of distribution, one that wants to distribute your product and welcomes your arrival on the scene.

WARNING OF THINGS YOU SHOULD AVOID

Warning 4a. Avoid using extensive distribution unless you have a marketing budget that will support such a system.

Warning 4b. Avoid using a long channel of distribution to reach your target market.

Warning 4c. Avoid pursuing a target market if it is served by a closed distribution system, or if it is not already being served by an existing channel of distribution that can be helpful to your new business.

---

5. Business and Consumer Product Classification Concepts

Marketing textbooks classify both business products and consumer products into useful categories, and describe the specific marketing and competitive characteristics associated with the products in each category. That information can be very helpful to anyone who is thinking of starting a small new business. By understanding and utilizing this readily available information, entrepreneurs can avoid starting a small new business with a product that is not compatible with a small marketing budget.[35]

Business Products Classifications

All products being marketed by one business to other businesses are considered to fall into one of five possible categories: raw materials, operating supplies, fabricating parts, installations, or accessory equipment.

Businesses Raw Materials and Operating Supplies

These two categories of business products tend to consist of commodities or commodity-like products. Steel, various chemicals, paper, paper clips, file folders and many similar products fall into these categories. A small new business that engaged in one of these product categories would not be able to offer significant differentiation compared to the products offered by numerous and well-established competitors. Even with a large marketing budget, a small new business entering into competition in any of these product markets is not likely to achieve even marginal success.

Businesses Fabricating Parts

These are products that become parts of some other, finished product. For example, a company uses raw materials to manufacture small motors which then become part of many appliances. Because such fabricated parts are typically sold directly from one manufacturer to another, it is often possible to keep distribution and promotional expenditures low. However, if a small new business intends to offer a fabricated part to mature business firms, more than likely the small new business will be targeting a mature market. When that is the case, warning 3b (earlier in this chapter) would apply; that is, a small new business should not enter a market where the products being offered are already in the mature stage of their product life cycle. Since established competitors will have well-developed relationships with customer firms, a small new business is likely to encounter long delays before persuading those firms to switch suppliers, if such a switch ever happens at all. In light of this reality, an entrepreneur would be well advised to avoid the fabricated parts market *unless he could offer something significantly better than current competitors' offerings.* If a small business can offer such a superior fabricated part, and if it can keep promotion costs low with direct (short) distribution, its market strategy could be somewhat compatible with a small marketing budget.

Business Installations

Large installations such as manufacturing plants, warehouses, or sophisticated materials handling facilities are beyond the means of all but a very few large businesses. However, smaller types of installations, such as specialty production or testing equipment, might be pursued by small new ventures. If a small business owner has designed extra or unique features into the product offering, targeted businesses may find it attractive. Distribution of these types of installations is usually direct, which might allow a small new business to handle its own distribution in an economical manner. Under such circumstances, offering some types of smaller business installations might be compatible with a small marketing budget.

Business Accessory Equipment

This category of products includes such things as office furniture, telephone systems, computer products, copy machines, and many other items not directly involved in the production operations of a firm. But well-established competitors already exist in each business accessory equipment category. If a small new business is going to enter into the business accessory field, more than likely it will be facing a number of well-established competitors in a mature market. That is not a situation favoring a small new business with a small marketing budget. Still, many business accessories can be designed with unique features that some target markets may find desirable. Since many business accessories are distributed directly or through short channels, it may be possible for a small new business to secure acceptable distribution quite economically. If the small new business's target market is well defined, relatively few in number, and not widely dispersed geographically, promotional expenditures may be kept a reasonable level. When these conditions exist, the business accessory market can be a fair match with a small marketing budget.

Consumer Products Classifications

All consumer products are classified into one of three categories: convenience goods, shopping goods, and specialty goods.

Consumer Convenience Goods

These are products found in grocery stores, drug stores, convenience stores, and many other outlets. We are all familiar with them: we buy them almost every day. Distribution of these products is extensive and uses long channels, two factors that are associated with large marketing budgets. Unless a small new business offers a really significantly different convenience product, it will encounter many active and aggressive competitors. To compete against them, the small new business would have to promote heavily—which again means having a large marketing budget at its disposal—in order to have even a small chance of succeeding. Because of the strong competition and potential distribution difficulties likely to be encountered, entering a consumer convenience goods market must be considered a mismatch with a small marketing budget.

Consumer Shopping Goods

This category of consumer goods includes fashionable apparel, furniture and home furnishings, large appliances, automobiles, and other products. They are called shopping goods because consumers go to retail stores selling such items, look at the different brands and models, and compare them with one another and with their own wants and needs before they buy them. They are "shopping," and this activity is very serious business to them.

Because some consumer shopping goods such as automobiles and major appliances require large marketing budgets, such products are not compatible with a small marketing budget. On the other hand, many apparel and home furnishing items are not well-known, heavily promoted major brands. Such products typically are sold (1) to many consumers in geographically concentrated markets (2) through short channels of distribution (3) using relatively few retail outlets (selective distribution). As pointed out earlier, all three of these conditions are fair or good matches with a small marketing budget. (See guidelines 1a, 4a, and 4b earlier in this chapter.) To have a reasonable chance of succeeding with a product in the consumer shopping goods category, a small new business owner would have to offer something very differentiated from what is currently available, and something that both the target market and the retailers serving them would find appealing. With an attractive product offering, a small new business may be able to gain the cooperation of selected retailers through short channels. If such circumstances are present, a small new business with a consumer shopping goods product can be a fair match with a small marketing budget.

Consumer Specialty Goods

These are tangible products "for which consumers have a strong brand preference and are willing to spend substantial time and effort in locating the desired brand."[36] Some brands of women's and men's apparel are specialty goods, as are certain brands of china and silverware. Expensive watches, certain electronic and photographic equipment, some automobiles and home appliances, as well as unique foods and health and beauty products can be specialty goods. For some consumers, Starbuck's coffee seems to belong to the category of specialty goods. It is important to note that specialty goods are ones for which consumers have a strong brand preference. Generally, specialty goods have been around for some time and have become both well known and desirable.

Three factors argue against a small new business trying to enter a specialty goods market. One is that specialty goods tend to require heavy advertising, which in turn requires a large marketing budget. A second negative factor is that the small new business's product will face strong, well-established competitors who will aggressively defend their market share. The third factor is that retail outlets are likely to be unenthusiastic about carrying a new brand *trying to become a specialty goods* before it has developed any reputation as such, especially if there is little evidence of it being heavily supported with promotions. Since specialty goods status for a product entails a significant investment in advertising and promotion, the consumer specialty goods market is just not compatible with the limited marketing budget typical of most small new businesses.

Marketing Strategies That Are Compatible with Small Budgets

Four types of product classifications can be compatible with a small marketing budget.

(1) Business fabricating parts that are significantly better than competitors' offerings.

(2) Small business installations with desirable special features not offered by competitors.

(3) Significantly improved business accessory products with important new features for well-defined target markets.

(4) Differentiated but very appealing consumer shopping goods in categories that are not dominated by major brand competitors.

(1) Fabricating Parts That Are Significantly Better than Competitors' Offerings

Wallace Leyshon's Appliance Control Technology, Inc. manufactured electronic control devices for makers of mid-price kitchen and laundry appliances.[37] Those control devices were business fabricating parts because they became an integral part of the finished appliances. It should be noted that the appliance industry was a mature market for fabricating parts suppliers when Appliance Control Technology, Inc. was formed. But ACT's electronic controls were a significantly better product than the electro-mechanical controls offered by established suppliers. They were less expensive, they made for higher-quality and more attractive appliances in the minds of consumers, and they helped reduce overall inventory costs. Because there were relatively few of those appliance manufacturers, ACT was able to operate with a small marketing budget.

(2) Small Business Installations with Desirable Special Features Not Offered by Competitors

Michael Kuperstein's new business was based on a small installation product. He founded Neurogen, Inc. because he wanted to design and market a computer-based system that could read handwritten numbers.[38] His first target market was banks, which daily had to process millions of personal checks handwritten by consumers. Kuperstein believed that if his system were installed in a bank's information processing system, it would reduce the banks' check processing costs by millions of dollars each year. Kuperstein's small business installation product offered the target market special features not available from any other supplier. Marketing strategies that display such characteristics can be compatible with small budgets.

(3) Significantly Improved Business Accessory Products with Important New Features for Well-Defined Target Markets

Paul Kittle founded Rusmar, Inc. for the purpose of selling foam to landfill operators to use as a cover for the trash that had been dumped each day in their landfills. They were required to do so by law.[39] Kittle also sold them the machines that could apply the foam on top of the trash. Applying foam—

instead of the traditional soil—allowed the operators to utilize more of their landfill's capacity, which translated into more revenue and profits for them. That made Kittle's machine an attractive accessory product for landfill operators. Kittle offered his well-defined target market an accessory product that helped them become more profitable. The presence of such conditions are often associated with compatibility with a small marketing budget.

(4) Differentiated but Very Appealing Consumer Shopping Goods in Categories That Are Not Dominated by Major Brand Competitors

When they were first introduced, New Balance athletic shoes targeted a market segment that was totally ignored by competing athletic shoe brands, and they did so by offering a differentiated but very appealing product. They pursued the aging baby boomer market, people 40 years of age and older. At the time, the average age of Nike's customers was early to mid 20s, while Reebok users averaged in their early to mid 30s. New Balance's customers were people who were old enough to start having serious foot problems, so much so that they visited podiatrists seeking help. Most competitors offered their shoes in only two widths—medium and wide. New Balance offered its shoes in a number of widths ranging from AA (very narrow) to the very wide EEEE. Not only did they promote their wider shoe models to their target market, they also promoted them to podiatrists who favored the wider models for patients who had to wear foot-supporting devices inside their shoes. None of the other shoe brands pursued either this target market or their podiatrists.[40] This marketing strategy enabled New Balance to operate with a much, much smaller marketing budget than that employed by Nike and Reebok.

What You Should Do

If you are offering a fabricated part for business use, you must design it in such a way that it will clearly be seen by your target market as having significant advantages over what they are currently using. Recall how Wallace Leyshon and Appliance Control Technology, Inc. created electronic control devices with such advantages. That is an example you can use as a guide. If you are offering a type of business installation or a piece of accessory equipment, you must make certain that your product's differentiated features are very important to your target market and can only be obtained from you. Michael Kuperstein and his Neurogen, Inc. were trying to achieve this with a type of business installation. Paul Kittle's foam and foam-applying machine are good examples of business accessory products with features that were very important to their target markets. Remember, for any new fabricating part, accessory, or installation to have a chance to succeed, it must be a significantly improved product with important advantages over competitors' offerings.

If your new business is to be based on a consumer product, your best bet by far is to offer a shopping good that is (1) differentiated from competitors' offerings in ways that are very appealing to your target market and the retailers serving your target market, and (2) not in a product category dominated by one or more major brand competitors.

Marketing Strategies That Are Not Compatible with Small Budgets

Four product classifications that are not compatible with small budgets are business raw materials, business operating supplies, consumer convenience goods, and consumer specialty goods.

Business Raw Materials and Operating Supplies

Both of these kinds of business products consist of commodities or commodity-like products. Furthermore, these products are almost always in the mature stage of their product life cycles, and are usually sold by industries whose type of market competition is oligopoly or nearly pure competition. All three of these factors are strongly associated with intense price competition that makes it almost impossible for a small new company to differentiate itself from established competitors. Such a situation is clearly not compatible with a small marketing budget.

Consumer Convenience Goods

Small new businesses based on consumer convenience goods face four conditions that are not favorable to small marketing budgets. Consumer convenience goods are sold in geographically dispersed markets. Competitors in consumer convenience goods markets often display oligopolistic characteristics. Most consumer convenience goods are in the late growth or maturity or decline stage of their product life cycle. Most such goods use an extensive distribution system. These four factors are clearly not compatible with the idea of a small budget marketing strategy.

Exceptions

It should be noted that occasionally a small new business based on a consumer convenience good can be successful. Such exceptions, though quite rare, typically involve a really significantly different product that consumers find very appealing. Ben & Jerry's ice cream is thought to be such an exception. Clearly, to many people, it is a significantly different kind of ice cream.

Consumer Specialty Goods

By definition, such products can emerge only after they have been very well promoted and, as a result have created a strong brand preference in the minds of their target market consumers. It is very difficult for a small new business to achieve such status for its product with only a small marketing budget.

Mistakes You Should Avoid

You should definitely not base a small new business on raw materials or business operating supplies or any other commodity or commodity-like product. Do not start a small new business based on a consumer convenience product unless it is truly and significantly better than products already on the market and unless you have a marketing budget that can support the introduction of such a product. Lastly, since it is not possible to create a consumer specialty product with a small budget, do not try to base a small new business on such a product.

The following is a *summary of guidelines and warnings associated with product classification concepts that are compatible with a small budget.*

YOUR MARKETING STRATEGY MUST SATISFY AT LEAST ONE OF THESE GUIDELINES

Guideline 5a. Offer a business fabricating part that is significantly better than current competitors' offerings.

Guideline 5b. Offer a small type of business installation with desirable special features not offered by competitors.

Guideline 5c. Offer a significantly improved business accessory product with important new features to a well-defined target market.

Guideline 5d. Offer a differentiated but very appealing consumer shopping product in a category that is not dominated by a major brand competitor.

WARNINGS OF THINGS YOU SHOULD AVOID

Warning 5a. Avoid entering product markets based on raw materials and operating supplies.

Warning 5b. Avoid starting a small new business based on a consumer convenience product unless it is truly and significantly better—not just a little better—than products already on the market.

Warning 5c. Avoid starting a small new business whose product will attempt to break into a consumer specialty market.

Carefully Evaluate All Marketing Strategy Elements

This chapter identified a number of potential marketing strategy elements that are likely to be incompatible with small marketing budgets. Given that hundreds of thousands of new businesses are started each year in the United States alone, it is very realistic to assume there are still other marketing strategy elements that are not compatible with small marketing budgets. For a person starting a new business, it would be most convenient if a complete list of all high-cost marketing strategy elements were readily available. Unfortunately, no such list is known to exist. Therefore, a person starting a small new business would be very prudent to (1) be aware that other high-cost marketing strategy elements may very well exist, (2) be alert for the possibility that one or more of the marketing strategy elements they are considering for use in their small new business may be one of those, and (3) to search for alternative low-cost marketing strategy elements to replace all those identified as high cost.

Summary

If your marketing strategy has satisfied both Screening Condition I and Screening Condition II, your new business should have a complete and synergistic marketing strategy that will not encounter any strategy execution delays. That means that your small new business has the potential of quickly achieving a growing sales revenue stream when it enters its launch period. But to achieve that potential, your marketing strategy also must avoid using marketing elements that are not compatible with a small budget.

Since practically all small new businesses have limited marketing budgets, people starting them should definitely avoid using marketing strategy elements that require a large marketing budget. If your small new business uses an expensive marketing element without having the budget to pay for it, you will not be able to execute your marketing strategy in a timely manner and/or in the manner intended. As a result, when the new business enters it launch phase, it will not begin to enjoy a growing stream of sales revenues. If the sales revenue stream is delayed long enough, the new business will fail.

If you are thinking of starting a small new business, this chapter identified 13 guidelines that can help you select marketing strategy elements that are compatible with small marketing budgets. You should strive to use in your marketing strategy only elements that are included in this list of 13. The chapter also presented 12 warnings identifying marketing strategy elements that tend to require large marketing budgets. You should avoid using those strategy elements. Both of those lists will help you identify inexpensive elements you will want to include in your marketing strategy, as well as expensive elements you will want to avoid. This is essentially Screening Condition III.

The high-cost marketing strategy elements identified in the chapter are a serious cause of small new business failures. Based on my research, I estimate that between one-half and three-fourths of all small new businesses use marketing strategies that include one or more elements that are incompatible with small marketing budgets. Essentially all such new businesses encounter serious operational and/or financial difficulties. The logical conclusion from this observation is that using marketing strategy elements that are incompatible with small marketing budgets is a serious mistake that contributes significantly to the failure of many small new businesses.

The 25 guidelines and warnings presented in this chapter fall into five general topic areas, one of which is *target market and market segmentation*. Target markets consisting of many geographically concentrated buyers are likely to be compatible with small marketing budgets, especially if there is an underserved segment in those markets. A few geographically concentrated buyers can also be compatible with a small marketing budget if the seller offers a significantly better product than those currently available. On the other hand, target markets consisting of many geographically dispersed buyers typically require that sellers have large marketing budgets.

The second general topic area discussed in this chapter is *type of market competition*. If a small new business hopes to succeed with a limited marketing budget, it should enter a monopolistic-competition market while offering a differentiated product that will appeal to a small but well-defined target market. If a small new business enters a market characterized as pure competition or nearly pure competition, or if it enters a market displaying oligopolistic characteristics, it will almost certainly need a large marketing budget to have any chance of succeeding.

The owner of a small new business should avoid entering a certain product market if the main product there is in the growth stage or the mature stage or the decline stage of its *product life cycle.* Such product markets almost certainly require a new business to have a large marketing budget to be able to compete successfully. If the small new business has only a limited marketing budget, it will have a much better chance of succeeding if it's product is just entering the introductory stage of its product life cycle. The best chance to succeed would come from pioneering a truly new product that would enjoy fast adoption by a well-defined target market that is not being well served by current suppliers.

The fourth general topic area is *channels of distribution.* With only a limited marketing budget, a small new business should use exclusive or selective distribution, and the channel should be both short and open. If a small new business wants to use extensive distribution, or a long distribution channel, or a closed vertical marketing system, the new business will encounter very serious difficulties without a large marketing budget.

With respect to the *business or consumer product classification* general topic area, the categories most compatible with a small marketing budget are business fabricating parts, small installations for businesses, business accessory products, and some consumer shopping goods. Product categories not compatible with small marketing budgets are business raw materials and operating supplies, consumer convenience goods, and consumer specialty products.

5

Screening Condition IV: Will Your Marketing Strategy Be Capable of Defending Itself Against Strong Counterattacks by Well-Established Competitors?

If your marketing strategy achieves all three of Screening Conditions I, II, and III, you will have made excellent progress toward identifying a successful marketing strategy for your small new business. Because of Screening Condition I, you will have identified a target market that is not currently being satisfied by competitors' offerings, and your new business will be offering that target market a product that it is eager to obtain. Your promotional communications will cause the individuals in your target market to fully understand and appreciate the advantages of what your new business has to offer. Compared with competitors' offerings, you will have priced your product to make it a very good value in the eyes of your target market individuals. Lastly, by arranging to distribute your product in a manner that is very convenient for your target market, your marketing strategy will be very synergistic because it has highly integrated the five elements of target market, product differentiation, promotional communications, price, and distribution. As a result of this integration, your marketing strategy should be both effective and highly efficient.

Since your marketing strategy also achieves Screening Condition II, it should not experience any strategy execution delays because it doesn't include any of the four types of undesirable characteristics described in Chapter 3. Consequently, your new business should begin enjoying a growing stream of sales revenues as soon as it enters its launch period.

Because your marketing strategy has also achieved Screening Condition III, it doesn't include any marketing elements that require a large marketing budget. You should therefore be able to execute your marketing strategy with the low level of marketing expenditures originally intended. By keeping good control of your marketing costs, your marketing strategy will soon be generating a sales revenue stream in excess of your costs, and your new business will be well on its way toward profitability and success.

So again, congratulations on making a great start toward achieving a successful new business. But don't rest on your oars yet, because there is still one more obstacle you'll have to overcome. If your new business starts enjoying sales successes and continues to grow, it will soon attract the attention of established competitors. There are at least two reasons for this. One is that they have observed your success and want to grab a share of that success before it is too late to do so. A second—but potentially more dangerous reason—is that they believe your business's success is causing them to lose sales. When that occurs, the established competitors are likely to consider your new business a serious threat and take some kind of action against it. And because they are well established and larger than your new business, they will most likely have the resources and marketing know-how to develop a strong counterattack designed to reduce, or even destroy, the effectiveness of your new business's marketing strategy. Because you don't want that to happen, you must make certain that your new business is capable of defending itself against such counterattacks when they occur. This is the essence of Screening Condition IV, which will help you evaluate your marketing strategy to determine if it possesses the characteristics it will need to defend itself against competitors' counterattacks when they do occur.

Examples of Counterattacks by Established Competitors

You have already been introduced to one striking example of a small new business being counterattacked by an established competitor in Chapter 3. The small new business was Legend Airlines, which was trying to start first-class-only business flights between Dallas' Love Field and both Los Angeles and Washington, D.C. The well established competitor was American Airlines. In fact, Dallas was their headquarters city. American Airlines didn't even wait for the small new airline to start operating. They clearly saw that Legend Airlines would attract some of their best customers once they began flying, so they counterattacked while the new airline was still in its prelaunch period.[1]

The American Airlines attack was broad and vicious. First they sued Legend Airlines, the city of Dallas, and the federal government with the goal of preventing or delaying the new airline from ever taking off. Then they paid for a radio advertising campaign supposedly from "concerned citizens" who were protesting the use of Love Field for commercial passenger flights. Their sales force offered Dallas business travelers special incentives if they remained loyal to American Airlines. In addition, American quickly leased the unoccupied terminal at Love Field that Legend Airlines had planned to use. That imposed costly delays on the new airline and forced it to spend precious financial resources on a new terminal and parking garage. American Airlines also used their newly acquired terminal at Love Field to begin offering the same kind of services that Legend had been planning to offer. The new airline did not survive, and its failure was due in great part to actions taken against it by the well-established competitor.[2]

Different Types of Counterattacks

There are three different types of competitive counterattacks that owners of small new businesses should be aware of. The first type, illustrated by American Airlines' attack against Legend Airlines, occurs when the established competitor sees that a new business—still in the process of being organized—has the potential of becoming a significant competitor if it becomes operational. In this type of counterattack, the established competitor undertakes to destroy the new business's marketing strategy even before it can be executed.

A second type of counterattack occurs as part of an established competitor's defensive plan, which is in place, ready and waiting to be used whenever a small new business attempts to steal its customers. In this type of situation the established competitor, expecting new competitors to emerge from time to time, has developed strong defensive measures to respond harshly to threats when they do emerge. The Batesville Casket Company, described below, is an example of this second type.

DISCOUNT CASKET RETAILERS VERSUS BATESVILLE CASKET COMPANY[3]

The Batesville Casket Company, a division of Hillenbrand Industries, Inc., was the leading manufacturer in the $1 billion U.S. casket market. Batesville's share of the market was approximately 40 percent, but they had a much larger share of the market for premium-priced caskets. Because operating margins were widely known to be very lucrative, the casket market frequently attracted small new retail businesses that would attempt to sell coffins at a discount. Batesville was able to fend off those small new competitors by selling its caskets directly to licensed funeral directors and by providing them with outstanding services.

Because of their marketing practices and customer services, Batesville created a mountain of goodwill and loyalty among funeral home operators. In turn, those funeral home operators cooperated fully with Batesville, and together they organized a distribution system for caskets that could not be easily penetrated by a small new business trying to sell coffins at a discount. How did Batesville accomplish such a closed distribution system? They used the following multifaceted strategy.

Batesville sold their caskets directly to licensed funeral directors. They did not sell to any wholesalers or retailers. In this way, Batesville's caskets were sold only at full list price, which was in the best interests of both funeral home directors and Batesville. For the funeral home directors, this resulted in markups of 200– 400 percent. For Batesville, it meant very happy and cooperative funeral home directors who were not interested in buying caskets from anyone but Batesville. Batesville also operated 68 company-owned distribution centers, which provided funeral homes with overnight delivery of caskets. Such delivery services saved funeral homes the costs associated with keeping an inventory of caskets. Batesville also financed the casket showrooms in funeral homes, which could easily cost $50,000 or more. Many funeral homes offered their customers pre-need funeral insurance, and Batesville was the largest underwriter of such insurance at the time.

Because they benefited so handsomely from Batesville as market leader, funeral homes also did their part to help maintain Batesville in that position. When a licensed funeral home director learned the names of the casket manufacturers who sold their products to discount coffin retailers, the director would share that information with other directors. This usually resulted in their boycotting those manufacturers, which clearly discouraged other casket manufacturers from selling to discounters. Some funeral homes reportedly contributed in another way to strengthen the Batesville distribution system—they would make repeated calls to a discount store's telephone number, thus tying up its telephone lines and preventing potential customers from getting through.

One small businessman who tried and failed as a discount retailer said: "My advice to anyone who wants to go into the casket business is: don't."

Based on the American Airlines and Batesville examples, one very important observation you should make is that well-established competitors have no doubt already faced—and defeated—a number of potential threats from small new businesses in the past. They are well-established competitors because they have had experience successfully fending off challenges by small new businesses. They know how to defend their businesses, and they are ready and well prepared to do so vigorously.

The third type of counterattack occurs after a new business has begun to enjoy some early sales successes. The established competitor notices the small new business's success, evaluates it, judges it to be a potential threat, and then designs a specific counterattack to eliminate the potential threat— or at least reduce it to an acceptable level. Two examples of this third type, one by Anheuser-Busch, another by food company giants, are described below.

MICROBREWERIES VERSUS ANHEUSER-BUSCH[4]

In recent years, many small independent breweries, or microbreweries, came into existence throughout the United States. They were attractive because they offered distinctive lagers and ales quite different from the beers made by Anheuser-Busch (A-B), Miller, Coors, and the other major domestic brewers. These microbreweries were local and small, and they grew very slowly at first; but eventually they gained 1 percent of the U.S. beer market, then 3 percent. Many of these microbrewery brands were distributed by A-B distributors. The owner of one such microbrewery said: "You got entree into every place immediately with an A-B distributor." At the same time, A-B beer sales remained essentially flat, while their profits fluctuated unevenly. If A-B wanted to increase their sales—and they did—they'd have to take sales from some else's brands. The most vulnerable competitors were the smaller brands, and the microbreweries were the most vulnerable of the smaller brands.

In response to the growing presence of microbrewies, A-B offered their 900-some distributors an "exclusivity" contract under which the distributors would agree not to carry brands of beer that competed with A-B's brands. By signing the contract, a distributor would receive a number of monetary and other incentives, including greater access to A-B credits and loans, an allowance of $1,500 per delivery truck for painting it with A-B logos and designs, a cash bonus of two cents for every case of beer sold, and the opportunity to be first in line when a new A-B territory became available. And there was one other incentive for signing the contract. If a distributor refused, there was no guarantee that their A-B distributorship would not be terminated. Reportedly, every distributor signed the contract.

The results of the exclusivity contract were quickly apparent and as favorable for A-B as intended. Once the A-B distributors stopped carrying the microbrews that competed with A-B brands, they started placing more emphasis on lesser A-B brands such as Red Wolf and Black & Tan Porter. They also began promoting Redhook Ale, a small brand partly owned by A-B.

The effects of the contract were very unfavorable—almost disastrous—for many microbreweries. Some industry analysts predicted that small breweries would go into decline. One microbrewery owner was quoted as saying: "We had eight Anheuser-Busch distributors at one time. Now we have two." He tried to find replacement distributors in areas where he had lost the A-B distributors, but was unable to do so: ". . . we just basically shut down in some of those areas."

Microbreweries were ignored when they were very small and not worth the trouble of taking seriously. But after awhile they got bigger, and the domestic beer market flattened out. The market and competitive conditions changed, and so did the attitude of the largest established competitor. The smaller breweries were now beginning to pose a threat that called for a counterattack.

MY OWN MEALS, INC. VERSUS FOOD GIANTS[5]

Mary Anne Jackson was 35 years old with CPA and MBA degrees and eight years of experience in planning with a huge food conglomerate. She had some guilty feelings about being a working mom while her little daughter was still preschool. She also found, after thoroughly searching food and grocery stores, that no one was supplying the kind of good quality children's meals she wanted for her daughter. So she was spending much of her weekends preparing and freezing wholesome meals the babysitter could feed her daughter during the upcoming week. Other women in similar employment-family situations, eager to prepare such healthy meals for their children, asked her about her meal preparation activities. Then, suddenly, Jackson's company was the victim of a leveraged buyout and Jackson was one of the many midlevel managers who were let go.

Jackson always thought she might start a company of her own one day. Since her work experience had been in the food industry, and since her personal experience had revealed that no company was marketing quality meals especially created for children, she decided she would start a new company to make wholesome meals for preschool children. The meals would be sold in plastic retort pouches that didn't need refrigeration. They could easily be prepared in less than two minutes in a microwave oven, or by placing the pouch in boiling water for four to five minutes. Given the number of working mothers with children, and the type of meals she was planning to produce, Jackson estimated that the size of the market was worth about $500 million per year.

She named her company My Own Meals, Inc. and, two years after becoming unemployed, she began distributing five different meals for children through two large food chains in Chicago that had agreed to carry her products. With the meals priced between $2.39 and $2.99, Jackson had expected sales of $1 million during her first year, a goal she reached and surpassed. Her line of meals was available in about 100 stores going into her second year, and in about 1,000 stores by the beginning of the third. Jackson had forecast sales of $10 million for the second year, and she expected sales to reach $60 million a few years after that.

Unfortunately, the growing market acceptance of My Own Meals—and the estimated market size of $500 million per year—had caught the attention of some of the major food giants. During Jackson's second year in business, both George A. Hormel & Company and ConAgra Frozen Foods entered the market with their brands of children's meals. Soon after that, Tyson Foods also introduced its own line of children's meals. Individual items in those competitors' product lines were priced between $1.09 and $1.29, considerably below the prices of My Own Meals.

Three years later My Own Meals had completely disappeared from supermarket shelves. Jackson's description of what happened was: "We got annihilated!"

These four examples clearly and strongly illustrate that small new businesses are very vulnerable to counterattacks by established competitors. Established competitors are very experienced companies that usually have the motivation, the resources, and the marketing know-how to successfully respond to the arrival of a small new competitor. They can preempt a small new business's marketing strategy, and completely disrupt its potential effectiveness, as American Airlines and Batesville caskets did. They can control the appropriate distribution channels to prevent or deny distribution to competitors they wish to destroy, as in the Anheuser-Busch and Batesville casket examples. Being larger and having greater resources, they can use lower prices to punish or destroy new competitors, as the food giants demonstrated. With their greater size and strength, they can usually forego profits for a longer period of time than a small new competitor. All four of the above examples display this characteristic. If you want your small new business to be successful over the long term, you must be ready and able to fend off a strong counterattack from an established competitor if and when it occurs. Screening Condition IV can help you prepare to do just that.

SCREENING CONDITION IV

Screening Condition IV consists of four characteristics that your marketing strategy must possess if it is to be capable of successfully defending your new business against an aggressive counterattack by a large competitor.

1a. Your small new business should not directly attack a large competitor. In fact, it should not even appear to threaten such competitors.

1b. If your small new business is based on a concept that eventually will cause it to either directly or indirectly engage a large competitor, you must be very certain that the competitor is vulnerable in some way that offers you a good chance for success. If the competitor is not vulnerable in some important way, your small new business will almost certainly fail.

2. Your new business's marketing strategy must be so designed that it neutralizes a large competitor's ability to disrupt or negate its effectiveness.

3. Your marketing strategy must include a significant and sustainable product and/or service advantage.

4. Your marketing strategy must incorporate a distribution component, or some other strong impediment, that provides your small new business with longer-term protection against competitors' counterattacks.

Each of these four characteristics *is in addition to* those already described in relation to Screening Conditions I, II, and III. They are discussed in great detail in the remainder of the chapter.

1. Do Not Attack a Large Competitor

In previous chapters you were introduced to three small new businesses that were on the road to marketing success. Neither Appliance Control Technology, Inc.[6] nor MicroFridge, Inc.[7] attacked large competitors—or any direct competitors—when they opened their doors. Glacier Nursery[8] chose a target market that large, distant competitors showed little interest in serving, so in a sense it also did not directly attack a large competitor. These three companies illustrate the merits of starting a small new business that does not directly attack a large competitor. When those new businesses are compared with the four examples presented at the beginning of this chapter, it should be perfectly clear why a small new business should not directly attack a large competitor.

Still, it is not easy for a small new business to avoid coming into contact with large competitors for any extended period of time. When some small new businesses begin to achieve growing sales, they often do so by taking sales away from established competitors. When that occurs, the small new business begins to be a threat to an established competitor. If that competitor is alert and sharply focused on what is happening in the marketplace, it will probably take determined action to neutralize the threat. Since it is already established in the marketplace, it will very likely use its financial and marketing resources to strongly counter the threat posed by the small new business. As the four foregoing examples illustrate, such counterattacks are often life threatening to a small new business. At the very least, such attacks will make life miserable for the owner of the small new business, who may come to regret wanting to compete against such an established rival.

On the other hand, there are times when an established competitor is intensely focused on some new internal development or is overconfident about its competitive position or is unaware of some inherent weakness or is concerned with some other very important business matter. When an established competitor finds itself under such distracting circumstances, it may fail to notice a small new company trying to enter its industry. Such a distraction or loss of focus may cause it to be vulnerable in the marketplace. That is, due to its circumstances the established competitor may not even be aware of the small new business or may not even want to be bothered by its existence. Or, the circumstances may be such that it won't or can't attack the new business. That is what I mean when I say that the established competitor may be "vulnerable." When something like that happens, a small new business may be able to gain some market successes for a short time period due to the established competitor's lack of response.

When Might an Established Competitor Be Vulnerable to an Attack?

If you are thinking of starting a small new business that might come into direct contact with an established competitor, how can you know if that competitor might be vulnerable to an attack? This is a good question, but not an easy one to answer. However, some researchers have explored this question by studying historical examples of attacks on large competitors whose circumstances at the time may have made them vulnerable.[9] In their findings, those researchers identified a number of circumstances that may cause large competitors to be vulnerable. That list is useful information for anyone thinking of starting a new business likely to confront an established competitor.

There seem to be 12 circumstances under which well-established competitors can be vulnerable to attack by smaller rivals. Those circumstances can be categorized under three broad headings: changing external forces, industry structure and/or market position, and the established competitor's behavior. The following explanations use historical examples of attacks on large competitors as illustrations.

Changing External Forces

There are four such forces. (1) A government agency is threatening or actually attacking the well-established competitor for some kind of legal, environmental, or other violation. (2) A new technology becomes available that gives small companies certain advantages over the established competitor. (3) The established competitor is subjected to some kind of external catastrophe. (4) A "new personality"—in a business or marketing sense—enters the industry.

(1) A Government Agency Attacks the Established Competitor

When the use of fluorocarbon-propelled aerosols was banned by the Food and Drug Administration, Gillette's Right Guard, the deodorant industry leader, lost significant market share as the public turned increasingly to roll-on alternatives.[10] Bristol-Myers became especially aggressive when this occurred. Their strong marketing efforts exploited Gillett's vulnerability and carried their Ban roll-on deodorant into the market leader position.

(2) A New Technology Weakens the Established Competitor's Dominance

Encyclopedia Britannica was the dominant market leader for years and years. But the arrival of CD-ROM technology quickly changed that.[11] Almost immediately new competitors entered the market with less expensive electronic encyclopedias that offered more features than traditional print versions.

(3) The Established Competitor Is Subjected to a Catastrophe

Perhaps the most notorious example of an external catastrophe occurred when seven people died after taking Tylenol tablets that had been criminally tampered with. The event quickly triggered increased marketing activity by a number of analgesic competitors. A similar increase in competition occurred when Procter & Gamble's new tampon, Rely, had to be withdrawn from the marketplace because of its association with a dangerous medical condition known as toxic shock syndrome.[12]

(4) A "New Personality" Enters the Industry

The number eight brewery in the United States in the 1960s was the Miller Brewing Company, whose sales had been declining for years due to anemic marketing and product development efforts. A "new personality" entered the domestic beer industry in the 1970s when the Philip Morris Company acquired that brewery.[13] The new marketing and management talent imposed on Miller by Philip Morris soon resulted in the introduction of new Miller Beer brands and much increased advertising expenditures. The suddenly intensified competition caused market leader Budweiser to focus strongly on Miller's new marketing activities, a distraction which allowed some of the other beer brands to take more aggressive actions than they might otherwise have taken.

Industry Structure and/or Market Position

This is the second main category of competitor vulnerability. A well-established competitor may be vulnerable to attack during any one of four industry structure and/or market position circumstances. (1) All established competitors, including the industry leader, are small. (2) The market leader has higher prices and costs because it emphasizes image and reputation and/or excellent quality and/or good service. (3) A new product positioning, product differentiation, or market segmentation opportunity can be identified and exploited. (4) Only the established competitor has national distribution, while other competitors are regional or local. When this condition is present, some distributors, retailers, and consumers are likely to welcome an acceptable new competitor.

(1) All Competitors Are Small

In the post–World War II era all motels, real estate agencies, and hamburger joints were small businesses. There were no large competitors, and certainly there were no dominant market leaders on a national scale in those business activities. When there is no dominant market leader, the door of opportunity is equally open to all, but all too soon, the savviest small competitors exploited those opportunities to become Holiday Inn, Century 21, McDonald's, and others. Similar examples of opportunistic small new firms becoming dominant market leaders can be found more recently in the fields of furniture and sporting goods retailing, and the eye care industry.

(2) The Market Leader Has Higher Prices and Costs Because It Emphasizes Image and Reputation, Excellent Quality and/or Good Service

In the late 1990s Verizon Communications, Inc. was using its *Yellow Pages* telephone directory as a cash cow to finance it competitive activities in the telephone service market. To maximize the cash flow, Verizon raised the rates it charged businesses for their advertisements in the *Yellow Pages*, a development that caused many small businesses to stop placing ads in that directory. A small competitor, *Yellow Book USA*, saw those alienated small businesses as a market waiting to be served, and they did so by offering them much lower rates than *Yellow Pages* was charging. Because Verizon was using their directory as a cash cow, it was hesitant to lower rates to more closely match those of *Yellow Book*. As a result, *Yellow Book USA* enjoyed tremendous revenue growth in the 10-year period from 1993 to 2003.[14]

(3) A New Product Positioning or Product Differentiation or Market Segmentation Opportunity Can Be Identified

For years Crest toothpaste dominated the market with the message that regular use of Crest would lead to very healthy teeth and gums. However, Beacham's market research showed that a sizeable market segment was looking for a toothpaste that offered breath-freshening qualities along with cavity prevention. When they developed such a product—Aqua-Fresh—and introduced it in the market, they were rewarded with a very warm reception. Beacham's identification and exploitation of a market segmentation/product differentiation opportunity allowed them to establish a new entrant in a field strongly dominated by two large, well-established competitors.[15]

(4) Only the Established Competitor Has National Distribution, While Others Are Regional or Local

The A&W brand was the long-established market leader in root beer when Barq's was only a small but popular brand in the New Orleans area. Throughout the nation, there was no strong number two brand that offered root beer drinkers an attractive alternative to A&W. Barq's thought it could expand its appeal into the areas immediately surrounding New Orleans, and some distributors and retailers gave full support to that notion. That successful initial expansion was followed by successive waves of similar expansions, and after several years, Barq's had become a well-established national brand.[16]

Established Competitor's Behavior

This is the third main source of an established competitor's vulnerability—the competitor's own behavior, specifically the following four types: (1) The established competitor is not an aggressive marketer on a regular and continuing basis. (2) It displays a significant weakness in its marketing strategy and/or cannot easily change its strategy to respond to changing competition. (3) The established competitor has offended an important channel of distribution or customer group. (4) It is in the process of diversifying.

(1) The Established Competitor Is Not an Aggressive Marketer

In the 1970s, American Chicle Company mounted a major marketing initiative when it noticed that Wrigley's, the gum market leader, lacked any significant product and marketing initiatives, thus leaving itself vulnerable to a market challenge.[17] Similarly, in the pickle business both Heinz and Borden's demonstrated little marketing aggressiveness, even though both had large market shares. Perhaps that was due to the fact that pickles were not an important part of their overall business. In any case, their complacency opened the door for Vlasic, which eventually captured market leadership.[18]

(2) The Established Competitor Displays a Significant Marketing Strategy Weakness

Market leader Hershey had a long-standing policy against using large national advertising campaigns, a noticeable marketing strategy deficiency. Hershey also displayed little aggressiveness when it came to introducing new products. Mars took note of Hershey's behavior, and through its advertising campaigns and new product introductions was able to move into the industry's number one position.[19]

(3) The Established Competitor Offended an Important Distribution Channel or Customer Group

Outboard Marine Corporation was a well-established competitor in the fishing boat market, especially bass fishing. But boat dealers, and bass fishermen as well, were clamoring for newer and more luxurious fishing boat models. Yet all of Outboard Marine's boats were old models and the company showed little interest in developing new ones. Earl Bentz, a former Outboard Marine employee, saw this demand for newer and better boats, and started his own new business to build just the kinds of boat models that dealers and fishermen wanted. Both of those parties eagerly welcomed Mr. Bentz's boats when he brought them to market.[20]

(4) The Established Competitor Is in the Process of Diversifying

In the late 1980s Epson was the dominant leader in printers for personal computers. Their dot matrix printers were everywhere. But Epson was also trying to break into the personal computer business, both because they saw it as a large and growing market of itself, and also because they believed personal computers would be a good companion product to their printers.

Their diversification efforts demanded large amounts of managerial and engineering time, as well as significant financial resources. When Hewlett-Packard's new ink jet printers came on the scene, Epson, distracted by its focus on diversification, paid little attention to the new competitor's product and failed to recognize right away that it was a serious rival.[21]

Two Additional Comments

First, it is quite possible—even probable—that there are more than 12 circumstances when an established competitor might be vulnerable to attack. Other critical circumstances may exist that have not yet been identified. If you are starting a new business that is likely to come into contact with an established competitor, it will be well worth your while to make a careful evaluation of that competitor's situation and circumstances. You just might find some good reason to suspect your competitor will have trouble counterattacking your new business once it has gotten started.

Second, there is no guarantee that every established competitor will be vulnerable to attack when it finds itself in one or more of the above 12 circumstances. Your small new business will still be taking a risk by entering a market with an established competitor, even if it is vulnerable. The crucial point is that you will face much less uncertainty if your small new business *does not attack* a well-established competitor.

What You Should Do

(1) The very best thing you can do is to enter a marketplace that is free of any direct competition. Your first and foremost goal should be to offer a differentiated product into a specific market in such a way that your small new business will not directly encounter an established competitor. Keep in mind the marketing strategies used by Wallace Leyshon and his Appliance Control Technology, Inc., and by Robert Bennett and his MicroFridge, Inc. Try, as they did, to enter a market in such a way and with such a product that your small new business will not face direct competition. (2) If your small new business is likely to confront an established competitor sometime in the not too distant future, however, be very certain that competitor is vulnerable in some important way. (3) Remember that there is no guarantee an established competitor will be seriously vulnerable even if it finds itself in one or more of the 12 circumstances described above. If you face a competitor—whether vulnerable or not—it might quickly and strongly counterattack your small new business, so you must be very certain that your marketing strategy also satisfies each

of characteristics 2, 3, and 4 of Screening Condition IV as described in the remainder of this chapter.

Mistakes You Should Avoid

Your small new business should not directly attack or threaten a large, well-established competitor. The danger of doing so has been painfully illustrated in the examples presented at the beginning of the chapter. You do not want your small new business to encounter the extreme competition experienced by Legend Airlines, by the discount casket retailers, by the microbreweries, or by Mary Ann Jackson's My Own Meals, Inc.

The following is a *summary of guidelines and warnings associated with the characteristic of not attacking a large competitor.*

YOUR MARKETING STRATEGY MUST SATISFY GUIDELINE 1A, OR BOTH GUIDELINES 1B AND 1C

Guideline 1a. Select a target market that is not being well served by a large, well-established competitor.

Guideline 1b. If your small new business is likely soon to engage an established competitor in the marketplace, be very certain that competitor is vulnerable in some important way.

Guideline 1c. If your small new business is likely to engage an established competitor sometime in the near future, be very certain that your marketing strategy also satisfies each of characteristics 2, 3, and 4 of Screening Condition IV.

WARNINGS OF THINGS YOU SHOULD AVOID

Warning 1a. Avoid directly attacking or threatening a large, well-established competitor.

Warning 1b. Avoid attacking any established competitor if that competitor is not vulnerable in some important way.

Three More Characteristics in Screening Condition IV

If your small new business enters its launch period without directly threatening large competitors, it will have satisfied the first characteristic of Screening Condition IV. And having done so, there is a good chance your business will not be exposed to aggressive, competitive counterattacks, at least not in the short run. But if your business enjoys early success and continues to build on that success, sooner or later its growing sales will attract the attention of a large competitor. When that occurs, your new business is likely to come under attack by that competitor, or at least be subjected to more competitive pressure than before. The four examples at the beginning of the chapter strongly suggest that all successful small new businesses will eventually come under attack by one or more large competitors. If you expect your small new business to enjoy early success, you should recognize this eventuality and make certain that your marketing strategy will be capable of defending against such counterattacks.

To achieve such a defensive capability, your small new business needs a long period of competitive peace in order to establish itself firmly in its target market and its distribution channel and gain the marketing and financial strength necessary to fend off counterattacks when they finally do occur. That is, your marketing strategy must have the ability of "buying time" in such a way that a large competitor *will be unwilling or unable to attack quickly*. Something in your marketing strategy must force the competitor to delay or abandon any notion of attacking your small new business. To have such a capability, your marketing strategy must also possess each of the other three characteristics constituting Screening Condition IV.

2. Your marketing strategy must be so designed that it neutralizes a large competitor's ability to disrupt or negate its effectiveness.

3. Your marketing strategy must include a significant and sustainable product and/or service advantage.

4. Your marketing strategy must incorporate a distribution component, or some feature that provides your small new business with longer-term protection against competitors' counterattacks.

These three characteristics are discussed below.

2. Neutralize the Competitor's Ability to Weaken Your Marketing Strategy

You saw in the four examples at the beginning of the chapter that all of the large competitors were able to do something in their counterattacks that essentially nullified the effectiveness of the marketing strategies of the offending small businesses. Those marketing strategies had been effective *only so long as the large competitors ignored them*. But they were rendered completely ineffective once the large competitors attacked them. Each of those small new businesses needed a stronger marketing strategy. Each needed something more in its marketing strategy. Each needed something that could have prevented the large competitor from destroying the effectiveness of its marketing strategy. What kind of thing could that be? What could those four small new businesses have included in their marketing strategies that could have thwarted the competitors' counterattacks from weakening or destroying their strategies' effectiveness?

There are five factors that can help a small new business blunt the efforts of a large competitor's disruptive attack:

- prevent or delay a large competitor's counterattack.
- create a superior reputation within the target market.
- maximize the product's attractiveness to the target market.
- select a target market that will prevent a counterattack.
- select competition that will not counterattack.

These five factors were identified by a number of researchers who studied the characteristics associated with successful marketing strategies for smaller businesses.[22]

Five Factors That Can Neutralize Large Competitors

Prevent or Delay a Counterattack

There are three ways you can try to incorporate something into your small new business's marketing strategy in order prevent or substantially delay a counterattack by a large competitor. (1) Do something to "change the rules of marketing." That is, use a marketing program that is different from the marketing programs established competitors have traditionally used in the past. Changing how the product is marketed can delay a competitor's response because (i) they are likely to doubt that the new marketing approach will be successful, (ii) they will not have experience planning and executing the new kind of marketing, and (iii) they may not be able to make an easy transition from their traditional marketing to the new marketing. (2) Significantly improve your product and/or service in a manner that cannot be easily adopted by competitors. (3) Create a barrier or an impediment to competitors by working closely with selected channels of distribution or by establishing strategic alliances with important customers or third parties. If done properly, such actions cannot be easily duplicated by the large competitor.

(1) "Change the Rules of Marketing"

Appliance Control Technology, Inc. (ACT) used a strategy that "changed the rules of marketing."[23] When ACT started marketing its electronic controls to manufacturers of medium-priced appliances, their competitors were offering those manufacturers standardized electro-mechanical control devices which they sold through distributors who called on the manufacturers' purchasing departments. ACT, on the other hand, called directly on those manufacturers' engineers and designers at the time they were planning new appliance models. ACT could supply those manufacturers with customized electronic controls that would be a better design match with the new appliance models than could be achieved with the standardized electro-mechanical control devices offered by the competitors. The result was a better overall appliance design, and one that was cheaper to produce as well. In effect, Appliance Control Technology changed the rules of marketing. It would not have been easy for the competitors to quickly change their marketing, even if they had wanted to do so.

(2) Significantly Improve Your Product and/or Your Service in a Manner That Cannot Be Easily Adopted by Competitors

By combining microwave, freezer and refrigerator functions in one device, MicroFridge is a shining example of such a product.[24] When compared with the three single purpose products available at the time to college students in dormitory rooms and budget motel operators, the MicroFridge was much more than just a significantly improved product. Meanwhile, companies selling electric hot plates, toaster ovens, and even microwave ovens and small refrigerators could not quickly develop, manufacture, and market a product to rival all the features and benefits of the MicroFridge.

Glacier Nursery was another example of a small new business offering a significantly improved and hard to duplicate product and service to its target market.[25] To offer trees and plants as hardy as those offered by Glacier Nursery, established competitors would have to open their own nurseries in some new harsh climate location like Montana. Even so, it would still be uneconomical for those out-of-state nurseries to try to duplicate Glacier Nursery's all-season-long delivery services to Montana's retail garden centers.

(3) Create a Distribution Barrier or a Strategic Alliance or Some Other Impediment That Will Prevent Competitors from Counterattacking

For an example of a strategic alliance, one can look again at Appliance Control Technology, Inc. and the relationship it was able to form with the manufacturers of medium-priced appliances.[26] By working closely with those engineers and designers when they were developing new appliance models, ACT helped them achieve appliances that were both more appealing in design and less expensive to produce. Clearly, the appliance manufacturers benefited significantly by their alliance with ACT. The previous suppliers to those manufacturers now faced the almost impossible challenge of finding a product or service they could offer those manufacturers that would be superior enough to cause them to forsake the benefits of the alliance with ACT.

Create a Superior Reputation Within the Target Market

This can be a very powerful factor for neutralizing a large competitor. Perhaps the most outstanding example of this factor is Starbuck's coffee. In less than 15 years Starbuck's grew from a small chain of seven stores in the Pacific Northwest to hundreds of stores across the entire United States. They did so by establishing an outstanding reputation for serving great tasting coffee in a comfortable atmosphere. Some competitors have tried to emulate their success, but no one has been able to negate the effectiveness of Starbuck's marketing strategy, which is strongly based on their tremendous reputation.

The Blackstone Bank and Trust Company is another example of a small new business that created a superior reputation.[27] It did so thanks to four things. It opened for business in Roxbury, a poor section of Boston so neglected by the banking industry that when it opened, Blackstone was the only bank in the community. It worked hard to provide fast and personal service to small business borrowers in the community. It gave all borrowers direct and easy access to the bank's two founders. And borrowers did not have to deal with a bureaucratic loan committee like those found in most banks, because there was none. No other bank was offering any of these services to the bank's target market of Roxbury's small business owners.

Maximize the Product's Attractiveness to the Target Market

This is the third of the five factors that can help small businesses resist a powerful competitor's attack. A small new business may be able to maintain its marketing strategy despite a competitor's attempts at disruption if it is able to make its product especially attractive to its selected target market. There are three ways this might be accomplished. (1) A small new business can so design its product that the competitors' offerings appear less and less attractive. (2) A new business might use product positioning and/or product differentiation to neutralize a competitor. The competitor may choose not to redesign its products to include features being offered by the small new business because significant effort and costs may be involved and also because of the uncertainty that the target market will respond favorably to such changes. (3) A small new business can also market a type of product that the competitor may not wish to offer because it would significantly cannibalize its already existing products and/or require a noticeable change in its advertising.

(1) Design the Product in a Manner That Causes Competitors' Products to Be Less Attractive

Glacier Nursery's products were home grown in the harsh climate of Montana. Homeowners who bought Glacier Nursery's products would be getting hardier trees and plants than those grown by out-of-state competitors in more moderate climates.[28] As a result, Glacier Nursery offered products that caused competitors' products to appear less attractive.

(2) Use Product Positioning and/or Product Differentiation to Neutralize Competitors

Appliance Control Technology, Inc. used both product differentiation and product positioning in their marketing strategy.[29] They were the only supplier of electronic control devices to actively pursue manufacturers of medium-priced appliances, and they did so by differentiating their controls to best meet the manufacturers' needs. Furthermore, they positioned their products as ones that would help those manufacturers achieve two very desirable goals: lower production costs and better-designed, more attractive appliances.

(3) Offer a Product That Competitors Will Not Duplicate for Fear of Cannibalizing Their Already Existing Products

When CD-ROM technology became a practical reality, several firms— including small ones—used it to introduce encyclopedias in electronic format rather than in print format. The dominant world leader at the time was *Encyclopedia Britannica*. It, too, had acquired CD-ROM technology, but it elected not to fully exploit it.[30] Had it done so, it would have severely cannibalized the sales of its printed encyclopedias and further hastened its loss of market leadership. As it happened, the advances made by the new competitors were sufficient to drive *Encyclopedia Britannica* off its once lofty perch.

Select a Target Market That Will Prevent a Counterattack

This fourth factor involves two ways a small new business can neutralize a large competitor through choice of target market. (1) It can select a market that established competitors have either ignored or not seriously pursued. Such markets are often considered too small and not worthy of their attention. An established competitor is less likely to go to the trouble of counterattacking over a market in which it has little interest. (2) A second way a small new business can prevent a counterattack is by selecting a market whose needs it can serve better than any competitor. When a small new business pursues such a strategy, the established competitor can either choose to do nothing, or it can somehow "gear up" to make itself more capable of competing in that market against the small newcomer. The significant investment of time, effort, and resources necessary to gear up may prevent the established competitor from launching a counterattack.

(1) Select a Market That Established Competitors Have Ignored or Not Seriously Pursued

When skateboarding and snowboarding were in their infancy, large sneaker marketers such as Nike and Reebok either ignored the youths who engaged in those activities entirely or considered that market too small to be worthy of attention. However, Van's, Inc., a very small player in the sneaker market, noticed that those skateboarders were growing in numbers and in enthusiasm for their sporting activities. When Van's managers saw that none of the large competitors had even established a foothold in that market, they undertook serious promotional activities directed at those board-riding youths, including sponsorship of many of their sporting events. Doing so helped them become the dominant sneaker supplier to those youths.[31]

(2) Select a Market Whose Needs Your Small New Business Can Serve Better Than Any Competitor

The small business owners of Boston's Roxbury neighborhood, and Montana's retail garden centers as well, had needs that were not being well served by established suppliers. Those markets offered opportunities to Blackstone Bank and Glacier Nursery. Two other markets whose "at-home" food preparation needs were not being satisfied were those of college students in dormitory rooms and guests staying in low-budget motels. Those markets represented opportunities for someone to exploit, and Robert Bennett and MicroFridge, Inc. did just that when they started marketing the combination microwave oven-freezer-refrigerator to them. A similar observation can be made with respect to Appliance Control Technology, Inc. and the relatively small and neglected market segment it chose to serve. These four small new businesses helped improve their chances for success by targeting relatively small and underserved market segments and offering them products and services that could satisfy their needs better than anything else available.[32] Their market selections probably deterred large competitors from launching counterattacks against them.

Select a Competitor That Will Not Counterattack

When a small new business selects a target market (as in the fourth factor discussed above), it is also choosing to face the competitors who are active in that target market. This fifth factor suggests that a small new business might do best *to focus on the competitor it wishes to compete against.* Thinking this way may help a small new business select a competitor that it will be capable of neutralizing. It might do this in two ways: (1) select a competitor with a history of not being an aggressive marketer, or (2) select a competitor that has as one of its markets a relatively unimportant segment that is not worth competing for when a small new business arises to pursues it as its own target market.

(1) Select a Competitor with a History of Not Being an Aggressive Marketer

The description of the first characteristic of Screening Condition IV included a discussion of when an established competitor might be vulnerable to attack. One such possibility occurs when all the competitors are small. The discussion pointed out that all motels, real estate agencies, and hamburger joints were still small businesses in the 1950s. There were no large competitors yet in those lines of business. The same is true still for other lines of business. If a small new business chooses to enter one of these markets, there is a very good chance that it will not be subjected to a counterattack because of the small size of all of the competitors.

(2) Select a Competitor Who Has as One of Its Markets a Relatively Unimportant Segment That It Will Not Defend If Targeted by a Small New Business

For quite a number of years the bottled pickle industry was led by Borden's and Heinz, each having approximately a 10 percent share of the market. Those two competitors historically had not been aggressive marketers, as evidenced by the absence of any significant promotional efforts. As pickles were a rather small business for both of these large companies, perhaps they were not given high priority for marketing expenditures, or even for managerial attention. This lack of competitiveness on the part of the two leaders eventually attracted the notice of the managers of Vlasic pickles. In seven or eight years Vlasic, a local pickle producer with less than 1 percent of the national market, was able to grow and become the U.S. market leader with almost one fourth of the market. Vlasic's growth occurred slowly, expanding first into one region, and then into another. Their growth came mostly at the expense of small local and regional producers, but it was made possible by the absence of any resistance from the two market leaders.[33]

What You Should Do

The foregoing describes 11 options a small new business can use to neutralize a large competitor's ability to disrupt the effectiveness of a challenger's marketing strategy. When you are starting your small new business, it is a matter of life and death importance that you recognize that your marketing strategy must incorporate this second characteristic of Screening Condition IV. You should try to include one or more of the above eleven options into your marketing strategy while your new business is still in its prelaunch stage. Failure to do so may result in a most undesirable outcome when your new business enters its launch stage. You have only to reflect on the four examples presented at the beginning of this chapter to visualize how unfortunate that outcome can be.

The last several pages have described what a number of small new businesses included in their marketing strategies to achieve the second characteristic of Screening Condition IV. Note especially that four of those new businesses utilized *more than one* of the 11 options presented. Although not completely described in the foregoing, Appliance Control Technology, Inc. in fact used five of the options, while Glacier Nursery used three, and MicroFridge, Inc. and Blackstone Bank each used two options. Why is this significant? The more of these 11 options your new business can include in its marketing strategy, the more barriers and obstacles you will be erecting to defend it from counterattacks by large competitors. You want to have as many of these obstacles and barriers in place as possible, forcing a large competitor to circumvent or surmount each of them before it tries to mount an attack on the effectiveness of your new business's marketing strategy. In short, the more of these options your new business uses, the stronger will be its defenses against a counterattack by a large competitor.

The following is a *summary of guidelines associated with the characteristic of neutralizing the competitor's ability to negate the effectiveness of your marketing strategy.*

YOUR MARKETING STRATEGY MUST SATISFY AT LEAST ONE OF THESE GUIDELINES

Guideline 2a. Use one or more of the three possible ways to prevent or delay a counterattack by a large competitor (change the rules of marketing; product improvement that cannot be easily copied; create a distribution barrier or impediment).

Guideline 2b. Create a superior reputation for your product among target market individuals.

Guideline 2c. Use one or more of the three possible ways to maximize your product's attractiveness to your target market (make competitors' products less attractive; use product positioning and/or product differentiation; offer a product that competitors won't offer because of cannibalization effects).

Guideline 2d. Use one of the two possible ways to make a target market selection that will prevent your small new business from being counterattacked by a large competitor (target market is too small or unworthy of attention; you can serve the target market better than any competitor).

Guideline 2e. Use one of the two possible ways to select a competitor that will not attack your small new business (competitor has a history of not being aggressive; competitor considers market not important enough to counterattack).

---

3. Have a Significant and Sustainable Product/Service Advantage

If you want to provide your small new business with the maximum amount of protection against counterattacks by large competitors, your marketing strategy must possess two more characteristics beyond those already discussed in this chapter. Having a significant and sustainable product and/or service advantage over competitors is one of them. If your new business has only a slight product and/or service advantage over established competitors, its sales revenues will probably not be large enough to ensure survival. Compared with the established competitors, your new business must have a significant product and/or service advantage if it is to attract customers in numbers large enough to generate a profitable cash flow. But even that might not guarantee survival.

Recall two of the four examples described at the beginning of this chapter. First, Legend Airlines, who planned to offer first-class-only flight service between Dallas' Love Field and both Los Angeles and Washington, D.C. Since Love Field was located near downtown Dallas, Legend Airline's first-class-only service would be very appealing to the Dallas business community, and no other airline was providing a comparable service. Clearly, Legend Airline was offering its target market a transportation service with a significant advantage over what was then currently available.

Second, My Own Meals, Inc., founded by Mary Ann Jackson to offer working mothers ready-made, high quality meals to provide their preschool children while the mothers were away at work. Her product offering was attractive, there was a large and accepting target market, and she had no competition when she started her new business. Jackson had identified a target market whose needs were not being satisfied, and she provided it with a product line that had significant advantages compared with the alternative offerings at the time.

When they first started, both Legend Airlines and My Own Meals had product/service offerings with significant advantages compared with what was available from competitors. But both soon failed. What both of them did not have was a *sustainable* advantage. That is why this third characteristic of Screening Condition IV states that a small new business's marketing strategy must include *a significant and sustainable product/service advantage.*

There are four possible approaches a small new business can take when trying to develop a significant and sustainable product/service advantage:

- offer product/service differentiation
- offer improved quality
- offer better value
- convince the target market to use the new business's brand name interchangeably with the product category

Patents and Sustainable Advantage

Some small new businesses are based on products never before conceived, designed, developed, and commercialized. Such products are called "new-to-the-world" products, and often the designers obtain patents on them. Having a patent on a product can protect it from being copied by others, but the patent does not necessarily guarantee that the product has a sustainable advantage. If a new product has a competitive advantage and is also protected by a patent, that advantage may prove sustainable for the entire period provided for by the patent. But not always!

How long does a patented product have a sustainable advantage? Robert Bennett invented the combination microwave over-freezer-refrigerator named the MicroFridge. Its design and construction was based on a patented switching device that prevented electrical power from being used by more than one of the three appliance components at any given time.[34] Based on that patent, Bennett and his MicroFridge might have a sustainable advantage for as long as the patent was granted protection. But if someone invented a better switching device that did not infringe on Bennett's patent, the MicroFridge would no longer have a sustainable advantage. In other words, Bennett's patent does not protect him from the possibility that someone else will invent a better switching device and thereby effectively eliminate the MicroFridge advantage.

Patents can be very useful helpmates when you are starting your new business, but don't make the mistake of thinking that having a patent guarantees your new business a sustainable advantage forever. If a patent does give your new business an advantage, be fully aware that it may not be sustainable even for the entire life of the patent.

Four Approaches to a Significant and Sustainable Advantage

Offer Product/Service Differentiation

Product and/or service differentiation represents one approach to gaining a significant and sustainable advantage. There are three ways a small new business can achieve such differentiation. (1) It can differentiate its product in a manner that makes competitive substitutes less acceptable to its target market. (2) It can offer a new form of a currently available product, where the new form offers the target market important new features and benefits not possessed by the old form. (3) It can offer different services that are meaningful to the target market. *It is important to note* that in each of (1), (2), and (3) the differentiation should be such that it prevents the large competitor from quickly copying the differentiation, either because it cannot do so or will not do so.

(1) Differentiate Your Product in a Manner That Makes Competitive Substitutes Less Acceptable to the Target Market

Both the electronic controls Appliance Control Technology, Inc. (ACT) offered to its target market of appliance manufacturers and the

MicroFridge Bennett offered to budget motel operators were differentiated products that made competitive substitutes less acceptable to those
customers. ACT's controls allowed the manufacturers to design more
attractive appliances at lower costs. Competitors that had previously supplied the manufacturers with electro-mechanical control devices were not
likely to quickly adopt the electronic controls technology that ACT was
using. If budget motel operators wanted to offer guest the benefits of a
MicroFridge in their room, they could choose to buy one MicroFridge,
or they could choose to buy one microwave oven *and* one refrigerator with
a freezer compartment. Furthermore, it was unlikely that manufacturers of
toaster ovens, electric hot plates, or even refrigerators or microwave ovens
would be able to quickly offer a product that could compete with the
MicroFridge. Even Brad Brown of Glacier Nursery offered his target market hardier trees and plants by growing them locally in Montana's own
harsh climate. Competing nurseries situated in more moderate climates
would have to move to harsher climates in order to duplicate what Brad
Brown was offering.[35]

(2) Offer a New Form of Product with Important New Features and Benefits

Perhaps the most dramatic example of offering a new form of a currently available product involves CD-ROM technology. One small new
business used the new technology to create an electronic version of an
encyclopedia that offered buyers several benefits over printed versions.[36]
Not only was the electronic encyclopedia much less expensive than the
printed ones, readers could activate sound recordings for selected topics
to enrich their reading and learning experience. Another practical benefit
to the owner of an electronic encyclopedia was that its storage did not
require the same shelf space as a printed encyclopedia. Meanwhile,
Encyclopedia Britannica shied away from marketing an electronic version
of its famous books because such a version would not be able to financially support its very large door-to-door sales force.

Of course MicroFridge, too, was a new form of currently available
product. Its benefits included all those associated with a refrigerator, a
freezer, and a microwave oven, but in a smaller size and at a lower price.
Similarly, to the manufacturers of medium-priced appliances, Appliance
Control Technology, Inc.'s electronic controls were also a new form of a
currently available product that offered those manufacturers important
new benefits.

(3) Offer New Services That Are Meaningful to the Target Market

The all-season-long delivery service that Glacier Nursery offered to Montana's retail garden centers was an important service to them, and one that was not available from out-of-state competitors. Paul Kittle's Rusmar, Inc. offered his landfill customers not only the useful foam product itself, but also a machine with which to apply the foam.[37] That machine was an important and very effective service component of Rusmar's offering. Several of Rusmar's customers considered it better than the competitor's machine.

Offer Improved Quality

A second approach a new business owner can use to attain a significant and sustainable advantage is to offer improved quality. This can be done in two ways. (1) A small new business can provide truly higher quality than that offered by competitors, or (2) it can offer a product which target market customers *perceive* as of significantly higher quality than the comparable currently available products.

(1) Provide Truly Higher Quality than Competitors

As noted earlier, Glacier Nursery was the only tree nursery located in the state of Montana. Because they were grown locally, Glacier Nursery's trees and plants were hardier and more capable of thriving in Montana's harsh climate than the offerings of competing nurseries located out-of-state in more moderate climates. Once Montana's retail garden centers recognized this characteristic of Brad Brown's trees and plants, they clearly appreciated the truly higher quality of his offerings.

Blackstone Bank and Trust Company offered its target market higher quality than what was available from competing banks.[38] Unlike any competitor, the bank was very conveniently located in the target market community, and it provided fast and personal service to its customers. In practice, this meant that customers had direct and easy access to the bank's founders. These features represented far higher quality banking service than anything available from the other banks.

(2) Provide a Product Perceived to Be of Higher Quality than Competitors' Offerings

Sometimes a small new business can offer a product that its customers simply perceive to be of higher quality than that offered by competitors.

Ben and Jerry's super premium ice cream appears to be an example of such a product. More recently, the small bottled water company, Glaceau, introduced a brand of enhanced health water called Vitaminwater. It took several years, but the brand was able to grow its distribution to over 50,000 outlets in the United States. Reportedly, many retailers credit the brand with creating a new product category that is providing them with very healthy margins (no pun intended). Vitaminwater seems to be another example of a small new business achieving a significant and sustainable advantage by offering perceived higher quality.[39]

Offer Better Value

This is a third approach to achieving a significant and sustainable advantage. Offering customers better value can be done in two ways. (1) A small new business could provide its target market with greater value by offer one or more extra product or service features while maintaining product prices comparable to the competitors'. (2) Offering a parity product at prices noticeably below competitors' prices will also afford customers better value, but this approach is viable *only if the price difference can be sustained long-term.*

(1) Offer Customers Extra Features at Competitors' Prices

Operators of budget motels easily recognized that buying one MicroFridge was a much better value than buying three small appliances separately—a refrigerator, a freezer, and a microwave oven. The MicroFridge's better value was further enhanced because the motel operator could gain added revenues from the sale of frozen meals, snacks, and drinks that could be stored and prepared in a MicroFridge. The motel operators also benefited because they could charge a higher rate for rooms that included a MicroFridge. For the manufacturers of medium-priced appliances, the electronic controls from Appliance Control Technology, Inc. were a better value than the competitors' electro-mechanical controls because the former contributed to improved appliance designs, lowered production costs, and reduced overall inventory costs.[40]

(2) Offer a Parity Product at Substantially Lower Prices That Can Be Sustained

Landfill operators could purchase foam for covering trash from Rusmar, Inc. or from Rusmar's competitor. On balance the two different foams were probably comparable in the extra landfill capacity they offered relative to ordinary soil. But Rusmar's prices were almost 50 percent cheaper than the competitor's prices, making his foam a much better value for the landfill operator.[41]

Convince the Market to Use the Brand Name Interchangeably with the Product Category

This is the fourth approach to achieving a significant and sustainable advantage. Jello and Kleenex are two well-known historical examples of a market adopting a new brand's name interchangeably with the product category. Another brand that achieved such status not too long after it came into existence was Federal Express (as in "FedEx" it). More recent examples of brands that may belong in this category are Xerox and Starbuck's coffee.

In this day of large advertising and promotional campaigns, is it still possible for a small new business to use this fourth way to achieve a significant and sustainable advantage? Perhaps at the annual convention of the association of budget motel operators one might hear some of the members using the term "MicroFridge" in their conversations without having to explain to one another that they are referring to a combination microwave oven-freezer-refrigerator. Reportedly, many food retailers believe that Vitaminwater created a new and lucrative category for their stores.[42] If these scenarios are true, these relatively new brands may have achieved a significant and sustainable advantage on the basis of their name recognition and acceptance.

What You Should Do

This section has described eight ways that a small new business can try to include a significant and sustainable product/service advantage in its marketing strategy. Your small new business must have a significant advantage over competitors in order to generate the profitable cash flow it needs to survive. But a significant advantage does not guarantee survival, as demonstrated by the examples presented at the beginning of this chapter. Your small new business must also have a sustainable advantage if it is to succeed.

In discussing this third characteristic of Screening Condition IV, four small new businesses were mentioned more than once. Glacier Nursery, Appliance Control Technology and MicroFridge were each mentioned three times, and Rusmar twice. This means that each of those four new businesses somehow incorporated more than one of the above eight options into their marketing strategies. By doing so, each of those new businesses was creating an even more formidable product/service advantage than would have been the case if their strategies had only included one of the above eight options. When you are planning your small new business you would be well advised to try to follow the examples of those four new businesses.

The following is a *summary of the guidelines and warnings associated with the characteristic of having a significant and sustainable product/service advantage.*

YOUR MARKETING STRATEGY MUST SATISFY AT LEAST ONE OF THESE GUIDELINES

Guideline 3a. Use one or more of the three possible ways to offer product and/or service differentiation (differentiate to make competitive substitutes less acceptable; offer a new form of product with important new features; offer different but meaningful services).

Guideline 3b. Use one or both of the two possible ways to offer improved quality (provide actual higher quality; offer perceived higher quality).

Guideline 3c. Use one or both of the two possible ways to offer better value (offer extra product or service features at competitive prices; offer a parity product at lower price).

Guideline 3d. Persuade your target market to use your brand name interchangeably with the product category.

WARNINGS OF THINGS YOU SHOULD AVOID

The following four warnings were presented in Chapter 2 with respect to achieving Screening Condition I. (See warnings 2a–2d in that chapter.)

Warning 3a. Avoid supposing your target market will want your differentiated product because you think it is a good idea.

Warning 3b. Avoid not making a critical comparison of the strengths/advantages and weaknesses/disadvantages of your product versus competitors' products.

Warning 3c. Avoid not confirming through testing and research that your target market actually believes that your product is different in some important way.

Warning 3d. Avoid thinking that the customer will install your product or arrange for someone else to install it.

4. Use Distribution or Some Other Impediment to Provide Longer-Term Protection Against Competitors' Counterattacks

If your marketing strategy successfully included one or more of the four approaches described in the third characteristic above, you should have confidence that it has achieved a significant and sustainable product/service advantage relative to the competition. Furthermore, if your marketing strategy has also achieved the second characteristic of Screening Condition IV, there is a very good chance it will result in a growing sales revenue stream once your small new business enters its launch period. Why is this likely to be true? Because your marketing strategy is offering your target market a product with a significant and sustainable advantage, *and* it includes one or more factors that prevent competitors from quickly attacking your new business.

But even if your marketing strategy achieves both characteristics two and three above and its sales continue to grow, it is unrealistic to believe that established competitors will never counterattack. Recall two of the examples presented at the beginning of this chapter. The microbreweries were well on their way to establishing themselves, and then Anheuser-Busch took notice and made changes that quickly disrupted their growing prosperity. My Own Meals, Inc. had had a successful first year of sales growth and was expecting an even better second year when a couple of food giants entered the market and quickly put an end to Mary Ann Jackson's dreams.

When a small new business begins enjoying sustained sales growth, it is almost certain that one or more established competitors will take notice. If the new business is taking sales from an established competitor, that competitor will more than likely be very unhappy with the situation and will look for ways to regain its lost sales. Or perhaps some well-established firm may simply notice the new business's prosperity and wish to get a share of that prosperity. Whatever the reason for the attack or counterattack, owners of small new businesses are doing themselves a great disservice if they are not well prepared for an eventual attack.

Because your marketing strategy has achieved both the second and third characteristics of Screening Condition IV, your new business should not experience competitive attacks during the early part of its launch period. Hopefully, such attacks won't occur until your new business is far into its launch period, or even later. But if you want to enjoy an even longer period without competitive counterattacks, your marketing strategy will also have to provide your new business with some kind of long-term protection. That is the purpose of this fourth characteristic of Screening Condition IV. You can create such protection if your marketing strategy includes a distribution component, or some other kind of impediment that will protect your new business's marketing successes from competitive retaliation for a longer period of time.

As mentioned in the above discussion of characteristic three, having a patent is an impediment that can provide a small new business with longer-term protection against attacks by established competitors. Both MicroFridge, Inc. and Rusmar, Inc. had patents that probably helped keep some potential competitors at bay. But in addition to patents, there are five other ways a small new business can use distribution to create an impediment that prevents or discourages competitors from counterattacking.

- improve logistics
- establish new relationships
- distribute directly to retail outlets
- offer a full product line
- provide new services

Five Ways to Provide Longer-Term Protection Against Counterattacks

Improve Logistics

If a small new business can offer faster delivery and/or less costly delivery and/or more reliable delivery, customers will view such delivery as improved service. If they value such service and wish to enjoy it on a continuing basis, it will tie them more closely to the small new business. With its all-growing-season-long delivery service, Glacier Nursery offered Montana's retail garden centers significantly improved delivery over what was available from out-of-state competitors. Improved logistics can also result by helping customers manage their logistics and inventory more efficiently. By working closely with the appliance manufacturers' designers and engineers, Appliance Control Technology, Inc. was able to help its customers reduce their overall inventory costs. In both these instances, improved logistics tied the customers more closely to the suppliers because they were helping them be more successful in their businesses. Any logistics improvements you can offer that competitors cannot quickly duplicate will provide your new business with a longer period of time free of competitive attacks.[43]

Establish New Relationships

If a small new business can establish exclusive relationships with dealers, distributors, and retailers, that will discourage them from taking on competing lines.[44] One new business designed an advanced type of distribution system for prescription drugs that created new relationships among five different groups of participants: health plan sponsors; insurance companies; pharmaceutical companies; doctors; and consumers.[45] Once the various relationships among those groups were established, they created barriers that competitors could not easily overcome. By working with its customers' engineers during the early stages in the design of new appliances, Appliance Control Technology, Inc. was able to establish relationships with appliance manufacturers that could not easily be disrupted.[46] Diaper Dan's Delivery Service tried to establish new and important relationships with recent mothers by guaranteeing that they would always get back the very same diapers their babies had been using all along—not someone else's, a feature greatly appreciated by mothers. Furthermore, by using women drivers, Diaper Dan expected to develop a woman-to-mother rapport than could not occur with male drivers.[47]

Distribute Directly to Retail Outlets

The microbreweries example presented at the beginning of this chapter illustrates how vulnerable to competitive attack a small new business can be if it does not control its distribution all the way into retail stores. If those microbreweries had had their own direct distribution into retail outlets, the retail availability of their products would not have been disrupted by Anheuser-Busch's new policies toward their distributors.

One small business even negotiated to set up the entire product category display in retail stores.[48] By taking on this logistic task, the company freed retailers of the responsibility and, in so doing, established a special relationship between itself and its retail customers. If a small new business can develop such a high level of in-store control, it can deter competitors from weakening or destroying its product's retail availability and display. When Vitaminwater first entered its launch period, for example, its founder often delivered his product into retail stores personally and helped set up its display.[49] When Hanes introduced its L'eggs hosiery, it delivered the hosiery right onto the free-standing displays it had provided to retailers. Hanes also sold the hosiery on consignment, which meant that retailers did not have to pay for the hosiery inventory on display in their stores. (See the L'eggs hosiery example in Chapter 2.)

In general, individuals starting a small new business should not lose sight of the distribution control that is associated with delivering directly to customers or using catalogs or the Internet as a means of being in contact with customers and distributing directly to them, or with distributing directly to customers through the mail or by using UPS, FedEx, or other delivery services. These are distribution options that cannot be disrupted by established competitors.

Offer a Full Product Line

The electronic controls that Appliance Control Technology, Inc. (ACT) manufactured were easily adapted to different models of the same appliance, and even to different appliances. Their controls had this versatility because the same piece of electronic hardware could easily be programmed for different appliances. Not only did this substantially reduce the customer's inventory, it also meant that ACT could offer every manufacturer a full line of electronic controls for all of the manufacturer's products. As a result, manufacturers did not have to deal with any other suppliers of controls, and that meant that they could make more efficient use of their time. Manufacturers often develop a greater loyalty toward suppliers who help them be more efficient.[50]

Provide New Services

If a small new business can identify, design, and provide new services that customers will highly value—services not currently available from competitors—that may well create an impediment that established competitors cannot or will choose not to challenge. Established competitors are usually larger organizations than a small new business, and that in itself may prevent them from introducing the kinds of services their upstart rival is offering. Or, because of the established competitor's large size, it may not be practical for them to offer such services to its large customer base.

Some small businesses have contributed to their success by providing customers with such new services as the design and management of in-store displays, managing the re-order and delivery and inventory functions, and even arranging for electronic fund transfers between customers and themselves.[51] We saw that Glacier Nursery strengthened its defensive position with its all-season-long delivery service, a service that probably was not economically practical for the out-of-state competitors to offer. Similarly, Appliance Control Technology, Inc. personnel consulted with appliance manufacturers' engineers when the latter were designing new appliances.[52] For the larger, more established competitors, it may not be possible or practical to attempt to duplicate such customized services.

What You Should Do

If your marketing strategy achieves both of characteristics two and three of Screening Condition IV, your new business should enjoy growing sales in the short run because your strategy offers an important product/ service advantage to your target market and it incorporates certain features that prevent competitors from quickly negating your strategy's effectiveness. Over a longer period of time, however, a large competitor that feels threatened may be able to organize an effective counterattack against your business if your marketing strategy does not provide for longer-term protection. This section has described five ways your marketing strategy can include a distribution component or some other type of impediment that can prevent the competitor from attacking for an even longer period of time. Each of those five tactics aims to develop a stronger and more loyal relationship between your new business and its distributors or customers. The stronger and more established the relationship becomes, the less success a competitor is likely to have if it attacks.

It was noted earlier in this chapter that some new businesses utilized more than one of the 11 options available to achieve the second characteristic. (See page 172.) By doing so, those new businesses were erecting more barriers and obstacles for competitors to overcome before they have any chance of succeeding in negating the effectiveness of the smaller rival's marketing strategies. Some of those same new businesses used more than one of the eight possible options for achieving the third characteristic. (See page 179.) By doing that, those new businesses were creating a much stronger, significant, and sustainable product/service advantage than if their strategies included only one of the eight options.

That same logic also applies to this fourth characteristic of Screening Condition IV. That is, a new business should try to incorporate more than one of the five options described above in order to create multiple barriers and obstacles that prevent or delay competitors from counterattacking. From the foregoing descriptions, you can see that Appliance Control Technology, Inc. used four of the impediment options available, and Glacier Nursery used two.

The following is a *summary of the guidelines associated with the characteristic of using distribution or some other impediment to provide longer-term protection against counterattacks.*

> ### YOUR MARKETING STRATEGY MUST SATISFY AT LEAST ONE OF THESE GUIDELINES
>
> Guideline 4a. Offer customers faster and/or less costly and/or more reliable delivery and/or help your customers manage their logistics and inventory more efficiently.
>
> Guideline 4b. Establish exclusive relationships with dealers, distributors, and retailers.
>
> Guideline 4c. Establish direct distribution into retail stores, and attempt to control your product's in-store shelf display.
>
> Guideline 4d. Offer dealers, distributors, and retailers a full product line in order to discourage them from turning to some other supplier who can do so.
>
> Guideline 4e. Offer dealers, distributors, and retailers highly valued new services that are not currently available from competitors.

Summary

If your marketing strategy has achieved each of Screening Conditions I, II, and III, your small new business will have a complete and synergistic marketing strategy whose elements should not cause any lengthy strategy execution delays. Furthermore, your marketing strategy will be quite compatible with a small marketing budget. Because your new business has such a strategy, it should begin enjoying a growing sales revenue stream as soon as it enters its launch period. However, you also want your marketing strategy to have the ability to defend itself against the competitive counterattacks that are almost certain to occur. That is why you must be certain that your marketing strategy also achieves Screening Condition IV. To do so, it should possess each of the following four characteristics.

Your new business should not directly attack a large competitor, or even give the appearance of doing so. If your new business will eventually bring you into contact with a large competitor, be absolutely certain that the competitor is vulnerable because of the presence of one or more of the 12 circumstances described in the first section of this chapter.

If you want your new business to be capable of defending itself against strong competitive counterattacks, your marketing strategy must possess a second characteristic: it must be designed so that it neutralizes a large competitor's ability to disrupt or negate its effectiveness. Your marketing strategy can achieve this by incorporating one or more of the 11 suggestions presented in the second section of this chapter.

Your marketing strategy must also have a significant and sustainable product/service advantage. That is the third characteristic associated with Screening Condition IV. A small new business can achieve this characteristic by integrating into its marketing strategy one or more of the eight options described in the third section of this chapter.

The fourth characteristic your marketing strategy needs in order to achieve Screening Condition IV is the use of a distribution component or some other type of impediment that will provide for longer-term protection against competitive counterattacks. You can make certain that your marketing strategy possesses this characteristic by following one or more of the five suggestions described in the fourth section of this chapter.

PART III

CREATING YOUR SUCCESSFUL MARKETING STRATEGY

6

Make Certain Your Marketing Strategy Will Have a Good Chance of Being Successful

You have now been introduced to the many details of the four screening conditions that can help you create a successful marketing strategy for your small new business. Your new business has been your passion for quite awhile—at least for a number of months, but perhaps for several years. You have already devoted much time, thought, effort, and financial resources to its creation. Clearly, you very much want it to succeed. To do that, you must have a successful marketing program to accompany all the other nonmarketing activities you have already engaged in and will engage in in the future.

To achieve that successful marketing program you must have a marketing strategy that satisfies each of the screening conditions described in the previous four chapters. You will also want your marketing strategy to display *richness* in achieving the four screening conditions because the more richness it possesses, the greater the chances that your small new business will be successful. These are the two topics discussed in this chapter.

Four Screening Conditions Help You Create a Successful Marketing Strategy

If your marketing strategy has successfully achieved Screening Condition I, your new business will have identified a target market whose wants and needs currently are not being satisfied by any competitor, and your new business will offer that target market a product that it is eager to obtain. You have planned a promotional communication that will cause the individuals in your target market to easily understand and fully appreciate that the advantages and benefits of your product offering far exceed those available from any competitor's. You have priced your product so that target market individuals clearly see it as a very good value when compared with the competitors' offerings. And you have arranged to distribute your product in a manner that makes it very convenient for individuals in your target market to purchase. As a result of these decisions, you have combined these five marketing elements in your marketing strategy in a way that makes it very synergistic and that will prove to be both very effective and very efficient.

If your marketing strategy has successfully achieved Screening Condition II, your new business will not encounter any lengthy strategy execution delays when it enters its launch period. Because your target market has been well defined and those individuals are looking for a product just like the one you will be offering, your new business should encounter no delays due to poor target market identification. And because you are very knowledgeable about the competition you will encounter and are certain that your new business can serve your target market better than they can, you should not encounter any strategy execution delays due to the competition. You have arranged for, and secured, the timely distribution of your product in all outlets where the target market will expect to find it. And you have researched all the environmental, legal, and governmental regulations that might affect your new business, you fully understand them, and you have complied with those that are applicable. Since your marketing strategy reflects all four of these considerations, your new business should not encounter any strategy execution delays and should begin to realize growing sales revenues as soon as it opens its doors to its customers. That sales revenue stream will be the first solid evidence that your new business is well launched on its path toward success.

If your marketing strategy has satisfied Screening Condition III, you've designed it to match your marketing budget. As a result, your new business will be able to execute its marketing strategy in a timely fashion and in the manner originally intended. These two conditions must be present in order to cause the growing sales revenues stream noted in the above paragraph. Thus, because your marketing strategy also has achieved Screening Conditions II and I, your new business should encounter no strategy execution delays, and your marketing strategy should show results shortly after you execute it. A sales revenue stream should begin to flow as soon as your new business enters its launch period and then continue to grow as more of your target market learns about your new business's excellent product offering.

The growing sales revenue stream your new business will be enjoying in the first 12–24 months of its launch period should continue if your marketing strategy has also achieved Screening Condition IV. Because of this condition, your small new business will not directly attack a large, well-established competitor. Your marketing strategy also includes three features that will further delay the possibility of competitive counterattacks. First, you have included something that will negate your competitor's ability to disrupt the effectiveness of your marketing strategy. This will prevent competitive counterattacks or at least delay them for some time. That delay will give your new business additional time to establish itself more firmly with its target market and its distribution channel. Second, your marketing strategy includes some significant advantage over your competitors, an advantage, moreover, that is *sustainable*. This factor will delay even further the emergence of a competitive counterattack. Third, your marketing strategy also includes a distribution component or some other kind of impediment that will provide your new business with even longer-term protection against competitive attacks. In effect, Screening Condition IV has erected these three protective barriers to fend off competitive attacks until your new business is far into its launch period. As a result, the sales revenue stream you have been enjoying should not be seriously threatened before your new business has become well established.

Successful Marketing Strategies Display *Richness*

After lunch or dinner, a person might order dessert of a single scoop of vanilla ice cream. Such a dessert could appropriately be called simple or plain vanilla. A second person might order a banana split featuring three scoops of flavored ice cream, a sliced banana, chocolate fudge topping, a large foamy spray of whipped cream, a generous sprinkling of nuts, a maraschino cherry or two, and perhaps still other goodies. This dessert could accurately be described as *rich*. In a similar way, a marketing strategy can be simple or it can be rich.

A rich marketing strategy—or a strategy that displays richness—is one that incorporates *more than the minimum number of guidelines* needed to achieve each screening condition. A rich strategy also clearly complies with all of the warnings associated with each screening condition. In other words, a marketing strategy that displays richness contains noticeably more features than the minimum number required for each of the four screening conditions, and disregards none of the warnings. In contrast, a plain vanilla strategy will incorporate only the minimum number of guidelines needed to achieve each screening condition.

What follows is a review of the details of three marketing strategies with which you are now well acquainted. Those details illustrate the concept of richness in marketing strategies.

Appliance Control Technology, Inc.

Appliance Control Technology, Inc. (ACT) was founded by Wallace Leyshon and two friends to design and manufacture microprocessor-based electronic controls for kitchen and laundry appliances.[1] Those controls were the buttons and panels people touch and push to operate their appliances.

Screening Condition I: A Complete and Synergistic Marketing Strategy

ACT *selected a target market* it could serve better than any competitor. Their target market comprised manufacturers of medium-priced appliances who at the time were being served only by suppliers of electro-mechanical controls. Compared with those suppliers, ACT offered the target market better controls with higher quality and more service, along with lower prices and overall lower inventory costs. Thus, ACT was able to better serve the target market in several ways, not just one. (See guidelines 1a–1d, and warnings 1a–1c in Chapter 2.)

ACT's electronic controls were *a differentiated product* that served the selected target market better than the electro-mechanical controls offered by existing suppliers. ACT's electronic controls were standardized—the same controls could be used in different models of the same appliance, and even in completely different appliances. This enabled the manufacturer to reduce both physical inventory and inventory costs as well. Two other advantages accrued to the manufacturers due to the product and service differentiation that ACT offered. Because of the close working relationship between ACT's engineers and the appliance companies' designers, the time required to move a new appliance model from conception to commercialization was greatly reduced. This brought down the manufacturer's development costs and created a marketing advantage for them since they could get their new models to market faster than before. Also, thanks to the close working relationship between supplier and manufacturer, the latter was able to offer more attractive new appliance designs, which consumers found more appealing. In effect, ACT's product differentiation offered customers a number of advantages over competing products, rather than just one. (See guidelines 2a and 2b, and warning 2b in Chapter 2.)

ACT *promoted* their products direct to appliance manufacturers' managers and designers. In doing so, they effectively communicated the four features and benefits they were offering. The appliance manufacturers understood and appreciated (1) ACT's product quality that resulted in better appliance models, (2) the improved delivery service, (3) the lower prices and overall reduction in inventory costs, and (4) the shorter new product design cycles. Here again, ACT's promotion was effective in several ways, rather than only one. (See guidelines 3a–3c and warnings 3a–3c in Chapter 2.)

Not only was ACT offering their customers improved control devices (compared with electro-mechanical controls), they did so *at lower prices*. But the appliance manufacturers also enjoyed additional cost savings through reduced inventories and shorter delivery times. Lastly, they also enjoyed savings due to the shorter new product design cycles resulting from their close working relationship with ACT. Overall, ACT offered their target market good value in several ways, rather than just a lower price for the control devices. (See guidelines 4a and 4c, and warnings 4b and 4c in Chapter 2.)

Distribution of ACT's controls directly to customers was faster and more reliable overall because standardized parts meant fewer parts, which in turn translated into fewer inventory problems. Because of the close working relationship between ACT's engineers and the appliance companies' designers, communication channels were very short and whatever problems arose could be quickly resolved. Thanks to its marketing strategy, ACT's distribution was more convenient for their customers in at least two ways that the competition could not easily match. (See guideline 5a in Chapter 2.)

Conclusion Regarding Screening Condition I   From the above observations, you can see that ACT's marketing strategy fulfilled Screening

Condition I in much more than a minimal way. Rather, their strategy displayed noticeable richness in each of the five elements that constitute a marketing strategy (target market, product differentiation, effective promotion, good value pricing, and convenient distribution).

Screening Condition II: Avoid Marketing Strategy Execution Delays

When he started his new business, Wallace Leyshon was already quite familiar with the kitchen and laundry appliance market, and he carefully selected the manufacturers of medium-priced appliances as ACT's *target market*. Those firms were not being served at all by the established suppliers of electronic controls, yet they represented a sizeable market whose control needs could be readily estimated. In addition, they were relatively few in number, and could easily be identified and contacted. Since ACT was offering them a significantly improved control product over what they were currently using, those manufacturers were very receptive to the communications they received from the small new business. (See guidelines 1a–1c, and warnings 1a–1d in Chapter 3.)

With regard to the *competition*, Leyshon knew that large suppliers of electronic controls had shown no interest in serving the manufacturers of medium-priced appliances because their controls were too expensive, compared with electro-mechanical controls. Since they couldn't serve that market, and current suppliers could only offer electro-mechanical controls, Leyshon clearly saw that ACT could serve that target market better than the competition. Leyshon knew that the four advantages ACT offered (described above) would be quickly recognized and appreciated by the target market as very desirable. For these reasons, ACT's marketing strategy encountered no strategy execution delays due to competition. (See guidelines 2a and 2b, and warnings 2a–2c in Chapter 3.)

By delivering their product direct, ACT's *distribution* was very convenient for its customers. Not only was if fast and reliable, but the good communications between ACT and their customers also contributed to faster problem resolution and fewer delays and shortages. Thanks to their direct distribution, ACT was able to avoid all strategy execution delays caused by distribution factors. (See guideline 3a in Chapter 3.)

ACT encountered no *legal, regulatory, or environmental* constraints or barriers. (See guideline 4a in Chapter 3.)

Conclusion Regarding Screening Condition II   Overall, ACT's marketing strategy was designed in such a way that it avoided any strategy execution delays whether due to target market factors or to barriers set up by competitors or to channel of distribution difficulties or to any complications caused by legal or environmental regulations. Furthermore, both the target market aspect and the competition aspect of ACT's marketing strategy demonstrated some degree of richness that probably further insured that the new business would not experience any serious strategy execution delays.

Screening Condition III: Marketing Strategy Is Compatible with a Small Budget

Wallace Leyshon selected a *target market* consisting of firms that were not being well served to the fullest extent. They were relatively few in number, so they represented a few geographically concentrated buyers. And ACT offered them a significantly better product than what they were using. These target market factors were very compatible with a small marketing budget. (See guideline 1b and warning 1b in Chapter 4.)

ACT entered a market where the *type of competition*—monopolistic competition—was compatible with a small marketing budget. They did so by offering a small, well-defined target market a very appealing, differentiated product with distinguishing features that resulted in both cost savings and more attractive new appliance models. (See guideline 2a and warnings 2a and 2b in Chapter 4.)

Because ACT's target market firms were still using electro-mechanical controls—which were in the mature phase of their *product life cycle*—the sudden availability of electronic controls essentially made them appear as new-to-the-world products to those firms. From their perspective, electronic controls were in the introductory stage of their product life cycle, a condition that is very compatible with a small marketing budget. (See guidelines 3a–3c and warnings 3a and 3b in Chapter 4.)

ACT *distributed* directly to its appliance-manufacturing customers, and such distribution does not require a large marketing budget. (See guideline 4b and warning 4b in Chapter 4.)

Microprocessor-based electronic controls for appliances are *business fabricating parts*, and ACT's electronic controls were of significantly higher quality than what the target market was currently using. These are conditions typically associated with a small marketing budget. (See guideline 5a and warnings 5a–5c in Chapter 4.)

Conclusion Regarding Screening Condition III   ACT's marketing strategy was so designed that none of its elements required a large marketing budget. Specifically, ACT's selection of its target market, of the type of market competition it chose to compete in, of its method of distribution, and of its type of product offering were all compatible with a small marketing budget. By pursuing a target market that would view electronic controls as a new product in its introductory stage, ACT's product offering was further able to compete with only a small marketing budget.

Screening Condition IV: Marketing Strategy Can Defend against Counterattacks

ACT *did not attack a large, well-established competitor.* But, to some extent, it did encounter a small, relatively new competitor. However, ACT operated and marketed in such a very different manner compared with that competitor that the two did not encounter one another in direct competition. (See guideline 1a and warnings 1a in Chapter 5.)

Wallace Leyshon designed his marketing strategy to include five elements that served to *neutralize a competitor's ability to disrupt or negate his strategy's effectiveness.* By offering electronic rather than electro-mechanical controls he prevented current suppliers from competing directly. He pursued a target market that was of little interest to the large, well-established suppliers of electronic controls. ACT engineers were working closely with the manufacturers' designers to come up with the best controls for their appliances. ACT's product differentiation and extra services made competitors' offerings much less acceptable to the target market. Lastly, ACT used marketing in ways that were quite different from the industry's traditional marketing, which had a delaying effect on competitors because of the extensive marketing changes they would have to undertake if they decided to compete in a similar manner. (See guidelines 2a, 2c, and 2d in Chapter 5.)

ACT's marketing strategy included three *significant and sustainable advantages.* One advantage derived from their engineers' close working relationships with ACT's customers. The higher quality of their product compared with electro-mechanical controls was a second advantage. ACT also offered better value to their customers through lower prices, inventory cost savings, and new product development cost savings. (See guidelines 3a–3c in Chapter 5.)

Leyshon designed ACT's marketing strategy to *use distribution and/or some other impediment to provide the company with longer-term protection.* Two different impediments were incorporated into the strategy. For one, Leyshon provided better and faster delivery services. The second impediment was the close working relationships ACT's engineers had with their customers' designers and engineers. Once those good relationships became well established, they became a barrier which competitors would find very difficult to overcome. (See guideline 4a in Chapter 5.)

Conclusion Regarding Screening Condition IV   Not only did ACT's marketing strategy avoid attacking any well-established competitor, it competed in a manner that precluded head-to-head conflicts with competitors. ACT's marketing strategy neutralized competitors by using five different tactics, and it achieved a significant and sustainable advantage in three different ways. Lastly, ACT's marketing strategy created at least two impediments that provided it with longer-term protection from competitor's counterattacks. As you can see, Wallace Leyshon designed ACT's marketing strategy to have great richness with respect to achieving Screening Condition IV.

Conclusion Regarding the Richness of ACT's Marketing Strategy

Wallace Leyshon's marketing strategy displayed notable richness in each of its five elements, and it clearly and strongly avoided any strategy execution delays. Also, each of the strategy's five elements was very compatible with a small marketing budget. And finally, ACT's strategy also did not attack any competitor, and it was very rich in features neutralizing competitors, in achieving significant and sustainable advantages, and in creating impediments that provided the company with longer-term protection against counterattacks. Overall, the strategy demonstrated great richness in every regard.

MicroFridge, Inc.

Robert Bennett and two partners formed MicroFridge, Inc. to design and market a miniaturized microwave oven-freezer-refrigerator combination that would run off a single electric cord plugged into an ordinary household electrical outlet without blowing a fuse or tripping a circuit breaker.[2]

Screening Condition I: A Complete and Synergistic Marketing Strategy

Given the MicroFridge's three main food-oriented benefits, and the fact that it could operate off a single electrical cord without causing an electrical short, two *target markets* that were a good fit were college students in dormitory rooms and guests staying in budget or economy motels. These markets were not being well served at all, they were easy to identify and contact, and there was no strong competitor pursuing either market. (See guidelines 1a–1d and warnings 1a–1c in Chapter 2.)

Compared with the products available on the market at the time, the MicroFridge was a very *differentiated product*. It took up less space and consumed less electrical power than did refrigerator-freezer combination and small microwave oven when purchased as separate units. (See guidelines 2a and 2b, and warnings 2a–2c in Chapter 2.)

Thanks to the uniqueness of the product, the *promotional element* of MicroFridge's marketing strategy benefited from much free and favorable publicity. Many good reports about the product appeared in the printed press and on radio and television as well. Bennett himself was interviewed by the media on a number of occasions. The two well-identified target markets readily understood and appreciated the MicroFridge's benefits, and they could easily be contacted by telephone, by mail, or in person by Bennett's small sales force. (See guidelines 3a–3c and warnings 3a and 3b in Chapter 2.)

At first the MicroFridge was moderately *priced*, too moderately priced, in fact, to judge by early sales. With a strong and growing demand trend and virtually no competition, Bennett raised the MicroFridge price twice within the first year of its launch. Despite the price increases, the continuing strong demand trend indicated that the MicroFridge represented a good value to its target market customers. (See guidelines 4a and 4c in Chapter 2.)

Because large appliance manufacturers were bypassing traditional appliance *distributors* to sell directly to large discount retailers, those distributors were looking for new products to sell and new markets to serve in order to bolster their stagnating sales. When they saw the MicroFridge—an exciting new product going into two markets (colleges and motels) that were new to them—they were eager to sign up as MicroFridge distributors. (See guidelines 5a–5c and warnings 5a, 5c, and 5d in Chapter 2.)

Conclusions Regarding Screening Condition I   Robert Bennett's marketing strategy included a very differentiated product that offered excellent benefits to target markets that were not being served at all, or were only being served poorly. The product and the target markets were an excellent match with one another. In addition to much free publicity, promotion of the MicroFridge was direct to target market individuals, either through distributors' sales forces or through Bennett's small sales force or via direct mail. The message of MicroFridge's benefits was easily communicated and easily understood and appreciated by potential customers. The price Bennett assigned to the MicroFridge clearly caused the target market to view it and its benefits as a good value. Distribution was convenient for the target market because MicroFridge's distributors were both experienced and eager to develop the new markets that the MicroFridge was introducing them to. Overall, MicroFridge's marketing strategy was both complete and synergistic, and displayed a noticeable degree of richness in its elements.

Screening Condition II: Avoid Marketing Strategy Execution Delays

Bennett identified two *target markets* that had a need for a product like the MicroFridge. Those target markets were easy to contact, their sizes were easily estimated, and at the time no competitor was trying to satisfy their needs. In the college dormitory market, whatever substitutes were being used were only marginally satisfactory at best. (Some colleges reportedly did not allow microwave ovens in dormitory rooms, but such prohibition did not seem widespread.) As for guests in budget motels, there was nothing at all that they could use to prepare inexpensive snacks or meals. Meanwhile, budget motel operators saw that room rates could be raised if the rooms included the convenience of a MicroFridge, and on top of that, they could realize additional revenues from the sale of microwaveable snacks and frozen meals to their guests. Overall, MicroFridge, Inc. did not encounter any strategy execution delays due to their target market selection. Rather, both target markets welcomed the arrival of the MicroFridge as a solution to a longstanding unsatisfied need. (See guidelines 1a–1c and warnings 1a and 1b in Chapter 3.)

When MicroFridge, Inc. entered its launch period, the only *competition* it faced were manufacturers of microwave ovens, small refrigerators, toaster ovens, and electric hot plates. At the time, none of those manufacturers had a product capable of competing against the MicroFridge. Because the MicroFridge faced no direct competitors, Bennett's new business did not encounter any strategy execution delays due to competition. Bennett's marketing strategy did a very effective job of avoiding such delays. (See guidelines 2a and 2b, and warnings 2a and 2b in Chapter 3.)

Since the major appliance manufacturers were increasingly bypassing traditional wholesalers to sell directly to large discount retailers, those traditional appliance *distributors* were open to adding new products and new markets to their portfolios. Consequently, they welcomed MicroFridge's arrival on the scene. Bennett's marketing strategy did not encounter any strategy execution delays due to distribution barriers. (See guideline 3a and warning 3a in Chapter 3.)

Because the MicroFridge consisted primarily of three very common household appliances that were powered by ordinary electricity, MicroFridge, Inc. was not subjected to any unusual *regulatory, environmental, or legal barriers*. Consequently, it encountered no strategy execution delays due to these forces.

Conclusion Regarding Screening Condition II   Robert Bennett's marketing strategy for his MicroFridge did not encounter any strategy execution delays due to the factors of target market, competition, distribution channels, or legal and environmental regulations. With the possible exception of some colleges not permitting microwave ovens in dormitory rooms, the strategy seemed to have avoided any barriers which might have prevented it from being executed in a timely manner. It solidly achieved Screening Condition II.

Screening Condition III: Marketing Strategy Is Compatible with a Small Budget

MicroFridge's *target markets* were underserved, but the thousands of budget motels and hundreds of colleges and universities were scattered in many locations across the country. However, each such institution was easy to identify, and relatively easy to contact. Futhermore, each college represented a potential for perhaps several hundreds of MicroFridges and each budget motel represented a potential of several dozens, or more. Since both of these institution types represented potential multiple-unit purchases, marketing expenditures to contact them would be allocated over a number of units sold, and thus prove to be economically justifiable. Bennett used personal selling on the college market in view of the high unit sales potential of each location. For the budget motels, more numerous and more widespread geographically, Bennett used direct mail and telemarketing. Overall, because MicroFridge was offering its underserved target markets a significantly better product, and because each target institution potentially represented multiple unit purchases, MicroFridge's selected target markets were compatible with a small marketing budget. (See guidelines 1a and 1b, and warnings 1a and 1b in Chapter 4.)

Regarding the *type of market competition* MicroFridge entered, it was neither pure competition nor oligopolistic competition. In a sense, since at the time there was no direct competition in either target market, MicroFridge had a monopoly. At the very least, the company had entered into a monopolistic competition where it had no strong competitors, only weak ones. This situation was very compatible with a small marketing budget. (See guideline 2a and warnings 2a and 2b in Chapter 4.)

The MicroFridge entered the market in the introductory phase of its *product life cycle*. No competing product existed at the time; nothing like it was available to colleges and motels. In addition, the MicroFridge, easy to understand and to use, addressed a need not previously satisfied. Based on those two observations, the MicroFridge was a new product—perhaps a true innovation—that was likely to be quickly and widely accepted by its target markets. These various conditions were quite compatible with a small budget. (See guidelines 3a–3c and warnings 3a and 3b in Chapter 4.)

The MicroFridge used a short *channel of distribution* that consisted of exclusive distributors eager to distribute the product because it was new and it introduced them to new markets they previously had not served. This channel of distribution arrangement was quite compatible with a small marketing budget. (See guidelines 4a–4c and warnings 4a–4c in Chapter 4.)

Robert Bennett was planning on selling his combined microwave over-freezer-refrigerator to colleges and universities and to budget motels, both of which were businesses. The MicroFridge was not essential to the operations of either type of business, but it could make those businesses more attractive to their markets. The MicroFridge therefore qualified as a piece of *business accessory equipment*, and a particularly desirable one, significantly better than any other similar product or combination of products available at the time. The selection of a business accessory item for his small new business was very compatible with a small marketing budget. (See guideline 5a and warnings 5a–5c in Chapter 4.)

Conclusion Regarding Screening Condition III   When Robert Bennett conceived his new business and it marketing strategy, he selected target markets and a type of product that were compatible with a small budget. His product was essentially in the introductory stage of its life cycle, his business was entering into a type of market competition that was either monopolistic or monopolistic competition, and he used a short, open, and exclusive channel of distribution. Because all these aspects of Bennett's marketing strategy were compatible with a small marketing budget, the strategy achieved Screening Condition III in a very solid way.

Screening Condition IV: Marketing Strategy Can Defend against Counterattacks

The MicroFridge *did not directly attack any competitor*, because no one was currently offering a combined microwave oven-freezer-refrigerator. (See guideline 1a and warning 1a in Chapter 5.)

Robert Bennett's marketing strategy used three different ways to neutralize *a competitor's ability to disrupt or negate his strategy's effectiveness.* The MicroFridge was a unique combination of different appliances with a patented device that would prevent it from blowing fuses or tripping circuit breakers. Bennett's strategy focused on two relatively small target markets. They and their needs were being completely ignored by the large appliance manufacturers, but the MicroFridge was very capable of satisfying those needs. The strategy further maximized the product's attractiveness to the target markets through product differentiation, which had the effect of making competitors' current product offerings even less acceptable than they already were. (See guidelines 2a–2e in Chapter 5.)

The MicroFridge had two *significant and sustainable* advantages. It was a new form of two or three common products combined into one compact product with only a single electric cord that would not blow fuses. It was very clear to potential customers that the MicroFridge was a differentiated product with important new features. In addition, by offering customers those extra, new features at an equal or lower price than the cost of three separate appliances, the MicroFridge gave customers better value for their money. (See guidelines 3a and 3c, and warnings 3b and 3c in Chapter 5.)

Bennett's marketing strategy *used distribution to provide his new business with longer-term protection against counterattacks by competitors.* He did this by establishing exclusive relationships with appliance distributors. MicroFridge's patented switching device was also an impediment that provided additional protection, at least for an intermediate time period, and perhaps even longer. (See guideline 4b in Chapter 5.)

Conclusion Regarding Screening Condition IV   Because the MicroFridge clearly did not attack any competitor, it certainly met the first characteristic associated with Screening Condition IV. Its marketing strategy neutralized the competition in three different ways, it gained a significant and sustainable advantage in two different ways, and it created impediments in two different ways. Thus, the MicroFridge marketing strategy also demonstrated a high degree of richness in achieving Screening Condition IV.

Conclusions Regarding the Richness of MicroFridge's Marketing Strategy

Robert Bennett's marketing strategy used five elements that were very synergistic and displayed a noticeable degree of robustness. The strategy clearly avoided any strategy execution delays due to its target market, competition, distribution channels, or any type of regulations. Everything about the strategy proved very compatible with a small marketing budget.

In addition, Bennett's marketing strategy did not attack any competitor; it neutralized the competition in several ways; it used two factors to gain a significant and sustainable advantage; and it used two different ways to create impediments that would provide longer-term protection. Bennett's marketing strategy displayed a high degree of richness in achieving Screening Conditions I and IV, while also strongly achieving Screening Conditions II and III.

Glacier Nursery

Brad Brown founded Glacier Nursery in Montana's Flathead Valley because there were no tree nurseries within the state of Montana, and he planned to grow "hardier" trees and shrubs than those grown by nurseries located in more temperate climates out-of-state.[3]

Screening Condition I: A Complete and Synergistic Marketing Strategy

Brown's primary *target market* comprised the 40 largest garden centers in Montana, which accounted for about 90 percent of the retail plant sales in the state. Because no tree nursery was located in Montana at the time, all of those garden centers had to obtain their supplies from out-of-state nurseries. Those nurseries served Montana's garden centers primarily during the spring peak selling season, then sharply reduced their delivery service during the remainder of the growing season. Brad Brown planned to provide Montana's garden centers with better service because he was closer to them and would serve them regularly throughout the growing season. And with his trees and shrubs having been grown in Montana's harsher climate, Brown also expected to sell a better product—hardier plants. Compared with the out-of-state competitors, Brown hoped to be able to serve Montana's retail garden centers better in these three ways. (See guidelines 1a–1d and warnings 1a and 1b in Chapter 2.)

Brown expected to establish exceptional *product differentiation* by offering five product and/or service advantages over the nurseries located outside of Montana. He would offer inexpensive and timely delivery services—even for small quantities—that competing nurseries could not match. He would offer delivery throughout the entire growing season. Because his trees and shrubs were Montana-grown, they would be hardier and have a greater survival rate than those from out-of-state growers. Being a smaller operator than his competitors, Brown believed his products would be of consistently higher quality. Lastly, being located closer to Montana's retail garden centers, Brown believed he could help them better manage their inventories—and inventory costs—by offering more frequent or when-needed delivery. These five factors strongly differentiated Glacier Nursery's product offering from those of competitors. (See guidelines 2a and 2b, and warning 2b in Chapter 2.)

From his previous experience as a foreman at a Christmas tree farm, Brown had become acquainted with all the owners/managers of Montana's retail garden centers. This greatly facilitated his *promotion* of Glacier Nursery, because much business in the nursery field is based on personal contacts and friendships. Brown personally visited all of Montana's garden centers to announce his newly opened Glacier Nursery and to promote its features and benefits, as described above. Because of their knowledge of, and experience with, the out-of-state growers, those garden center operators fully understood and appreciated the advantages of Brown's offerings. In addition to sending some free samples to a handful of garden centers each year, he kept in touch with operators through telephone calls and personal visits. Overall, the promotional element of Brown's marketing strategy was closely integrated with his target market and product offering. (See guidelines 3a–3c and warnings 3a and 3b in Chapter 2.)

At the start, Brown *priced* his products about 10 percent below the competition, but he hoped to bring his prices up to competitive levels after Glacier Nursery had established a good reputation among customers— perhaps after two years or so. Still later, when he expected to have demonstrated his nursery's superior services and higher quality, hardier trees and shrubs, he would be able to charge a slightly premium price, while still having customers view his offerings as good value. By helping the retail garden centers to better control their inventories and to reduce their inventory costs, Brown further enhanced Glacier Nursery's image of offering good value. (See guidelines 4a–4c and warning 4a in Chapter 2.)

Regarding *distribution*, Brown arranged to use three local trucking companies to deliver his trees and plants throughout Montana, and to do so in a timely manner throughout the entire growing season. This element of his marketing strategy was closely integrated with the elements of target market, product differentiation, and promotion, thus making it a highly synergistic marketing strategy. Additionally, by offering much better delivery services than competitors, Brown expected to develop a reputation for superior service, a factor which would allow him eventually to charge premium prices. (See guideline 5a and warning 5a in Chapter 2.)

Conclusion Regarding Screening Condition I   Brad Brown's marketing strategy for his Glacier Nursery identified three ways it could service its target market better than competitors, and it developed five ways it could offer the target market improved product differentiation, including delivery services. The nursery's promotion was sharply focused on its 40 main customers, and clearly communicated its advantageous offerings through direct personal and telephone contacts, which were supplemented by free samples. With its pricing slightly below competitors' pricing, the nursery clearly created good value and tied all five marketing elements into a complete and synergistic marketing strategy. In short, Glacier Nursery's marketing strategy clearly achieved Screening Condition I, with ample richness evident among and between its five elements.

Screening Condition II: Marketing Strategy Avoids Strategy Execution Delays

Brad Brown selected a *target market* with which he was already very familiar. He knew most of the garden center operators personally, and he knew why they were dissatisfied with their current suppliers—Montana's garden center operators were just not very important to the large out-of-state nurseries supplying them. Because those operators knew they were not being well served, they were ready to welcome any legitimate and reliable nursery that could serve them better. An integral part of Brown's marketing strategy exploited his competitors' weaknesses, and turned them into competitive advantages for Glacier Nursery. As a result, Glacier Nursery did not encounter any strategy execution delays due to its target market selection. (See guidelines 1a–1c in Chapter 3.)

The out-of-state *competitors* were willing to serve Montana's retail garden centers during the spring selling season because their large purchase orders could justify delivering to customers so far away. After the peak spring selling season, however, those growers were less interested in delivering small, "fill-in" orders to distant customers. Those smaller fill-in orders opened the door for Glacier Nursery to make inroads into the Montana market, because the large competitors saw them as being too small to contest. Thus, those competitors had no incentive to establish barriers that would cause Glacier Nursery to experience strategy execution delays. (See guidelines 2a and 2b, and warnings 2a and 2b in Chapter 3.)

Brown's marketing strategy used direct *distribution* from his nursery to his customers. There was nothing that competitors could do to disrupt Glacier Nursery's shipments or to establish barriers that would hamper Glacier Nursery's ability to provide timely delivery services. (See guidelines 3a and 3b, and warning 3a in Chapter 3.)

Glacier Nursery encountered no *legal, environmental, or regulatory barriers* that caused it to experience strategy execution delays.

Conclusion Regarding Screening Condition II   Brad Brown's target market selection—along with his selection of the competitors serving that target market—helped his new business avoid any barriers or disruptions that might have caused strategy execution delays. His use of direct distribution further prevented competitors from causing Glacier Nursery to suffer strategy execution delays due to distribution barriers. And because his was a tree nursery business, it did not encounter any such delays due to legal or environmental regulations. His marketing strategy did a nice job of achieving Screening Condition II.

Screening Condition III: Marketing Strategy Is Compatible with a Small Budget

Brown's marketing strategy *targeted* some 40 retail garden centers, all located in Montana. Although Montana was not a small geographically concentrated domain, those garden centers were relatively few in number, they were not being well served, and they were not so widespread that marketing to them would be unwieldy. Because of those three factors plus the fact that Glacier Nursery was offering better products and services than competitors, Brad Brown's marketing strategy was compatible with a small marketing budget. (See guidelines 1a and 1b, and warning 1a in Chapter 4.)

The *type of market competition* Brown entered was neither pure nor oligopolistic. Neither was it monopolistic in the traditional sense. However, as the only nursery in Montana, Glacier Nursery displayed some characteristics of a monopolistic competitor who was offering his customers better products and services. Throw in the fact that Brown was offering hardier plants at below-market prices, and you had a situation where Glacier Nursery clearly seemed to have significant advantages over faraway competitors. Such situations are quite compatible with a small marketing budget. (See guideline 2a and warnings 2a and 2b in Chapter 4.)

Nationwide, tree nurseries were in the mature stage of their *product life cycle*. But Montana had yet to experience the development of such businesses as a local industry sector. So in a sense, tree nurseries in that state had not yet reached maturity, and apparently had not even entered into the growth stage of their product life cycle. This fact, along with a relatively small number of customers and the lack of in-state competition, made Brown's marketing strategy quite compatible with a small marketing budget. (See guidelines 3b and 3c in Chapter 4.)

Brad Brown *distributed* his trees and shrubs directly to the garden centers he was serving. To do so, he used three local trucking firms who were pleased to receive the work, and that arrangement proved very compatible with a small budget. (See guidelines 4a–4c and warning 4b in Chapter 4.)

Glacier Nursery sold trees and shrubs to other businesses, which then used them as components of landscaping projects. Under these circumstances, those trees and shrubs were in effect, *business fabricating parts*, a product type that is quite compatible with a small marketing budget. (See guideline 5a in Chapter 4.)

Conclusion Regarding Screening Condition III   Brown's marketing strategy satisfied or followed guidelines in each of the five areas described in Chapter 5: market segmentation or target market, type of market competition, stage of the product life cycle, channels of distribution, and business or consumer product classification. Consequently, the strategy solidly achieved Screening Condition III and so could be executed with only a small marketing budget.

Screening Condition IV: Marketing Strategy Can Defend against Counterattacks

Brad Brown's marketing strategy *did not directly attack a major competitor* because established competitors did not view Montana's garden centers as important markets. They were willing to ship large orders of trees and shrubs to Montana in the spring, but they had little interest and incentive to do so at other times of the year. Glacier Nursery's marketing strategy definitely satisfied the characteristic of not directly attacking a large competitor. (See guidelines 1a–1c and warning 1b in Chapter 5.)

Glacier Nursery's product and service differentiation was quite extensive, and *served to neutralize a competitor's ability to disrupt or negate its marketing strategy.* (See the above discussion on Screening Condition I that described how Glacier Nursery's marketing strategy was able to achieve five product and/or service advantages over out-of-state competitors.) By incorporating those advantages, Brown's marketing strategy effectively "changed the rules of marketing," compared with the traditional marketing practiced by the competitors. Brown was also creating a superior image based on hardier plants and better delivery service. These things had a strong neutralizing effect on competitors—it would be very costly for them to duplicate Glacier Nursery's accomplishments. Glacier Nursery's selection of a small target market of little interest to far-off competitors also had a neutralizing effect on competition. (See guidelines 2a–2e in Chapter 5.)

Several of Glacier Nursery's product and service differences represented *significant and sustainable advantages*. Hardier trees and shrubs, delivery services throughout the growing season, and help with inventory cost control were three significant benefits to Montana's garden center operators that far-off, out-of-state competitors would not find economical to try to duplicate. Thus, these advantages were likely to be sustainable for some time. In addition, for the first few years, Brown intended to keep his prices slightly lower than competitions'. (See guidelines 3a–3c and warning 3b in Chapter 5.)

Brown used distribution and other impediments to provide Glacier Nursery with *longer-term protection against competitor's counterattacks*. Glacier Nursery's more frequent and timely delivery service throughout the entire growing season was an important benefit that out-of-state growers could not economically duplicate. And Brown established good relationships with all 40 of Montana's garden center operators, which again was not practical for competitors to attempt. He also offered a fuller product line as time went by. All of these things represented impediments that the competitors would have to overcome if they were going to mount a serious counterattack against Glacier Nursery. (See guidelines 4a, 4b, 4d, and 4e in Chapter 5.)

Conclusion Regarding Screening Condition IV   Glacier Nursery did not directly attack any large competitor. Rather, it chose to compete in a small market segment that was not of primary interest to any competitor. In addition, Glacier Nursery neutralized competitors by using five product and/or service advantages, and it used three different ways to gain a significant and sustainable advantage over competition. Lastly, Glacier Nursery used several distribution and other impediments to provide itself with longer-term protection against counterattacks by competitors.

Conclusions Regarding the Richness of Glacier Nursery's Marketing Strategy

Brad Brown's marketing strategy was very synergistic and showed notable richness among and between its elements. It was very effective both in avoiding all possible strategy execution delays and in being very compatible with a small marketing budget. Brown's strategy did not directly attack any large competitor; it used several advantages to neutralize competitors; it used three different ways to gain a significant and sustainable advantage; and it used several impediments to serve as longer-term protection against counterattacks. Overall, like the marketing strategies of

ACT and MicroFridge described above, the Glacier Nursery strategy displayed impressive richness.

Conclusions on Richness in Successful Marketing Strategies

Marketing strategies can be simple, plain vanilla, or they can be rich and robust. The strategies used by ACT, MicroFridge, and Glacier Nursery are particularly good examples of the latter type. Such strategies employ more guidelines than the minimum number needed to achieve each screening condition. A rich marketing strategy will make a small new business stronger and more competitive because those guidelines represent advantages over its competitors and barriers or obstacles against any competitor's counterattacks. Richly designed strategies also clearly and completely follow all the warnings related to each screening condition. Consequently, they do not have any inherent weaknesses that competitors can easily exploit to harm the small new business.

How important is such richness to you and your new business? Very important! You should strive to achieve high degrees of richness in your marketing strategy because doing so will greatly increase your small new business's chances of success.

Summary

Chapters 2 through 5 introduced you to the things you must include—and not include—in your marketing strategy in order to achieve each of Screening Conditions I through IV. Chapter 6 described how you should use what you learned in Chapters 2–5 to evaluate whether or not your marketing strategy has a good chance of being successful. Two major topics were discussed.

The first part of this chapter reviewed the purpose of each screening condition and the contribution it makes to creating a successful marketing strategy for your small new business. If your marketing strategy achieves all four screening conditions, it will be very synergistic, it will not encounter any strategy execution delays, and it will be compatible with a small marketing budget. In addition, it will include elements that will make your small new business able to fend off counterattacks by established competitors. With these four strengths built into your marketing strategy, it should have a very good chance of being successful.

The second part of this chapter described how successful marketing strategies display a richness in achieving the four screening conditions. That is, rich strategies do not achieve each screening condition in just a minimal way. Rather, they do so by incorporating more than the minimum number of guidelines for each screening condition. The more specified guidelines your marketing strategy employs, the richer it becomes, and the richer it is, the stronger and more competitive your small new business will be, thereby giving it an ever greater chance of succeeding. For that reason, you want to make your marketing strategy as rich as it can be.

Good luck to you creating a rich marketing strategy that will guide your small new business to great success!

Notes

Chapter 1

1. Bounds, Gwendolyn, "Lessons of Success and Failure," *Wall Street Journal*, July 12, 2004, pp. R1, R6.

2. "Economic Focus: Life After Debt," *The Economist*, April 16, 2005, p. 68.

3. Bjerke, Bjorn and Claes M. Hultman, *Entrepreneurial Marketing: The Growth of Small Firms in the New Economic Era* (Cheltenham, UK: Edward Elgar Publishing Ltd, 2002), pp. 5 and 12.

4. Same source as note 3.

5. Same source as note 3.

6. Carson, David, Stanley Cromie, Pauric McGowen, and Jimmy Hill, *Marketing and Entrepreneurship in SMEs: An Innovative Approach* (London: Prentice-Hall, 1995), p. 160.

7. Same source as note 6, pp. 86, 90.

8. Stasch, Stanley F., "Three Common Marketing Causes of Small New Business Failures," in *Research at the Marketing/Entrepreneurship Interface*, G. E. Hills, S. Attaran, F. Beuk, B. Kochuveli, and J. Mollner, eds. (Chicago: The University of Illinois at Chicago, 2007).

9. Attributed to Ron Reilly, senior vice-president/executive media director, Ogilvy & Mather, Los Angeles, California; see "What the Experts Say" section attached to Edward O. Welles, "A Whole New Game," *Inc.*, April, 1990, pp. 58–69.

10. Lawton, Christopher, "A Liquor Maverick Shakes Up Industry with Pricy Brands," *Wall Street Journal*, May 21, 2003, pp. A1, A9.

11. Richman, Tom, "Made in the U.S.A.," *Inc.*, January, 1989, pp. 47–53.

12. Turrettini, John, "Cut the Partners," *Forbes*, July 26, 2004, p. 136.

13. Lambert, Emily, "His Own Beat," *Forbes*, July 5, 2004, p. 140.

14. See Stasch, Stanley F., "Screening for Successful Low-Budget Marketing Strategies for New Ventures," *Journal of Research in Marketing and Entrepreneurship* 4, no. 3 (2002): pp. 229–267, and Stanley F. Stasch, "Identifying Successful Low-Budget Marketing Strategies for New Ventures: A Proposed Evaluation Procedure," in *Research at the Marketing/Entrepreneurship Interface*, G. E. Hills, S. Attaran, F. Beuk, B. Kochuveli, and J. Mollner, eds. (Chicago: The University of Illinois at Chicago, 2004); see also Stanley F. Stasch and John L. Ward, "Evaluating Aggressive Marketing Strategies for Smaller-Share Firms," *Marketing Intelligence Planning in Action* 7, no. 7/8 (1989): pp. 4–15, and Stanley F. Stasch, Ronald T. Lonsdale, John L. Ward, and Dawn A. Harris, "Characteristics of Share-Gaining Marketing Strategies for Smaller-Share Firms: Literature Review and Synthesis," *Journal of Marketing Theory and Practice*, spring 1999, pp. 1–13.

Chapter 2

1. These happenings were associated with the publication, E. J. McCarthy, *Basic Marketing* (Homewood, IL: Richard D. Irwin, 1961).

2. Murphy, Anne, "Inventions 'R' Us," *Inc.*, June 1991, pp. 82–91.

3. Finegan, Jay, "Grown in Montana," *Inc.*, January 1991, pp. 62–69.

4. "Miller's Fast Growth Upsets Beer Market," *Business Week*, November 8, 1976, pp. 58–67.

5. Singer, Harvey and F. Stewart Debruicker, "L'eggs Products, Inc.," in Star, et al., *Problems in Marketing*, 5th ed. (New York: McGraw-Hill, 1977).

6. Richman, Tom, "Made in the U.S.A.," *Inc.*, January 1989, pp. 47–53.

7. Mamis, Robert A., "Small Chill," *Inc.*, February 1990, pp. 66–73.

8. Welles, Edward D., "Decisions, Decisions," *Inc.*, August 1990, p. 82.

9. Brown, Paul B., "Plastics," *Inc.*, June 1990, p. 71.

10. Welles, Edward D., "Sound Strategy," *Inc.*, May 1991, p. 48.

11. Spragins, Ellen E., "Child's Play," *Inc.*, February 1991, p. 64.

12. Same source as note 6.

13. Same source as note 7.

14. Brokaw, Leslie, "Play by Play," *Inc.*, September 1989, pp. 64–71.

15. Fisher, Anne B., "House Calls," *Inc.*, July 1989, pp. 72–79.

16. Fraser, Jill Andresky, "Broadcast News," *Inc.*, January 1990, pp. 70–75.

17. Same source as note 11, p. 70.

18. Same source as note 10.

19. Posner, Bruce, "Seeing Red," *Inc.*, May 1989, p. 58.

20. Same source as note 6.

21. Same source as note 7.

22. Same source as note 2.

23. Same source as note 8.

24. Same source as note 14.

25. Same source as note 11, p. 70.

26. Same source as note 15, p. 78.

27. Same source as note 6.

28. Same source as note 7.

29. Same source as note 9.

30. Same source as note 14.

31. Same source as note 19.

32. Same source as note 6.

33. Same source as note 7, but see also "It Runs Hot and Cold—Who Wants It?" *Inc.*, February 1995, p. 67.

34. Brown, Paul B., "Cookie Monster," *Inc.*, February 1989, p. 57.

35. Case, John, "Hot Seats," *Inc.*, June 1988, pp. 82–83.

36. Same source as note 15.

37. Same source as note 11, p. 70.

38. Hopkins, Michael S., "In Search of the Perfect Business," *Inc.*, March 1989, pp. 52–63.

39. Finegan, Jay, "Burning Ambition," *Inc.*, August 1991, pp. 44–49.

Chapter 3

1. Richman, Tom, "Made in the U.S.A.," *Inc.*, January 1989, pp. 47–53.

2. Mamis, Robert A., "The Small Chill," *Inc.*, February 1990, pp. 66–73; see also "It Runs Hot and Cold—Who Wants It?" *Inc.*, February 1995, p. 67.

3. Finegan, Jay, "Grown in Montana," *Inc.*, January 1991, pp. 62–69.

4. Murphy, Anne, "Inventions R Us," *Inc.*, June 1991, p. 84.

5. Brown, Paul B., "Plastics," *Inc.*, June 1990, p. 76.

6. Welles, Edward O., "Decisions, Decisions," *Inc.*, August 1990, p. 82.

7. Ibid., p. 89.

8. Fisher, Anne B., "House Calls," *Inc.*, July 1989, p. 78.

9. Welles, Edward O., "Sound Strategy," *Inc.*, May 1991, p. 48.

10. McCartney, Scott, "American Plays Hardball with a Start-Up Over All-First-Class Flights," *Wall Street Journal*, January 9, 2000, pp. B1, B4.

11. Ibid., p. B1.

12. Same source as note 2.

13. Same source as note 1.

14. Same source as note 3.

15. Welles, Edward O., "Decisions, Decisions," *Inc.*, August 1990, p. 86.

16. Same source as note 9.

17. Case, John, "Hot Seats," *Inc.*, June 1988, p. 83.

18. Ibid., p. 83.

19. Same source as note 1.

20. Same source as note 2.

21. Same source as note 3.

22. Hopkins, Michael S., "In Search of the Perfect Business," *Inc.*, March 1989, p. 63.

23. Sprigins, Ellyn E., "Child's Play," *Inc.*, February 1991, p. 70.

24. Ibid.

25. Ibid.

26. Same source as note 9.

27. Hyatt, Joshua, "Cheap Counsel," *Inc.*, September 1988, p. 106.

28. Ibid.

29. Posner, Bruce G., "Class Pictures," *Inc.*, May 1990, p. 83.

30. Posner, Bruce G., "Seeing Red," *Inc.*, May 1989, p. 58.

31. Finegan, Jay, "Down in the Dump," *Inc.*, September 1990, p. 96.

32. Ibid., p. 98.

33. Finegan, Jay, "Burning Ambition," *Inc.*, August 1991, p. 44.

34. Same source as note 27, p. 107.

35. Fisher, Anne B., "House Calls," *Inc.*, July 1989, p. 74.

36. Brokaw, Leslie, "Anatomy of a Start-Up Revisited," *Inc.*, March 1990, p. 83; see also Kahn, Joseph P., "The Money Game," *Inc.*, October 1988, pp. 106–111.

37. Brokaw, Leslie, "Anatomy of a Start-Up Revisited, *Inc.*, June 1991, p. 89.

Chapter 4

1. Stasch, Stanley F., "Three Common Marketing Causes of Small New Business Failures," in *Research at the Marketing/Entrepreneurship Interface*, G. E. Hills, S. Attaran, F. Beuk, B. Kochuveli, and J. Mollner, eds. (Chicago: The University of Illinois at Chicago, 2007).

2. Stasch, Stanley F., "When Might a New Venture Succeed with a Low Budget Marketing Strategy," in *Research at the Marketing/Entrepreneurship Interface*, G. E. Hills and R. P. Singh, eds. (Chicago: University of Illinois at Chicago, 2000), and Stasch, Stanley F., "Characteristics of Successful Low Budget Marketing Strategies for New Ventures: Analysis of Selected Cases," in *Research at the Marketing/Entrepreneurship Interface*, G. E. Hills, D. J. Hansen, and B. Merrilees, eds. (Chicago: University of Illinois at Chicago, 2001).

3. Kahn, Joseph P., "The Money Game," *Inc.*, October 1988, p. 106–111.

4. Mamis, Robert A., "The Small Chill," *Inc.*, February 1990, pp. 66–73; see also, "It Runs Hot and Cold—Who Wants It?" *Inc.*, February 1995, p. 67.

5. Richman, Tom, "Made in the U.S.A.," *Inc.*, January 1989, pp. 47–53.

6. Spragins, Ellen E., "Child's Play," *Inc.*, February 1991, pp. 62–71.

7. Welles, Edward O., "Sound Strategy," *Inc.*, May 1991, pp. 46–56.

8. Same source as note 5.

9. Same source as note 4.

10. Finegan, Jay, "Grown in Montana," *Inc.*, January 1991, pp. 62–69.

11. Posner, Bruce, "Good Vibrations," *Inc.*, July 1988, pp. 64–69.

12. Same source as note 7.

13. Case, John, "Hot Seats," *Inc.*, June 1988, p. 80.

14. Ibid., p. 83.

15. Most textbooks on the principles or fundamentals of marketing, or on marketing management, offer lengthier discussions of the product life cycle concept.

16. Most textbooks on the principles or fundamentals of marketing, or on marketing management, offer lengthier discussions of the diffusion of innovation theory.

17. Same source as note 5.

18. Same source as note 4.

19. Same source as note 10.

20. Posner, Bruce G., "Seeing Red," *Inc.*, May 1989, pp. 48–59.

21. Fisher, Anne B., "House Calls," *Inc.*, July 1989, pp. 72–79.

22. Same source as note 6.

23. Same source as note 7.

24. Same source as note 13.

25. Same source as note 4.

26. Same source as note 5.

27. Same source as note 10.

28. Johnson, Robert, "Mr. Bentz's Pursuit of Ideal Bass Boat Irks His Ex-Employer," *Wall Street Journal*, December 8, 1999, pp. A1, A12.

29. Martinez, Barbara, "Inside Job," *Wall Street Journal*, May 21, 1998, pp. R23, R25.

30. Welles, Edward O., "Educating Octavia," *Inc.*, June 1989, pp. 84–93.

31. Brown, Paul B., "Cookie Monster," *Inc.*, February 1989, p. 57.

32. Hyatt, Joshua, "Cheap Counsel," *Inc.*, September 1988, pp. 102–107.

33. Fraser, Jill A., "Broadcast News," *Inc.*, January 1990, pp. 70–75.

34. Hopkins, Michael S., "In Search of the Perfect Business," *Inc.*, March 1998, pp. 52–63.

35. Etzel, Michael J., Bruce J. Walker, and William Stanton, *Marketing*, 14th edition (Irwin/McGraw-Hill, 2006), pp. 208–214, but especially Tables 8-1 and 8-2.

36. Ibid., p. 210.

37. Same source as note 5.

38. Welles, Edward O., "Decisions, Decisions," *Inc.*, August 1990, pp. 80–90.

39. Finegan, Jay, "Down in the Dump," *Inc.*, September 1990, pp. 90–100.

40. Pereira, Joseph, "Sneaker Company Tags Out-of-Breath Baby Boomers," *Wall Street Journal*, January 16, 1998, pp. B1, B2.

Chapter 5

1. McCartney, Scott, "American Plays Hardball with a Start-Up Over All-First-Class Flights," *Wall Street Journal*, January 9, 2000, pp. B1, B4.

2. Trottman, Melanie, "Legend Air Ends Operations After Love Field Battle," *Wall Street Journal*, March 6, 2001, p. A4.

3. Lubove, Seth, "Dancing On Graves," *Forbes*, February 28, 1994, pp. 64–65.

4. Ortega, Bob and John R. Wilke, "Amid Probe, Anheuser Conquers Turf," *Wall Street Journal*, March 9, 1998, pp. B1, B8.

5. Richman, Tom, "The New American Start-up," *Inc.*, September 1988, pp. 54–63; Mary Beth Sammon, "From Unemployed to Entrepreneur," *Family Circle*, November 7, 1989, pp. 153–155; Leslie Brokaw, "Anatomy of a Start-Up Revisited: My Own Mission," *Inc.*, January 1990, p. 75; and Suzanne Oliver, "The Shiksa Chef," *Forbes*, May 24, 1993, pp. 66–68.

6. Richman, Tom, "Made in the U.S.A.," *Inc.*, January 1989, pp. 47–53.

7. Mamis, Robert A., "The Small Chill," *Inc.*, February 1990, pp. 66–73; see also "It Runs Hot and Cold—Who Wants It?" *Inc.*, February 1995, pp. 67.

8. Finegan, Jay, "Grown in Montana," *Inc.*, January 1991, pp. 62–69.

9. This section is based on the article by John L. Ward and Stanley F. Stasch, "When Are Market Leaders Most Likely to Be Attacked?" *The Journal of Consumer Marketing,"* Fall 1986, pp. 41–48.

10. Ulman, Neil, "Time, Risk, Ingenuity All Go into Launching New Personal Product," *Wall Street Journal*, November 17, 1978, pp. 1, 19.

11. Samuels, Gary, "CD-ROM's First Big Victim," *Forbes*, February 28, 1994, pp. 42–44.

12. Wysocki, B., "Punching Is Furious in Tylenol-Datril Fight for Non-Aspirin Users," *Wall Street Journal*, May 24, 1976, pp. 1, 17; and *Business Week*, "A Painful Headache for Bristol-Myers," October 6, 1975, pp. 78–79; also Rotbart, Dean and John A. Prestbo, "Taking Rely Off Market Cost Procter & Gamble a Week of Agonizing," *Wall Street Journal*, November 3, 1980, pp. 1, 20.

13. *Business Week*, "Miller's Fast Growth Upsets the Beer Industry," November 8, 1976, pp. 58–67.

14. Latour, Almar, "Amid High-Tech Turf Battle, Baby Bells Feel Heat on Cash Cow," *Wall Street Journal*, April 13, 2004, pp. A1, A16.

15. Crew, Bob, "A Tale of Two Products: Crunchy Nut and Aqua-Fresh," *Marketing Communications*, April 1981, pp. 30–31.

16. *The Times-Picayune*, "Bubble Barq's Hits No. 2 in National Root Beer Market," October 10, 1993, Money section, p. F1.

17. *Business Week*, "Turning Warner-Lambert into a Marketing Conglomerate," March 5, 1978, pp. 60–64.

18. *Forbes*, "Who's Got Heinz in a Pickle?" August 15, 1977, pp. 63–64.

19. *Forbes*, "Hershey Steps Out," March 17, 1980, p. 64.

20. Johnson, Robert, "Mr. Bentz's Pursuit of the Ideal Bass Boat Irks His Ex-Employer," *Wall Street Journal*, December 8, 1999, pp. A1, A12.

21. Yoder, Stephan Kreider, "How H-P Used Tactics of the Japanese to Beat Them at Their Own Game," *Wall Street Journal*, September 4, 1994, pp. A1, A6.

22. The discussions of characteristics 2, 3, and 4 of Screening Condition IV are strongly based on E. P. DiMingo, "Marketing Strategies for Smaller-Share Players," *The Journal of Business Strategy*, January–February 1990, pp. 26–30; M. Magnet, "Meet the New Revolutionaries," *Fortune*, February 24, 1992, pp. 94–101; M. E. Porter, "How to Attack the Industry Leader," *Fortune*, April 29, 1985, pp. 153–165; M. E. Porter, "Know Your Place," *Inc.*, September 1991, pp. 90–93; and Stanley F. Stasch and John L. Ward, "Evaluating Aggressive Marketing Strategies For Smaller-Share Firms," *Marketing Intelligence and Planning* 7, no. 7/8 (1989), pp. 4–15.

23. Same source as note 6.

24. Same source as note 7.

25. Same source as note 8.

26. Same source as note 6.

27. Kahn, Joseph P., "The Money Game," *Inc.*, October 1988, pp. 106–111.

28. Same source as note 8.

29. Same source as note 6.

30. Samuels, Gary, "CD-ROM's First Big Victim," *Forbes*, February 28, 1994, pp. 42–44.

31. Pereira, Joseph, "Board-Riding Youths Take Sneaker Maker on a Fast Ride Uphill," *Wall Street Journal*, April 16, 1998, pp. A1, A8.

32. Same sources as notes 6, 7, 8, and 27.

33. *Forbes*, "Who's Got Heinz in a Pickle?" August 15, 1977, pp. 63–64.

34. Same source as note 7.

35. Same sources as notes 6, 7, and 8.

36. Same source as note 30.

37. Finegan, Jay, "Down in the Dump," *Inc.*, September 1990, pp. 90–100.

38. Same source as note 27.

39. Bounds, Gwendolyn, "How a Small Beverage Maker Managed to Win Shelf Space in One of the Most Brutally Competitive Industries," *Wall Street Journal*, January 30, 2006, pp. R1, R3.

40. Same source as notes 6 and 7.

41. Same source as note 37.

42. Same source as note 39.

43. Same source as notes 6 and 8.

44. Porter, Michael E., "Know Your Place," *Inc.*, September 1991, pp. 90–93.

45. See the Medco example in M. Magnet, "Meet the New Revolutionaries," *Fortune*, February 24, 1992, pp. 94–101.

46. Same source as note 6.

47. Finegan, Jay, "Diaper Dan," *Inc.*, March 1991, pp. 80–90.

48. See the Newell Company example in M. Magnet, "Meet the New Revolutionaries," *Fortune*, February 24, 1992, pp. 94–101.

49. Same source as note 39.

50. Same source as note 6.

51. Same source as note 48.

52. Same sources as notes 6 and 8.

Chapter 6

1. Richman, Tom, "Made in the U.S.A.," *Inc.*, January 1989, pp. 47–53.

2. Mamis, Robert A., "The Small Chill," *Inc.*, February 1990, pp. 66–73; see also "It Runs Hot and Cold—Who Wants It?" *Inc.*, February 1995, p. 67.

3. Finegan, Jay, "Grown in Montana," *Inc.*, January 1991, pp. 62–69.

Index